W9-AIA-267

SMASHED!

Folsom Lake College Library

SMASHED!

The Many Meanings of Intoxication and Drunkenness

Peter Kelly, Jenny Advocat, Lyn Harrison and
Christopher Hickey

MONASH University
Publishing

© Copyright 2011
All rights reserved. Apart from any uses permitted by Australia's
Copyright Act 1968, no part of this book may be reproduced by
any process without prior written permission from the copyright
owners. Inquiries should be directed to the publisher.

Monash University Publishing
Building 4, Monash University
Clayton, Victoria 3800, Australia
www.publishing.monash.edu

This book is available online at
www.publishing.monash.edu/books/smashed.html

ISBN: 978-0-9806512-8-7 (pb)
ISBN: 978-0-9806512-9-4 (web)

Design

Les Thomas

Printer

Griffin Press

Contents

About the authors

Peter Kelly is an Associate Professor/Principal Research Fellow in the Alfred Deakin Research Institute at Deakin University. He has published extensively on young people, youth at-risk and the practice of Youth Studies. His research is currently focused on exploring the emergence of new work identities, obligations, and responsibilities in a globalised risk economy, and the ways these concerns find expression in discussions about new work ethics in populations such as young workers.

Jenny Advocat is a Research Fellow in the Southern Academic Primary Care Research Unit (SAPCRU) in the School of Primary Health Care, Monash University. With a background in Medical Anthropology and Health Sociology, she has researched and published in a variety of areas, including around the use of the Internet for research and treatment, young people and alcohol use, work/life balance and complementary medicine.

Lyn Harrison is an Associate Professor in the School of Education (Faculty of Arts and Education) at Deakin University, and coordinates the university's Graduate Certificate in Higher Education. Her research interests lie in exploring youth subjectivity and the production of risks in late modernity, particularly in relation to health, well-being and sexuality.

Chris Hickey is an Associate Professor and Deputy Head in the School of Education at Deakin University. His research has focused on youth studies and the links between identity and issues of social cohesion and exclusion. His work investigating the behaviours of young males as members of peer groups within sport, physical education and popular culture is recognised internationally. He maintains a strong interest in the translation of research into practice and has enjoyed extensive work with schools and sporting clubs. He is currently Chief Editor of the *Asia-Pacific Journal of Health, Sport and Physical Education*.

Acknowledgments

This book had its beginnings in a literature review that was commissioned by *DrinkWise* Australia Ltd with funding provided by *DrinkWise* Australia and the Australian Government Department of Health and Ageing.

Dr Jo Lindsay was a significant contributor to that review, as were Dr Karin Barty and Dr Andrew Padgett who did much of the literature searching and collating. The work done in that review was also greatly assisted by the support of Monash University librarians Ms Sue Little and Ms Janet McGarry. We also greatly appreciate the administrative support of Ms Ros King who, at that time, was the Business Development Manager in The Faculty of Arts at Monash University.

We also thank Nicola Pitt for her admirable editing/formatting of the final version of this book.

Prelude

In mid-2009 a brief story appeared on the web site of *The Australian* newspaper (No Author 2009). Under the heading 'Victorian Premier John Brumby says booze is too cheap, as Melbourne reels from escalating street violence', The story painted a disturbing picture of the claimed relationship between readily available cheap alcohol (in the form of cheap white wine), underage drinking and drunkenness, and increasing street violence. The sentiment, the concerns and the content could be found, as we will argue, in many other spaces and places in the industrialised democracies at the start of the twenty-first century.

The story suggested that an Australian Federal Government Preventative Health Taskforce was examining an array of measures including the introduction of a so-called sin tax on alcohol, changes to liquor licensing regulations, and changes to the marketing of alcohol. John Brumby, then the premier of the Australian state of Victoria, was quoted in his responses to questions about these policy discussions: like many a politician in this context, Brumby voiced his concerns about alcohol and binge drinking, saying that: "'It is a fact at the moment that some of the cheap, very cheap white wine – colloquially known, I think, as goon – you can buy for as little as 50 cents a drink… and I would say that's a very, very cheap price indeed'".

The story went on to say that the former premier thought the problems of violence that were 'gripping' the streets of Melbourne were the result of drunkenness and 'swarming gangs'. According to Brumby:

> "They're people who can hardly stand up, they're people who've had 20 or 30 drinks and they're in a state where they're just not in control of their senses and I think some of them unwittingly are involving themselves in violence and alcohol is the sole cause of that".

In the UK, meanwhile: 'A blonde student lifted her glazed eyes to the camera, held up her drink and smiled. She was wearing stockings with a lace slip and had ripped her T-shirt in half to reveal her bra'. So begins a story in the UK newspaper *The Observer* in September 2008 (Asthana 2008). In the article the author reports on a debate in the UK about the responsibilities that university student unions have to promote responsible drinking, and to take steps to curb intoxication and drunkenness among young people at events staged and/or promoted by the unions. The story posits that one dimension of the debate is related to claims by student unions that various companies and promoters irresponsibly target the university population in the form of drinks promotions, pub crawls and organised binge sessions. The blonde female student given a starring role in the story was apparently on an 'organised pub crawl in which hundreds of undergraduates lurched from bar to bar as they cheered, laughed and downed drink after drink', an event not uncommon in university towns, the article implied.

The National Union of Students claims to be trying to encourage a responsible approach to drinking, and has criticised the companies running the pub crawls, saying that 'they encouraged young people to binge-drink'. The union targeted one particular event organiser, Carnage UK, whose university pub crawls are 'staged in 15 different cities and will host 300,000 students over the next university year'. Such companies and events were 'putting "hurdles" in the way of their attempts to encourage responsible drinking', the students claimed.

The Observer article suggests, however, that student unions may indeed be on a less than stable (high) moral ground:

> … the company that runs Carnage UK hit back by releasing a list of events organised by unions across the country that advertised cut-price drinks and appeared to promote heavy drinking. According to the research, many student unions continue to run or promote nights such as "drink the bar dry", a "pound a pint" and "trebles for singles".

Leaving aside, for the moment, the competing claims about who is promoting a culture of binge drinking, intoxication and drunkenness in UK universities, the article cites Professor Ian Gilmore, the president of the Royal College of Physicians, on the risks to health and well-being, and the potential negative social consequences, of intoxication and drunkenness:

> "Although alcohol is legal, it is still a drug. It should not be used as a loss-leader like soap powder." He said there was still a university culture that revolved around alcohol, and warned that binge-drinking could lead to violence, date rape, unwanted pregnancies and serious injuries.

Back in Australia, at the annual Earle Page lecture at the University of New England in September 2009, Tony Abbott (2009), the former Australian Federal Government Health Minister and the then Opposition Shadow Minister for Families, Housing, Community Services and Indigenous Affairs, devoted a deal of space to commentary on the ways in which successive Australian governments had attempted to deal with a range of chronic, seemingly intractable, health, well-being, housing, education, work and life-expectancy issues in remote Indigenous communities. Much of this commentary focused on what Abbott and others, including leading Aboriginal Affairs academics, have identified as a 'paradigm shift' in the ways that these issues are conceptualised, a shift echoed in the title of Abbott's lecture, 'The end of the disaster narrative and the new consensus on Aboriginal Affairs'. In the lecture, he stated:

> Sutton has noted the pressure on the new government from "within Labor and certain Aboriginal circles to water down" the intervention. A progressive politics, he said, has "dulled our instincts about the sanctity of indigenous people's right also to be free of violence, abuse, neglect, ignorance and corruption". In most Aboriginal towns' special circumstances, the right of children to a good night's sleep and of women to be free from drunken violence should trump the normal right of adults to drink alcohol... the right of children to have food on their table should trump adults' normal right to spend their money on cigarettes and gambling, especially when that money is not actually earned. As Warren Mundine has frequently said, it would be better to extend welfare quarantining to all welfare dependent families with children than to lose its benefits for Aboriginal people because it might seem to some like racial discrimination.

Introduction

This book emerges from particular times, spaces and places. In many of the advanced liberal democracies at the start of the twenty-first century there is a great deal of public, policy and academic interest in the problems that are seen to be connected to alcohol-related intoxication and drunkenness. As our opening anecdotes suggest, in the United Kingdom (UK) and Europe, in the United States of America (the US), in Australia and New Zealand – and in a number of other countries around the globe – a variety of public health issues, crime and justice concerns, debates about young people and violence or anti-social behaviours, and a range of similar and related problems are understood and responded to in ways that link them to intoxication and drunkenness.

As we will discuss throughout this book, the ways in which this diverse array of concerns, issues and problems are connected to the use of alcohol at levels that result in intoxication and drunkenness are problematic. Indeed, from the outset we will claim that definitions and understandings of intoxication and drunkenness; explanations and descriptions of the causes and consequences of intoxication and drunkenness; interpretations of the symbolic, cultural, moral, legal and political meanings that attach to, and shape, these understandings are things that are uncertain, ambiguous and subject to debates that appear to not be resolvable.

While we situate this book in particular configurations of time, space and place we also argue that much of what passes for, or appears as, contemporary debate about these issues also shares strong connections to a long history of concerns about alcohol, its uses by certain groups and populations, and the results and consequences of intoxication and drunkenness. In some respects there is much that is not new in these debates. At the same time new technologies of measurement, calculation, quantification and definition are deployed in a variety of settings to *better*, more *accurately*, identify both the extent of intoxication throughout broader populations and within more specific populations, and to determine levels of individual intoxication.

In this context we argue that any debate and discussion about intoxication and drunkenness needs to situate these competing claims, ideas, understandings, definitions and measurements in particular historical, social, cultural and political contexts. Intoxication and drunkenness need to be understood and defined with due regard to these contexts, and with an appreciation for the influences of various social processes and categories such as social class, gender, ethnicity and race, and geography. In other words, we make a strong claim for the need to acknowledge that intoxication and drunkenness will mean different things to different people, different organisations, and different groups of commentators, politicians, policy professionals, and different expert, scientific, communities.

Importantly, the problems and meanings that become associated with intoxication and drunkenness suggest different things if and when they are discussed as a health issue; a legal issue; a youth issue; an Aboriginal issue; an inner-city issue related to clubs/venues; a licensing issue; an issue for sporting clubs; an issue for rural communities; a welfare issue; and/or an issue for privileged, middle-aged business people.

In this book we present the results of an extensive, multi-disciplinary review of a variety of understandings and definitions of the terms *intoxication* and *drunkenness* from the perspective of the individual. These individual understandings and responses are located in and alongside a range of expert, policy, public health and media representations, definitions and understandings of intoxication and drunkenness. We develop an approach to examining the meanings and understandings of intoxication and drunkenness in different places and at different times which is grounded in culture and the knowledge that they are embedded in systems of meaning. As Becaaria (2003, 101) argues, research into 'alcohol use, drugs and intoxication presents theoretical problems relating to the objective nature of intoxication, and cultural distinctions within the social sciences as well as the philosophy of subjective meaning and understanding'.

In our discussion and analysis we document how individuals in Australia, New Zealand, the UK, Europe, the US and other contexts define intoxication and drunkenness. A key feature of this discussion is that we compare, contrast and locate individual, *lay* understandings of intoxication and drunkenness in relation to those held by *experts* in key fields and disciplines. We examine the definitions of intoxication and drunkenness used in Australian and international policy guidelines, and those held by experts in key fields including medicine and public health, politics and law, sociology and criminology, anthropology and cultural studies.

A key claim we make here is that these descriptions and definitions are contextual and contingent. As we have already suggested, individuals, experts, organisations, news media and governments define and describe intoxication and drunkenness in ways that are related to particular purposes, outcomes and ends. These may include responding to community concerns about violence and anti-social behaviour. It may be that the individual and public health outcomes of intoxication and drunkenness – for particular populations, or the population in general – are a primary concern. Whatever the focus of these concerns, we witness the development and deployment of an array of strategies, tactics, campaigns and laws in ways that are designed to support these purposes. It may be that tactics and campaigns, and purposes and ends in one context and framework of understanding may support those in other settings. However, they may often also contradict and act against each other.

Public health researchers, for example, call for increased awareness about the amount of alcohol it takes for an individual to become intoxicated – focusing on either the number of drinks consumed or the volume of alcohol ingested. Other disciplines, such as criminology and legal theory take as their starting point for understanding intoxication more philosophical notions of personal responsibility, choice and free will – particularly when trying to make judgments about the range of consequences that flow from states of intoxication and drunkenness. Located in between these differing, sometimes contradictory, interpretations are a variety of understandings and strategies that both experts working in an academic framework as well as individuals going about their daily lives utilise to make sense of the meanings, characteristics and consequences of intoxication and drunkenness.

In presenting the discussion in the chapters that follow we have a number of purposes, and make a number of claims. For instance, we suggest that given the nature of the debates and discussions that we have briefly introduced to this point there is some need to present, as we do in this book, an overview, review and critical discussion of the diversity of approaches to identifying, measuring, understanding and responding to intoxication and drunkenness. Indeed, we claim that one of the strengths of the discussion we present here is the work that it does in setting out a contemporary account that crosses over and traverses a number of disciplines. In addition to this multi-disciplinary overview – which because of its very nature must sacrifice some detail and depth in the pursuit of a broad review – we attempt to locate the ways in which non-expert, lay populations and individuals attach meaning and purpose to intoxication and drunkenness, the contexts and relations in which these occur, and the roles that they play in an array of social settings and occasions. So, for example, we find that intoxication is more readily defined by experts through calculable, measurable, biological and physiological criteria. Yet even among experts in a similar field, such as biomedical science, there are different ways of defining intoxication for different purposes. Importantly, we identify an imperative for biomedical and public health researchers to seek to more precisely define and calculate intoxication and drunkenness in ways that locate intoxication and drunkenness as the outcome of individual practices.

However, our discussion and review suggests that individuals tend to define their own intoxication and drunkenness with reference to feelings, observable behaviour and social actions. In addition, in most cases, for most individuals, drinking alcohol is an inherently social activity involving different practices, conventions and relationships for men and women, and different social groups. In this sense intoxication and drunkenness are firmly located in social spaces and attention to these spaces is essential if we are to better understand the diverse roles that alcohol and, specifically, intoxication and drunkenness play in individuals' lives – in the social, cultural and symbolic spaces in which humans generate, and give meaning to their lives.

In framing our presentation of this account we have indicated a sense that the many meanings of intoxication and drunkenness need to be situated historically, socially and culturally. At this stage we also make a case for acknowledging and working with the complexities and ambiguities that accompany, even produce, these many meanings. We will return to what we might do with this complexity and ambiguity in our concluding chapter. At this point we want to make a number of points to guide the reader through this complexity and what it means for how we present our account. In some respects these are important methodological and theoretical elements for what follows. Annemarie Mol and John Law (2002, 1), in their *Complexities: An introduction*, suggest that over the past few decades, in many branches of the social sciences, there has been 'a revolt against simplification. The argument has been that the world is complex and that it shouldn't be tamed too much'. In reading what follows it should be apparent that we have some sympathy for this position. Mol and Law are themselves cautious about both complexity and simplification and what these mean for what we can know – about anything. If things are too complex can we make any sense of them? If we simplify things too much what do we leave out? To begin the task of dealing with the always present dilemmas of *simplification* and *complexification*, Mol and Law suggest a starting definition of complexity: 'There is complexity if things relate but don't add up, if events occur but not within the processes of linear time, and if phenomena share a space but cannot be mapped in terms of a single set of three-dimensional co-ordinates'. For our purposes this definition enables us to say that the many meanings of intoxication and drunkenness bear some relation to each other but in no way add up to a coherent, non-problematic, unified whole; that across different co-ordinates of time, space and place an array of events, ideas, forms of knowledge and other processes and practices attempt to make sense of intoxication and drunkenness. In doing so they produce not something that is simple and agreed upon, but things that are complex, ambiguous and ambivalent. And something that is subject to constant and ongoing debate about meanings, measurements, consequences, responsibilities, obligations and rights.

Mol and Law (2002, 7–13) outline some tactics for dealing with complexity in the work that social scientists do as they write about the things that they engage with or seek to explore and/or explain. A number of these tactics provide a model for how we present our discussion in this book. At one level they suggest that *lists* of things can be made without necessarily imposing an order on them: lists 'assemble elements that do not necessarily fit together into some larger scheme'. In our discussion we tend to provide lists of an array of orientations, understandings and meanings associated with intoxication and drunkenness. We also write in ways that include *multiplicities*: Mol and Law suggest that when 'investigators start to discover a variety of orders – modes of ordering, logics, frames, styles, repertoires, discourses – then the dichotomy between simple and complex starts to dissolve'. This certainly happens in what follows. Finally, for now, they make a distinction between *mapping* as a mode of ordering that makes – sometimes forces – connections and relations between things, maps that in some cases may assist us to make sense of a direction, but at a different scale may be less useful, and *walking*, which suggests a different relationship to the ways we encounter the world and its complexities – a way of encountering and making sense of the world in which a map may be more or less useful. So, in our discussion we do provide some directions, and some sense of purpose but we don't provide a comprehensive map that, ultimately, would enable us to make sense of the complexities and ambiguities we encounter in this engagement with the many meanings of intoxication and drunkenness.

Structure of the book

With these general observations and preliminary statements in mind we have structured the remainder of this book in a way that develops the discussion and analysis of these observations in more detail.

In the following chapter we present a historical account of a range of issues related to the problems of intoxication and drunkenness that focuses on a number of themes that appear to recur – often in different, but related forms – at a number of points during the seventeenth, eighteenth and nineteenth centuries. In the late twentieth and early twenty-first centuries we continue to experience and respond to echoes of these concerns. These themes include the following: the ways in which understandings of intoxication and drunkenness become attached to, and articulated with, particular concerns about sinfulness, delinquency and/or vice; the shifting and unstable ideas about the responsible, autonomous self who may be more or less accountable for states of intoxication and drunkenness and a range of consequences that might flow from these states; the ways in which personal and social consequences of intoxication and drunkenness – often related to concerns about health, public order, the regulation and licensing of the production, distribution, sale and consumption of alcohol, and ideals associated with prohibition and temperance movements – have tended to be filtered through concerns about the supposed moral delinquency of certain groups, social classes, and ethnic populations.

In the final sections of that chapter we present an account of the ways in which the news media produces, comments on and translates contemporary concerns and difficulties associated with the problems of intoxication and drunkenness. The discussion there will provide an outline of the analysis and commentary that will be developed in greater detail in the following chapters.

In Chapter 2 we present a discussion of the ways in which psychological, biological and medical expertise struggles over definitions of intoxication and drunkenness. In these struggles we see different forms of expertise attempting to develop more sophisticated ways to identify, define, measure and quantify states of intoxication and drunkenness. In these attempts we see an emphasis on what might be called objective, quantifiable, generalisable, 'scientific' measures, and the applications of these in various medical and psychological contexts in which the physical and mental health and safety dimensions of intoxication and drunkenness are of primary interest. As the discussion in that chapter demonstrates, these attempts are not very successful in removing ambiguity, uncertainty and debate from definitions, measurements, and calculations.

Chapter 3 provides an account of the ways in which disciplines such as sociology, anthropology and human geography understand intoxication and drunkenness. Our aims in this account are to explore some of the cultural, social and symbolic dimensions that shape differing understandings of intoxication and drunkenness. In this chapter we suggest that drinking styles can vary according to cultural background. For example, it is often suggested that southern European drinking is typified by moderate drinking of wine with meals whereas British and northern European drinking is typified by 'bingeing' or drinking beer or spirits to achieve rapid intoxication. Anxieties and ambivalences about drinking cultures that value intoxication are often the subject of media commentary. In such commentary simplified cultural stereotypes are drawn – such as the bingeing British and Australians or the easygoing southern Europeans and sensible Nordic countries – to criticise public behaviour and imagine alternative cultural arrangements. However, the research literature raises questions about these stereotypes, and suggests that processes of globalisation may make the distinctions between 'wet' and 'dry' cultures less than useful.

In that chapter we also identify cross-cultural variation in both biomedical and lay definitions of intoxication and drunkenness. Lay understandings of intoxication and drunkenness are distinct from scientific biomedical and public health definitions. Lay definitions tend to focus on feelings, observable behaviour and short-term effects whereas scientific definitions most often focus on calculations of amounts of alcohol consumed and blood alcohol content. Intoxication and drunkenness are frequently social rather than individual practices and getting drunk with others is valued in some social groups and settings. Our discussion suggests that some drinking settings are strongly linked to drunkenness and intoxication – particularly the night-time economy in post-industrial cities which is a complex and contradictory space. Here, for example, we suggest that the new culture of intoxication identified in the UK literature involves large numbers of young people drinking rapidly to intoxication as a means to achieve pleasure, escape and loss of control.

In Chapter 4 we review media commentary and the research literature that focuses on different populations and the problem of intoxication and drunkenness. Included there is a discussion of young people as a population who present particular concerns in relation to intoxication and drunkenness. We also present a limited account of media commentary and research on the raft of issues that are associated with understandings of intoxication and drunkenness and Indigenous populations (in this case in Australia). These issues present a minefield for review and discussion. The political, cultural, social and economic dimensions of the history of colonialism, dispossession, and marginalisation of Indigenous populations in Australia are things that make an appearance in this commentary and research. We also present a discussion of the research literature on gender differences related to intoxication and drunkenness. The discussion there makes it clear that different rules and moral codes still apply to the ways in which men and women drink, often to levels of intoxication and drunkenness. For the most part intoxication and drunkenness appear to be expected of males and are seen as deviant in females. This is not to say that male intoxication and drunkenness is not seen as a problem and particular groups are the targets of legal interventions, particularly related to issues around public safety. There is evidence, however, that young women are adopting more traditionally male drinking styles and the reasons for this are not yet well known.

Finally, in Chapter 5 we present a discussion of the ways in which the problems of intoxication and drunkenness are understood, interpreted and acted upon when they become issues or concerns to be managed, regulated or subjected to legal considerations and judgment. In that chapter we provide an account of some of the ways in which media commentary tends to focus on the anti-social, even criminal, consequences of intoxication and drunkenness, and, for the media, the always incomplete, problematic and ineffectual ways that governments respond to and attempt to manage these issues. This background discussion leads to a review of the legal and criminological research and commentary on issues such as: the ways in which intoxication and drunkenness may mitigate personal responsibilities and accountabilities; the particular nature of choice, consent and responsibility in cases of sexual assault when intoxication is a factor; the dilemmas associated with various regulations related to the promotion and policing of the Responsible Serving of Alcohol (RSA) in various contexts; and the relationships between intoxication, violence and gender.

Research notes

There are two important additions at the end of this book that indicate the scope and nature of the literature that we reviewed, and a further reading list. In Appendix A we describe the research methodology that has guided our review, and we include descriptions of the ways we searched both the academic literature and news media commentary. Appendix B is a 'further reading' section, which includes two types of literature which are not included in the references list. First we include references that are cited within citations in this book. Secondly, we include articles that were located during our search but which, at the time, we considered of marginal relevance for inclusion. These may provide a useful resource for those with an interest in the discussions and debates we present here.

Chapter 1

The problems of intoxication and drunkenness: A brief background and history

I therefore turned my attention more particularly to the young; and as my residence was, for some years previous to 1816, on the south side of the river, the most direct way to which lay through the Saltmarket, the very "St Giles of Glasgow", my eyes and ears were shocked several times a day by the profanity, indecency, filth, and vice, which were exhibited by hordes of young and old, and even infants, who were growing up pests to society, and ruined in themselves, for whose souls or bodies no one seemed to care, and whose wretchedness was enough to disgrace a professedly Christian community. Could nothing be done to stem this torrent of vice and ungodliness? [...] My object was to seize a dozen of these wild human beings on the streets, and try what, by the blessing of God, might be done with them. (David Stow, nineteenth century social reformer, cited in Hunter 1994, 10–11; see Appendix B)

An evening stroll in Sydney in the early 1990s: It was as if William Hogarth's Gin Lane stretched for blocks. The streets were littered with drunks, some vomiting where they stood. The footpaths outside the hotels were strewn with broken glass. People argued with and hurled abuse at one another. Others with vacant eyes stood mumbling soundlessly to themselves, arms whirling like aimless windmills. Through the streets surged packs of feral teenagers with brutish faces and foul, mindless mouths. (Graham Goodman, journalist/commentator in *The Bulletin* [not referenced], cited in Eckersley 1992, 7; see Appendix B)

Introduction

The problems of intoxication and drunkenness – of their definition from different perspectives for different purposes; of their measurement; of the regulation, policing and management of their causes and consequences; of the ways in which they impact on different populations and groups; of the often moral dimensions and concerns that attach to them – are not unique to the late twentieth and early twenty-first centuries. Yet, in the often frenzied, often sensationalist, often politicised, often morally charged contemporary commentaries and public debates about intoxication and drunkenness there is a sense that these problems have sprung freshly from what is also, often, seen as the uniquely problematic, even declining, morally bankrupt, permissive social, cultural and economic landscapes of our times. Our opening quotes in this chapter attest to some of the problems with imagining the problems of intoxication and drunkenness in this way.

As indicated in the introduction to this book, a key concern of the discussion here is to identify, map and review the ways in which intoxication and drunkenness present as particular problems in different contexts and from a variety of perspectives. In order to provide a degree of contextual detail to this discussion this chapter will provide some background to these problems – both historical and contemporary. In saying this, our aims here are somewhat modest. There are any number of more detailed, in-depth historical accounts of the sorts of problems and issues that we have identified as being associated with intoxication and drunkenness. Included here might be accounts such as those of Eric Burns (2004) in his *The Spirits of America: A Social History of Alcohol*; Iain Gately's (2008) *Drink: A Cultural History of Alcohol*; John Greenaway's (2003) *Drink and British Politics Since 1830: A Study in Policy-Making*; or Mack Holt's (2006) *Alcohol: A Social and Cultural History* (see Appendix B). In addition, a number of these accounts might have a particular focus on a particular period, certain populations, or limited geographical/national contexts. We do not have these intentions or outcomes in mind here.

Alongside these qualifications about the extent and detail of our historical analysis we also want to make clear that in sketching some of the contours of the contemporary landscape from which these issues emerge, we draw extensively on diverse accounts in a number of key, mass circulation newspapers in the US, the UK, Australia and New Zealand. As we indicate in Appendix A, our reasons for this approach are largely pragmatic and, determined by the fact that the print media presents a readily searchable archive in relation to these concerns. In addition, within these media spaces we are able to identify a number of concerns that will be examined in greater detail in subsequent chapters. The benefit of introducing a number of these problems at this time and in the form of media commentary is that in some important respects the various media platforms, and in this instance the *print* media, provide a more accessible space – but also, often, a less-restrained and less-scholarly space – in which problems associated with intoxication and drunkenness are aired, debated and translated from more specialised, arcane, expert contexts that, by definition, are not as readily accessed by the general, lay public.

With these qualifications in mind this chapter presents a historical account that focuses on a number of themes that appear to recur – often in different, but related forms – at a number of points during the seventeenth, eighteenth and nineteenth centuries, and which continue to echo through the late twentieth and early twenty-first centuries. These themes include the following: the ways in which understandings of intoxication and drunkenness become attached to, and articulated with, particular concerns about sinfulness, delinquency and/or vice; the shifting and unstable ideas about the responsible, autonomous self who may be more or less accountable for states of intoxication and drunkenness and the range of consequences that might flow from these states; the ways in which personal and social consequences of intoxication and drunkenness – often related to concerns about health, public order, the regulation and licensing of the production, distribution, sale and consumption of alcohol, and ideals associated with prohibition and temperance movements – have tended to be filtered through concerns about the supposed moral delinquency of certain groups, social classes, and ethnic populations.

In the final sections of this chapter we present an account of the ways in which the media produces, comments on and translates contemporary concerns and difficulties associated with the problems of intoxication and drunkenness. As we have just indicated, our discussion at that time sketches much of the background to the analysis and commentary in chapters that will follow.

Historical roots?

The story goes that the night before the Battle of Hastings King Harold's soldiers stayed up drinking while the Normans were at prayer and William of Malmesbury claimed that the success of the Normans can at least be partly put down to the drunkenness of the English soldiers, which led them to take on the Norman army "more with rashness and precipitate fury than with military skill" (quoted by Barr, 1995, p. 26 [see Appendix B]). Malmesbury went on to note that the Normans soon adopted the English habits of drinking and eating to excess. Although Barr does sound a word of caution about the bias of the Norman William of Malmesbury he also notes that: "...there is no doubt that the new Anglo-Norman nation that was formed by force in the eleventh century retained the reputation for drunkenness that had been created by its purely English predecessors" (Barr 1995, p. 26). (Herring et al. 2008a, 477)

Of course, alcohol, intoxication and drunkenness have been a part of human society for thousands of years (Ben-Noun 2002). How alcohol is used, individual and societal responses to it, and the consequences of intoxication and drunkenness change through time and place. In 1989 and 2006 Nordlund (2008), for example, conducted a follow-up study on an initial survey conducted in Norway in 1964. In this study she concluded that 'the general view on alcohol use and abuse has changed radically in the last 40 years or so. People today accept both heavier and more frequent intoxication before they call it abuse and this applies whether the drinking takes place among friends or in solitude' (Nordlund 2008, 90).

In Herring et al.'s (2008a) review of the historical precedents for the recent increased media attention and policy obsession with binge drinking in the English context, they argue, drawing from Barr (1995), that 'heavy drinking has always been part of the British character and moreover this has distinguished the inhabitants of Britain from its continental neighbours'. Drawing again from Barr (1995, 25) they reach back to the eighth century to:

> missionary and reformer Saint Boniface who although born in Britain spent most of his life in Europe, [and who] in his old age wrote to Cuthbert, the Archbishop of Canterbury, with reports claiming that: "In your dioceses the vice of drunkenness is too frequent. This is an evil peculiar to pagans and to our race. Neither the Franks nor the Gauls nor the Lombards nor the Romans nor the Greeks commit it". (Herring et al. 2008a, 477)

So, are the various problems associated with intoxication and drunkenness recent phenomena? Do current concerns just revisit old ones? What might be novel about these issues? A useful starting point for this discussion can be found in the ways in which, at the start of the twenty-first century, sections of the media try to explain the issues related to the problems of intoxication and drunkenness in settings such as Australia, the UK and the US. A key theme in these discussions by media commentators (though not the only one) is a reference to the historical roots of these issues. Here there a sense that there are some national, culturally based traits or attributes that pre-dispose the English, or the Australians, or, often by inference or by comparison, some others – such as Mediterranean Europeans – to understand, think about or use alcohol in ways that lead to intoxication and drunkenness, or, indeed, to guard against these possibilities.

Sections of the British and American media, for example, consider Britain to be the archetype of a problem drinking culture. According to Julie Burchill (2001), the English are 'a hedonistic, freebooting, swashbuckling race who, when not allowed to go around the world conquering other people, drown our sorrows any way we can, crouched out here on our cold, little island; as lonesome, untamed and hardcore as the Corsicans or Cypriots on theirs'. The inevitable result of such drinking is violence. As one teenage drinker told *The Guardian*, 'it's what Britain is all about at the weekend... getting pissed, causing a bit of trouble, having a laugh' (Morris 2001; see also Lyall 2007; Midgley 2001a). And Sarah Lyall (2006) writes in *The New York Times*:

> Britons have long been known for their love of alcohol and their belief that among the naturally repressed, drinking is an essential prelude to relaxation and joie de vivre... But Britons are just as notorious for their tendency to segue seamlessly from drinking into brawling, to overdo it and then behave like loutish hooligans.

Annie Britton, an epidemiologist studying the drinking habits of British civil servants, has observed that drunkenness is 'certainly a national characteristic. Other countries, for example, tend to be ashamed or mortified by drunkenness. The UK is unique in glorifying it with programmes such as the appalling Booze Britain. And our drinking habits have got worse' (*The Guardian* 2006). In an effort to find an historical precedent for the British drinking culture, Frank Boyce, writing in *The Guardian*, invokes the memory of Saint Pyr, a Welsh abbot, who 'got so bladdered one night in AD520, he fell down a well and drowned' (Boyce 2004), while Tristram Hunt, writing in *The Times*, describes the 'British love of drink' as 'one of the great historical truisms' (Hunt 2004). A review of a book on the history of wine even suggested that drunkenness only emerged as a cultural trait in the Dark Ages, and mainly in Britain, whose: 'Anglo-Saxon inhabitants... were the worst offenders of all: there are more references to intoxication there than to the rest of Europe combined' (Lourie 2002).

In the US, some media commentary seeks to explain and understand Americans' drinking by pointing to historical figures who led successful lives despite their drunkenness. Writing in *The New York Times* Pollan (2003), for example, constructs a narrative of the history of the United States in terms of its struggle against alcohol abuse. This narrative begins with the denunciation of 'the excesses of the "alcoholic republic"' by several of the founding fathers, including George Washington, Thomas Jefferson and John Adams, and continues through to Ulysses S. Grant, who was forced out of the Army because of drunkenness (Ramos 2000), only to redeem himself by leading the Union to victory in the Civil War, and ultimately to become President (see also Remini 2000; Brennan 2002; Felten 2006).

For Caleb Carr (2000) writing in *The New York Times*, Grant's emergence from the scourge of drunkenness is reflected in the history of New York, which is celebrated for its ability to succeed in spite of the drunkenness of its residents. Carr (2000) writes, for instance, that one of the 'enduring mysteries' of New York is how it has 'consistently produced some of the great engineering marvels of the world', despite being 'eternally plagued by drunkenness, filth, disease, violence and corruption'. One such plague, writes Kevin Baker (2001a), was the Five Points slum – at one time 'the world's most notorious slum' – which was blighted by prostitution and public drunkenness.

Some sections of the Australian media also seek to frame their discussion of the Australian drinking culture in a historical context. Australia, too, is described as 'a culture that elevates intoxication to national myth' (Farouque 2007). These myths however, are understood and handled in an ambiguous, uncertain way:

> In overall drinking, Australia's population is not the worst in international rankings… We're about in the middle for total per capita consumption among English-speaking countries. "This doesn't mean that there is no problem in Australia, but rather that we, and other comparable countries, have become used to a good deal of problematic drinking as a part of ordinary life". (Farouque 2007)

John Mangan (2004) suggests that the British 'heritage' underpinning Australian culture includes 'Puritanism, drunkenness, pragmatism and distrust of theory, philistinism, dislike of anything showy, theatrical, arty or "too serious", British good sense and the British sense of humour'. For Chris Middendrop (2004), writing in *The Age*, what Germaine Greer calls Australia's long tradition of "ruinous drinking habits" can be traced back to white settlement. It began during initial settlement because white Australians couldn't cope without alcohol. 'It was accepted', Greer writes, 'that without alcohol life in the Great South Land would be unbearable'. In this sort of narrative it is claimed that Australians took to drink as a coping mechanism because they couldn't comprehend the Indigenous people or deal with a surreal landscape.

Drunkenness in Australia is also described as being 'entangled in the legend of male mateship', and is traced to the use of rum as a 'colonial currency' in New South Wales (NSW), and to the nineteenth century gold rush (Farouque 2007; see also Farrelly 2007; Higson 2008). The 'faint stirrings of the nation's social conscience' are attributed to punishments handed out for drunkenness in the new colony (*New Zealand Herald* 2006b), while Middendorp (2004) writes that 'the conspicuous consumption of booze seems to have been one of early Melbourne's more notable attributes'.

While the focus of much of the discussion of a history of drunkenness in the British and Australian print media has been to reflect upon their nation's drinking cultures, they do so not only to revere it, but also to identity points of tension within it – especially with regards to drunkenness amongst young people and women. In nineteenth century Australia, the debates about women and drunkenness emphasised the frailty of women's bodies. It was argued that feminine dispositions 'made them especially prone to… lascivious [behaviour], and hence a danger to themselves and to men (both in terms of their condition in the temporal world and their future in the afterlife)' (Killingsworth 2006, 362). The dangers to/for women in terms of drunkenness were not only framed in biological terms, but, Killingsworth (2006, 362) argues:

> In the case of wives, it was felt that drunkenness reduced women's capacity to (passively) manage and further the family's material and spiritual interests: a drunk woman would not be capable of attending to her children and her husband; and, just as importantly, women who drank were deemed incapable of setting a good moral example for their family (drunken women were often placed with prostitutes at the bottom of the social/moral scale).

Women were not the only concern in relation to drunkenness in Australian history. Graycar (2001, 1–2) argues that nearly half of all convictions in Magistrates' Courts in the first years of the twentieth century were for drunkenness: 'From 1901 to 1906 the number of convictions fell from 57,212 to 45,843 – though convictions as a proportion of cases remained constant at around 90%. It can be seen that a great deal of police and court resources at the beginning of the century were devoted to drunkenness'. At the start of the twenty-first century, public drunkenness has been decriminalised in most parts of Australia, though Graycar argues that drunkenness is still a problem: 'In the first half of the century drunkenness was seen as a crime in itself. Today it is seen as a precipitating factor'.

Paul Kingsnorth (2005) laments the disappearance of traditional pubs, which have 'long been the cornerstone of British culture'. He writes fondly of the Luppitt Inn, which is little more than the front room of 84-year-old Mary Wright's stone farmhouse, and which he describes as 'one of the last custodians of a dying tradition'. He references the French poet Hilaire Belloc's observation that pubs were 'closer to the nation's pulse than the monarchy, the Church of England or the mother of parliaments'. The pub was the 'institution of the ordinary people', the 'indefinable something' of 'discussions... games... drunkenness, the foibles of the landlord, the conviviality, the unpredictable gathering of diverse people'. This is the culture that is lost, writes Kingsnorth, to 'identikit' bars and pubs which promote the kind of mass-drunkenness for which Britain's youth are renowned.

Polly Toynbee (2005), writing in *The Guardian*, confesses that 'British drinking culture as we know it is already repulsively uncivilized'. As it is described by *The Guardian*, the drinking culture in Britain today, especially amongst young people, is particularly problematic. The paper describes young Britons as 'men and women who are fully committed to the cause of alcoholic annihilation', emptying 'both their bladders and stomachs' in 'the streets of capitals across mainland Europe' (*The Guardian* 2004b). And this is despite evidence that:

> the damage done by drink is increasing [in the UK], as alcohol-related deaths from cirrhosis, hepatitis and alcohol poisoning have soared by 18% over the past five years. Those figures are dwarfed by the 22,000 violent drinking deaths in car accidents and pub stabbings, with half of violent crime due to drink. Last week's figures showed under-age "drunk and disorderly" prosecutions up by 25%. (Toynbee 2005)

Barton (2007) seeks to balance out such reports with evidence that Britons' drinking habits are changing. He cites transformations in the ways in which cider is understood, branded and used as an example. Whereas cider was once 'the tipple of bus stops, a route to quick, cheap drunkenness' – 'the preserve of teenagers', who were attracted by ciders' 'exciting names and bright packaging' (Morris 2001) – it has now been 'made respectable'. Today, cider is 'no longer swigged lukewarm from cans, it comes in glass bottles and is served over ice, while the emphasis is placed maturely upon the apple flavour, not cider's ability to get drinkers inebriated at pace' (Barton 2007). Here it might be considered that cider represents a certain maturation of

British drinking culture, while also containing within it a source of the problems with that culture.

And as Leo Benedictus (2007) points out, studies suggest that cider might actually provide a counter to the health problems caused by alcohol abuse. Citing the *Journal of Agricultural and Food Chemistry*, he argues that cider 'contains high concentrations of phenolics and antioxidants', which are thought to play a part in preventing heart disease and some forms of cancer. However, Benedictus also suggests that cider contains far higher concentrations of cheap alcohol, leading to outbreaks of particularly energetic rural drunkenness on an epic scale. As a result, even though cider itself has transformed into a drink that is positioned as more sophisticated, the habits of its drinkers may not have matured in the same ways. Benedictus (2007) claims that 'when the new season's plastic flagons appear on shelves in the south-west, something takes hold of local men'. These men 'take to the streets to celebrate together, and finally to fight one another, in scenes seldom seen elsewhere in Britain since the darker days of the hundred years war'.

Gin, ale, vice, sinfulness and personal responsibility: The changing face of the problem of intoxication and drunkenness

In this section we want to explore in a little more detail the ways in which concerns about intoxication and drunkenness take a particular shape at certain points in history. Our focus here will be on highlighting some of the shifts in understanding the causes and consequences of intoxication and drunkenness. These movements include changes in the ways in which the individual is held to be responsible – legally and morally – for their conduct and behaviours: both in terms of being and becoming drunk, and for what the person might do when drunk.

Herring et al. (2008a, 478) make a strong claim that current concerns about binge drinking are not new and that there is a long history of attempts to regulate consumption and the purchasing of alcohol. They argue, for example, that the first licensing act dates back to Henry VII's reign in 1494. They identify three patterns of governmental responses to alcohol use in England at this time:

> First, there is a discernable pattern of periods of inactivity interspersed by periods of heightened concern and activity, often in the form of legislation. Second, these periods of activity are usually the result of concerns about the socioeconomic impact of alcohol – generally

drunkenness and especially public drunkenness. Third, women's drinking is often singled out as a matter of particular concern.

A couple of centuries later, between 1720 and 1751, the gin epidemic, or gin craze, emerged as the 'first modern moral panic over intoxication' (Nicholls 2006, 133). At this time 'gin consumption in England rose from half a gallon in 1688 to 19 million gallons in 1742' (Barr 1995, 189; cited in Herring et al. 2008a, 479). In this moral panic alcohol use emerges as a marker of the supposed moral character of different social classes. It was gin more than ale, or any other alcoholic beverage, which raised the alarm bells of government concern:

> One of the most famous public debates regarding alcohol concerned the relative merits of drinking beer or gin. This debate was underpinned by spatial metaphors of Gin Lane (a place of immoral behaviour – particularly by women – violence, slum life, disorder and potential revolution), and Beer Street (a place of joviality, business success, progress, modern civilized streets, houses and shops; see O'Malley and Valverde, 2004, [Appendix B] for a detailed overview). Gin was cheap and plentiful and hence was the favoured drink of the working classes. At the time, beer was considered to be a healthier alternative; hence gin became central to middle-class anxieties over working-class drunkenness, immorality and unruly crowds, and thus a necessary focus of legislation and taxation that ultimately led to reduced usage. (Jayne et al. 2006, 454)

While not focusing on divisions between social classes, Herring et al. (2008a, 479) argue that 'gin drinking was an issue of grave concern for the contemporary policy makers and opinion formers' and that 'concerns were primarily around public drunkenness, high morbidity and mortality rates and the neglect of children by their drunken mothers'. In eighteenth century England 'gin was seen as producing a new kind of drunkenness', described by some as causing '"a Kind of instantaneous Drunkenness, where a Man hath no time to recollect or think whether he has had enough or no" (Tucker 1751, 21; quoted by Nicholls 2003, 129)' (cited in Herring et al. 2008a, 481). We can see echoes of these forms of thinking in twenty-first century concerns with products like *alcopops* and energy drinks mixed with alcohol.

Understandings of intoxication and drunkenness have a long history of being linked to debates about individual responsibility. In England in the late seventeenth century, drunkenness was firmly associated with sin, and crime pamphlets of the time proclaimed the potential '"chain of sin" that would lead a person from a lesser infraction such as swearing or Sabbath breaking to fighting, theft, and the most heinous of crimes, murder' (Rabin 2005, 457). At this time, the threat was perceived for both rich and poor, however, Rabin (2005, 457) argues that 'English representations of the relationship between alcohol and crime shifted between the late seventeenth century and the middle of the eighteenth century'. A new discourse arose, Rabin argues, in which rich and poor were considered differently affected by alcohol, with implications for the evolution of the notion of responsibility and the acceptability of the excuse of intoxication in a court of law. Of course, at various points in time, legal theory draws from social, political and economic contexts, and it is that which we focus on here. Rabin (2005, 457) argues that:

> Drunkenness among the wealthy was often described as a private vice, while drunkenness and addiction to alcohol among the laboring poor were said to pose "political mischiefs" that increased crime and threatened to break down gender roles and the structure of the family. The rise of this new discourse about alcohol did not displace older explanations for crime, but it did affect definitions of responsibility.

Rabin's (2005, 459–461) discussion highlights how, in the context of intense religious faith, drunkenness was understood as a particularly evil behaviour in pamphlets published during the seventeenth and eighteenth centuries. Drunkenness was identified 'as "cursed and abominable," the "queen" of sins, "the root of all evil, the rot of all good"'. Given the seriousness of the sin of drunkenness, 'the crimes that followed... were to be punished severely with no room for mitigation or pardon'. However, Rabin argues that as ideas about an individualised, autonomous, responsible self began to emerge during the seventeenth century Enlightenment, the understandings of intoxication – particularly the notion of 'responsibility for acts committed while intoxicated' – also underwent a transformation. While intoxication was not considered a legitimate excuse for criminal behaviour, it can be found mentioned in court proceedings, and begins to be seen as a mitigating factor in understanding and punishing certain criminal behaviours:

> defendants argued for acquittal, mitigation, or pardon based on their sense that drunkenness reduced their level of responsibility for crime. The number of cases in which drunkenness was mentioned rose between 1681 and 1751, but the proportion of cases did not. The rate of acquittal

and mitigation for cases in which drunkenness was mentioned ranged from 50 percent to 100 percent, with an average of 71 percent over the whole period. (Rabin 2005, 466)

In spite of these transformations, not everyone agreed that intoxication was a reasonable excuse for criminal behaviour. Rabin (2005, 461–462), for example, comments on the liberal philosopher John Locke's interpretation of such an excuse:

> Locke cited the coexistence of sanity and insanity in the same person as "making them two persons". For the insane, Locke argued that legal responsibility for crime was suspended because the "self was changed" and "the self-same person was no longer in that man". Unlike the mad person, however, the drunken offender was held accountable for all of his behaviour. Within Locke's understanding of a contingent self, displaced by circumstance, madness was the unique exception to legal accountability. Locke explained that the law could not excuse an offence committed under the influence of alcohol because human laws "cannot distinguish certainly what is real, what is counterfeit; and so the ignorance in drunkenness or sleep is not admitted as a plea". For Locke, the fact that a jury could not corroborate a state of mind exposed the limits of law and disqualified the excuse of drunkenness.

Locke's discussion of the problems of intoxication and responsibility contributed to more public debate about these issues at the time. These concerns were also addressed by the eighteenth century German philosopher Immanuel Kant who proposed the importance of using reason to balance our interpretation of experience. Nicholls (2006, 136) argues that: 'By muddling up our sense of our selves and our capacity for rational thought, in addition to undermining our will (both in terms of the choices one makes when drunk and the decision whether to drink or not), drunkenness should be anathema to a Kantian'. However, as Nicholls (2006, 136) shows:

> Kant himself was often remarkably indulgent towards alcohol – describing wine-parties, for example, as "merry, boisterous, and teeming with wit" (Kant, 1978: 60 [see Appendix B]). While insisting that "all stultifying drunkenness, such as comes from opium or brandy... which does not encourage sociability or the exchange of thought, has something shameful about it" (1978: 59). Kant only condemns specific forms of intoxication which he ascribes to specific intoxicants. He also asserts that the "openheartedness" that drink produces is a "moral quality" (1978: 71).

Rabin's (2005, 476) discussion and analysis highlights the shift from the characterisation of drunkenness as a sin, to an approach that focused on the ways in which drunkenness should be considered in punishing criminal behaviour associated with it. In the seventeenth century so-called murder pamphlets 'depicted drunkenness as a sin that signalled a criminal fate, threatened the social order, and demanded the most severe punishment'. During the next hundred years there was a shift in thinking about drunkenness, its consequences, and the nature of individual responsibility under its influence. Rabin (2005, 469) discusses how drunkenness was used in the courts as a mitigating factor, a situation that speaks directly to the ways in which the autonomous, responsible self of the Enlightenment – a self held to be ultimately responsible for its own behaviours and destiny – is compromised by states of drunkenness:

> Drunkenness appeared as an excuse for a wide variety of crimes in pretrial depositions and trial transcripts. Along with the most common crime, theft, defendants introduced drunkenness as an excuse when charged with attempted rape, sedition, and arson. The alcohol plea was used to explain accidental deaths resulting from quarrels as well as domestic disturbances and other erratic, violent behavior. Defendants blamed the mental state induced by alcohol for relatively harmless effects such as memory loss and for more serious conditions in which a defendant's intoxication made him or her susceptible to persuasion to commit a crime. Two kinds of excuses emerge: in the first, a simple drunkenness plea, offenders argued for diminished responsibility. The second linked the effects of intoxication with insanity.

So, by the eighteenth century, as Rabin (2005, 477) identifies:

> Despite the legal commentators' insistence that legal and moral responsibility had to be understood separately where drunkenness was concerned, testimony of participants in the courtroom reflected a belief that drunkenness could mitigate the offender's guilt. Judicial authorities and defendants alike considered alcohol powerful enough to leave them "incapacitated" and "insensible with the effects of liquor".

Rabin (2005, 477) argues that court reports reflecting questions 'about both the defendant's and the victim's level of intoxication and capacity to reason reflected the court's interest in the subject'. Further, this eighteenth century legal and judicial concern with reason reflected a Lockean 'preoccupation with mental states and those circumstances that might compromise or displace one's rational capacities'. In the courtroom, defendants and witnesses attempted 'to separate a generally innocent character from a specific criminal act'. In these attempts to imagine a separation between the crime and the criminal 'there was undoubtedly a connection between the kind of crime committed and the explanation attached to it'. However, a state of intoxication was not equally applicable to all criminal acts:

> The excuse of drunkenness suited certain opportunistic offenses better than others: a brawl in an alehouse, a seditious toast to the Pretender, or an impulsive theft might more readily be explained with a defense of drunkenness. In all cases, defendants claimed that their mental state, induced by alcohol, absolved them from at least some of the responsibility for their crimes. The use of drunkenness as a mitigating circumstance was possible because the law had long recognized that various sorts of mental states were exculpatory. (Rabin 2005, 477)

While not working to completely free a defendant from guilt:

> In this eighteenth-century dialogue of mitigation, the plea of drunkenness emerged as an important trope, a formula through which defendants and judicial authorities negotiated mitigation. Rather than absolute guilt, the plea of drunkenness suggested notions of partial responsibility, a spectrum of culpability in which drunkenness might place one closer to the excusable end without implying innocence. Judicial authorities may have agreed, and as attested by the high rate of mitigation in cases where drunkenness was mentioned, they often accepted this explanation; it did not serve as grounds for acquittal, but it frequently justified a less severe punishment based on the defendant's "fuddled mind". (Rabin 2005, 477)

Various literary and artistic figures from the eighteenth and nineteenth centuries provide other interpretations of the character of intoxication and drunkenness at this time, and of the ways in which different individuals might understand these states. Alcohol, and specifically intoxication, was seen as providing an outlet for rebellion against *bourgeois sensibilities* and a way to participate in something bigger than oneself:

> Oscar Wilde's quip that "a glass of absinthe is as poetical as anything in the world" for example, sums up the increasing use of intoxication among Romantic and early Modernist artists as a trope for the rejection of bourgeois sensibilities, the pursuit of "ironic transcendence"... and

the celebration of all sorts of "higher pleasures". George Moore, in his memoirs of life in bohemian late 19th century Paris, described the tavern as "a snort of defiance at the hearth"… while Charles Baudelaire ascribed the desire for intoxication to a highly refined, "yearn[ing] for the infinite". (Nicholls 2006, 144–145)

Yet, as Rabin (2005, 466) argues, the ramifications of drinking to intoxication for rich and poor were not alike and, again, we find ourselves back in the courtroom. By the mid-eighteenth century:

> excessive drinking among the poor was [seen to be] more serious and had more ominous ramifications than drinking among the wealthy. The notion that the poor had less of an ability to control the effects of alcohol on their emotions and their behavior was applied in the courtroom where defendants, their witnesses, lawyers, and even prosecutors introduced evidence about alcohol as a factor that could mitigate one's responsibility for crime.

The courts both reflected changing public understandings of intoxication and drunkenness and influenced thinking of the time. In addition there were other influences, including governmental acts and laws which influenced the use of alcohol. As Mason (2001, 109) argues these Acts and Laws, which can be understood as both leading, and emerging from, social, cultural and political understandings of the problems associated with alcohol use and consumption – including drunkenness – were influential in shaping changes in the use of alcohol in nineteenth century England:

> On July 23, 1830, Parliament passed "An Act to permit the general Sale of Beer and Cyder by Retail in England." Commonly known as the Beer Act of 1830, this law called for a major overhaul of the way beer was taxed and distributed in England and Wales. In place of a sixteenth-century statute that had given local magistrates complete control over the licensing of brewers and publicans, the Beer Act stipulated that a new type of drinking establishment, the beer shop, or beer house, could now be opened by any rate-paying householder in England or Wales (Scotland and Ireland had their own drink laws).

Mason (2001, 109) argues that this new permit was welcomed and its use spread quickly throughout England: 'So attractive was the idea of the beer house to both retailers and consumers, in fact, that within six months of the Beer Act's taking effect, over 24,000 beer houses had sprung up throughout

England and Wales'. Again, the possible range of consequences of this new permitting system was understood largely in terms of apparently *self-evident* difference between the social classes. The self-evident nature of working class vices is, from this perspective, heightened by the ways in which beer and ale were made available and regulated. Mason (2001, 110) argues that:

> From the moment the new law took effect on October 10, 1830, many members of England's privileged classes complained about the widespread debauchery the law had supposedly incited. In a steady stream of sermons, poems, crime reports, and stump speeches, the beer house came to represent intemperance, idleness, and a lack of discipline – in short, all the self-destructive vices of the working class.

Mason (2001, 110) also argues that evidence indicates that the Beer Act not only 'initially increased levels of drunkenness among England's working class'. Even more significantly, he argues that its long-term consequence was in its effect on the perceptions of working class drunkenness. Put simply, the long-term legacy of the Act was that the middle and upper classes saw drunkenness as a problem of the working classes:

> From 1830 until the 1870s, it was counted as something of a truism in middle- and upper-class society that the Beer Act had touched off an irreversible course of working class drunkenness. Social commentators of all political persuasions, ranging from the conservative Henry Mayhew to the communist Friedrich Engels, viewed the Beer Act as a defining moment in the fortunes of England's working class.

Was this a new kind of drunkenness, or a new set of ideas about the nature, causes and consequences of drunkenness as a social problem, or was it just a continuation of the Gin Craze from years before? One element of difference that appears clear is that the context or spaces of drinking events had shifted: 'A working-class culture previously centered around the home, the church, and the work-site now quite clearly found its focal point in the neighborhood beer house' (Mason 2001, 111). Drawing on the commentary of Friedrich Engels (1844; see Appendix B), Mason (2001, 121) points out that 'beer shops had become the hubs of Manchester's slums' and the outcome of the Act was effecting the working class most prominently.

Engels, a colleague of Karl Marx, and commentator on the conditions of the English working class during the depths of the Industrial Revolution, was quick to note that the blame for working class drunkenness lay not with the workers themselves, but with the nation's leaders and the system they had created. In ratifying the Beer Act, Engels argued, Parliament 'facilitated the spread of intemperance by bringing a beerhouse, so to say, to everybody's door' (cited in Mason 2001, 152). As Mason (2001, 121) suggests: 'Although he stops short of arguing, as some Temperance workers were wont to do, that the Beer Act was little more than a conspiracy of the rich to subjugate the poor, Engels insists that the poor should not be held accountable for conditions over which they have no control'. In many respects this is a markedly different view of intoxication and drunkenness than we find in religious and philosophical accounts which emphasise ideas of sinfulness and personal responsibility.

Not only can drunkenness in the late nineteenth century be understood through the prism of class, but also through geography and public space (though of course all of these three are related). Beckingham (2008, 306), for example, argues that the English city of Liverpool was considered the drunkenness 'shock city' of the nineteenth century. In this instance statistics and geography are used to explore various ways of understanding drunkenness:

> Liverpool's unenviable position can be seen in the evidence collected by the House of Lords Select Committee on Intemperance in 1878. Data from annual police reports presented to the committee revealed a clear north–south divide, with northern towns revealed as 3.5 times more drunken than southern towns and Liverpool as the most drunken town in England and Wales. The committee was presented with a cartographic realization of this data that located drunkenness firmly north of a line from the Severn to the Humber. Crucially, drunkenness was felt to threaten society as much as it did the drunkard.

It can be argued, however, that particular definitions of drunkenness, as both a 'vice' and as a 'public offence' actually provided statistics that 'were both grounded in and helped to reinforce a problematic geography of drunkenness' (Beckingham 2008, 306). For Beckingham (2008, 302–309) it is the public aspect of drunkenness that raised concerns: 'drunkenness only became a problem, and therefore a statistic, when it became a public problem'. In his discussion Beckingham questions the reliability of statistics such as those which define levels of public drunkenness because, he argues, not only is such a state difficult to define objectively but also record keeping practices change from place to place and over time. As such, he argues that different cities have different approaches to drunkenness, and in order to understand it, intervention practices and magisterial actions must also be mapped, concluding that, 'any statistics, therefore, are dependent upon contingency and context'.

Beckingham (2008, 309) goes on to illustrate the many contingencies of understanding drunkenness and intoxication in a particular time and place. He quotes a head Constable, Leonard Dunning, who claimed that:

> Drunkenness may or may not amount to an offence against the law, if it does it may or may not come under the notice of a police-man, if it does he may or may not think fit to interfere either by arresting or reporting the offender, if he does his superiors may or may not consider the case a proper one for prosecution: to measure intemperance as a vice by the numbers of offences against public order which survive all these "ifs" is about as logical as it would be to measure the number of people who break their legs in the city as a whole by the number picked up in the streets by the police ambulances.

The difficulties associated with defining and identifying an individual's state of drunkenness was acknowledged in the nineteenth century in England when it fell to individual police officers to make this call:

> In 1871 the Liverpool Critic called for clarity from magistrates on what could be considered "drunk". It noted that different people might appear to be drunk when staggering along the street but might be clear in the head, while others might be cloudy in the head but walking without trouble. (Beckingham 2008, 307)

The lesson from history here is one, as Beckingham (2008, 310–311) argues, related to the problem of defining, mapping and quantifying the problem of drunkenness. In nineteenth century England, as at other times in history: 'statistics for drunkenness reflected the nature of policing, and therefore of public and governmental pressures applied through the Watch Committee, the body of councillors responsible for organizing the policing of the town'. Beckingham's point is worth quoting at length here for its relevance to the approach taken to dimensions of the problems of drunkenness and intoxication today:

> The greater issue is the use made of those statistics. Those uses did not just tell facts based on geography; the geography of drinking was there in the production of the epistemological "fact" of drunkenness. Significantly, deciding when reason and responsibility is lost such that that person enters the statistical food-chain remains discursively constructed

today. Hence maybe it is just as useful to reassert the importance of contextualizing twenty-first century drinking and drunkenness in an understanding of discretionary and uneven policing of spaces of alcohol consumption. When this is done for the nineteenth-century, we discover that the numbers behind those 'facts' of drunkenness tell us more about their compilers and campaigners than about those who, as numbers, are recorded in them.

In a similar vein, Jayne et al. (2006, 455) recall a study by Monkkonen from 1981 (see Appendix B) which draws a distinction between official statistics of arrests for public drunkenness and life on the ground in 22 cities in the US between 1860 and 1920. Official statistics are connected with political concerns and the changing nature of definitions:

> Despite statistical sources identifying a general decline over the period, Monkkenon shows that some cities (such as San Francisco, St Louis, Buffalo and Louisville) saw consistent growth in arrests for drunkenness and a further nine cities also showed increases at various times throughout this period. He also challenges the picture provided by such statistics by suggesting that, rather than drunken disorder significantly declining, it was political concerns and associated changing legal definitions (and different policing in different localities) that explain these statistics.

Temperance and prohibition: Some reflections from the United States

In this section we do not propose to provide a detailed history of temperance movements and of prohibition campaigns in the US. Again, such an account is beyond the scope of our discussion. Our purpose, instead, is to briefly sketch some of the tensions and understandings of alcohol and intoxication and drunkenness that gave temperance and prohibition movements their particular character in the US – up until the start of the twentieth century. This discussion references a number of the points we have developed to this stage. Namely, that the problems of intoxication and drunkenness take on different characteristics in different times, spaces and places, and in relation to the behaviours and dispositions of different groups and populations. These characteristics, however, can echo far beyond these times, spaces and places.

A point of entry into this discussion is provided by Stolberg's (2006, 41–46) discussion of Alexis de Tocqueville's observations about the always ambivalent and ambiguous ways in which alcohol was understood in colonial and post-revolutionary America. As Stolberg argues, 'Alcohol was a pervasive part of the early American pharmacopoeia'. However, as in England at the time, drunkenness was, in many contexts, understood in terms of sinfulness: 'alcohol tolerance was apparently widespread among Americans since despite relatively high levels of consumption, public drunkenness was rare'. The religious language of sinfulness was prominent in making sense of the problems that arose from drunkenness:

> Drunkenness, perhaps influenced by Puritanical traditions, was regarded as a sin, as a "wicked example". For example, Alexis de Tocqueville (1835/2002: 38 [see Appendix B]), in reviewing the legal codes of early America, noted that in the Connecticut Code of 1650 that drunkenness was severely punished; in addition, innkeepers were prohibited by the Code of 1650 from supplying their customers with more than a certain amount of wine (Tocqueville, 1835/2002: 38). Magistrates who "were guilty of drunkenness" were targets of early American social reformers.

This religiously shaped environment appears to have been influential in containing public displays of drunkenness. However, de Tocqueville notes a particularly American aspect of the relationship to drunkenness which led to viewing drunkenness in increasingly medicalised ways:

> In a note to his *Democracy in America*, Tocqueville (1835/2002: 232) observed that more than 270,000 Americans were members of temperance societies and had pledged to abstain from strong liquors. He concluded that the tendency of Americans to engage collectively in associations, such as temperance societies to combat drunkenness, was a distinguishing feature of their democracy. There were, accordingly, ambivalent and, at times, contradictory views held during the seventeenth, eighteenth, and nineteenth centuries on the roles of alcohol in healing, in society generally, and toward problems associated with alcohol consumption in America. While alcohol consumption was an accepted part of early American life, including the medicinal roles of alcohol in health and healing, habitual excessive drinking was increasingly becoming a recognized problematic area of concern. (Stolberg 2006, 49)

Ferentzy (2001, 365) argues that in seventeenth century America a sense of 'compulsion or loss of control is not central to pre-industrial ideas about drunkenness'. Indeed, a discouragement of drunkenness was only one aspect of religious-based moderation: immoderation was a sin with regard to the excess use of, or attachment to, many things – not just alcohol. In other words, the concept of alcoholism did not exist as something separate from so-called 'diseases' of sin. Ferentzy cautions against reading terms such as 'sickness' or 'disease' in relation to drunkenness in the same medicalised way that we would understand them today. As Ferentzy argues, 'passionate preachers', might have used these terms to denote any number of things that they considered immoral or sinful.

In framing drunkenness as a moral issue, alcoholism, or chronic drunkenness, was initially not considered a disease. Instead early temperance movements 'looked to legislation as a way to control use' (Stolberg 2006, 84). The medicalisation, or initially, the scientific interest in chronic drunkenness nonetheless developed out of early temperance movements. In the late eighteenth century, 'Rush was the first American physician to identify chronic drunkenness as a distinct disease with a progressive nature and accompanying personal and social complications' (Stolberg 2006, 42). The full history of the development of alcoholism as a specific disease is beyond the scope of our discussion. However, it is interesting to note here that there is indeed a history to this idea, and that it has not always been considered a specific medical phenomenon. Indeed, Stolberg explains that 'by the late nineteenth century, it could also be observed that: "Many physicians, especially specialists who make treatment of drunkenness a business and source of profit, are positive it is a disease"' (Stolberg 2006, 84). For our purposes here, to understand drunkenness and intoxication in a historical context, it is worth mentioning that drunkenness in itself was not considered the defining characteristic of alcoholism. Instead, 'it was recognized from a medical standpoint that: "It is the internal craving for alcoholic liquors, and for their intoxicating effects, that constitutes the disease, and not the fact of drunkenness"' (Stolberg 2006, 84).

Ferentzy (2001, 367) is concerned with the idea of 'chronic drunkenness' and considers this in relation to historical understandings of addiction. Ferentzy argues that understandings of chronic drunkenness as a loss of control over one's drinking habits 'first appeared at the end of the eighteenth century'. However, 'in colonial America, large amounts of alcohol were consumed, and few considered drunkenness especially problematic'. As Ferentzy suggests, those who were most concerned were businessmen worried about productivity and clergymen worried about morality. Increasingly widespread concerns with drunkenness during the eighteenth and nineteenth centuries were formalised and given an institutional dimension through the development of organised temperance movements. Ferentzy draws from Levine (1978; see Appendix B) to argue that Enlightenment principles of autonomy, responsibility and rationality had an effect on the ways in which drunkenness was understood and dealt with. That is, 'the changing conceptions of habitual drunkenness in America were related to a societal shift toward increased demands for self-control' (Stolberg 2006, 88). Instead of being an inherently sinful self, the Enlightenment individual, as we have already discussed, was understood in ways that incorporated ideas of a free will and an essentially good human nature into decision-making. In this way 'deviance' came to be interpreted as 'unnatural' and as something that required intervention, disciplining and correction in this worldly life (Ferentzy 2001, 370).

As in England with the distinction between Gin Alley and Beer Street, the American temperance movement considered spirits more dangerous. For example, in 1885, the United States Brewers' Association called for a 'high tax on ardent spirits while asserting that the consumption of beer was a way to prevent drunkenness, and also the best way to secure temperance' (Stolberg 2006, 62). Whilst the differences between classes were a defining feature of English approaches to drunkenness, in the US, drunkenness was also understood in terms of ethnic, or so-called racial characteristics: 'Drunkenness, along with disease, poverty, and immorality, were, at one time or another, identified as characteristic of most immigrant groups, such as the "Irish race"' (Stolberg 2006, 78). However, some ethnic groups were associated more with temperance than with drunkenness: 'a study of industrial workers in Worcester, Massachusetts between 1870 and 1920, found that Irish Americans tended to engage in agitation against temperance, while Scandinavian Americans tended to agree with advocates of temperance (Stolberg 2006, 78). The relations between alcohol, drunkenness, temperance and cultural background were never clear cut, were never un-ambiguous: 'Italians and Jews, for instance, were two ethnic groups characterized as drinking in moderation...' Yet they were considered by some to be *un-American* in their 'temperate home drinking practices'. Indeed, they were, in this sense, seen to threaten the 'future of that most American of social institutions, the saloon' (Stolberg 2006, 78).

We conclude this discussion of certain elements of the temperance and prohibition movements in the US during the eighteenth and nineteenth centuries with a reference to concerns with drunkenness and intoxication in the military at the beginning of the twentieth century: 'One large sector of American society routinely scrutinized by Progressive reformers for warning signs of moral decay was the military' (Stolberg 2006, 76). Not only were temperance societies involved in petitioning the military to change its ways, but various levels of the Federal government held positions on these issues that were influenced by temperance discourses. Temperance movements used a number of strategies to articulate their positions on alcohol and drunkenness to various national security concerns. These included, as Stolberg argues (2006, 76–77), the following:

- **The possibilities of corruption, debauchery and moral decay among soldiers exposed to the temptations of alcohol:**

  In 1910, the U.S. Surgeon General suggested that temperance societies be formed within the military (Brandt, 1987: 98 [see Appendix B]). In 1916, reports were filed on the proximity of saloons to military bases and of the concomitant frequency of drunkenness among soldiers and sailors (Brandt, 1987: 53–55). The Secretary of War at the time, Newton Baker, recognized that excessive alcohol use could weaken the military (Brandt, 1987: 55–56) and, consequently, our national preparedness for war, a growing political concern. In March 1917, New York State banned liquor distribution near the army camp at Plattsburg (Brandt, 1987: 59).

  General John J. Pershing, Commander-in-Chief of the American Expeditionary Forces (AEF) largely accepted Progressive medical ideals, including those concerning the prevention of venereal disease, which accepted the causative association between intoxication and patronizing prostitutes (Brandt, 1987: 103). For example, in General Order Number 77, issued by Pershing to the AEF, troops returning from leave intoxicated were mandated to undergo initial treatment for venereal disease (Brandt, 1987: 103). "Drunkenness was seen as the first step on the road to the brothel and subsequent infection" (Brandt, 1987: 107–108).

- **The demands for raw materials for the war effort in World War I:**

  With respect to conservation, it was reported "that it requires almost one pound of coal to brew one pint of beer". In fact, it was asserted that in 1917, American brewers consumed 3,250,000 tons of coal and over 3,000,000,000 cubic feet of gas. The implication clearly was that these resources could be better used elsewhere. Industry supported these efforts, as stated in the Manufacturers' Record: "Every interest of the nation and of the world demands the closing of every saloon and the total Prohibition of the manufacture of alcoholic drinks during the war". The WCTU and the Anti-Saloon League grasped the need to conserve grain to push for the wartime prohibition of alcohol as a patriotic conservation measure.

- **The framing of patriotic sensibilities by opposing German brewing interests:**

  Progressive reform efforts commensurately accelerated as American preparation for war led to our actual military involvement in World War I. The national mobilization accompanying World War I was an opportune time for progressive reformers to push forward with alcohol prohibition, both as a form of conservation, as grain not used in brewing and distilling could be used to feed the troops, and as an act of patriotism, as the major American beer brewers, particularly Busch, Pabst, and Schlitz, had clear German roots. For instance, a full-page advertisement in the New York Times taken out on November 3, 1918 by Dr. J. H. Kellogg proclaimed: "We are fighting three enemies–Germany, Austria and Drink". In fact, in June 1917, William Faunce, then president of Brown University, had delivered this message in his speech to the graduating class titled: "Patriotism Spells Prohibition".

The point to draw from this sort of listing is the ongoing, often strategic (and not just in a military sense) mobilisation of various concerns to support a temperance or prohibition agenda. In this sense we can again see the often conflicting, but also complementary relation between medical, religious, political and moral ambitions in defining the problem of intoxication and drunkenness.

Setting the agenda? Media commentary and twenty-first century concerns with intoxication and drunkenness

In this final section we want to move from sketching some of the historical dimensions to the social, cultural, economic, political and moral issues associated with intoxication and drunkenness. Much of the remainder of this book will be located in the ambiguous, unclear, and uncertain spaces in which experts, lay populations and individuals discuss, debate and argue about the meanings, causes and consequences of intoxication and drunkenness; and how, exactly, it might be possible to agree on the rules of engagement in this debate. Or the terms on which it might be conducted. Once again, we suggest that the public, mediated spaces of the major newspapers are a useful place to identify and map out the contested terrain of these debates.

In a very general sense in media coverage of intoxication and drunkenness we see evidence of the ambivalence, uncertainty and confusion that accompanies any debates about the issues that we are discussing here. Many of these ambiguities rest on the problem of defining what constitutes intoxication and drunkenness. Here the two terms often take on distinct, separate meanings. In many instances, the news media views intoxication as a scientific, legal and policy issue that can be defined empirically. In this context the media often draws on expert testimony in discussing intoxication. In contrast, the news media generally discusses drunkenness as the cultural correlate to intoxication. It cannot be measured empirically. Moreover, in the case of drunkenness the media rarely draws on 'expert' testimony, resorting instead to describing it in lay terms.

So, intoxication is often identified in the following ways: as a formal definition of how impaired a person is, in terms of their blood alcohol level, which is useful for legal and policy purposes; and as a generic term that describes the effect of illicit as well as licit drugs. In this sense media commentary often imagines 'intoxication' as the object of an academic study of alcohol (Lange 2000) – it is what experts tell us it is. On the other hand 'drunkenness' is regarded as the cultural correlate of intoxication – it is what people do, or the state that people end up in.

Media commentary might discuss intoxication as a practice engaged in by certain groups in society, such as celebrities (White 2002; Shepherd 2008; Jesella 2008; Frankel 2005; Satel 2001; Barron 2008; *New Zealand Herald* 2008a; Blundell 2005; Scott 2003; Dixit 2005; Kurtz 2006), musicians (Heaney 2003; *The Sunday Times* 2004), and as 'a profound state' or 'total peace' sought after by clubbers (Benedictus 2004; see also Britten 2007). Such commentary might also employ the term 'intoxication' as a catch-all term for the very worst effects of alcohol consumption. These are the 'bitter rewards of intoxication', as John Patterson (2005) writes. Discussions of the damaging effects of alcohol on the drinker's health are sometimes framed not in terms of 'drunkenness', but in terms of the possible consequences of 'acute alcohol intoxication' (Chrisafis 2004; Bennett 2005). So Mike Barnes (2009) and Rebecca Hardy (2008) can claim that the *gig-goer* is in danger of doing damage to their health 'not so much because [they] might be trashed and put their head in a bass bin – although that certainly wouldn't help' – but because 'intoxication impedes the protective mechanisms of the inner ear' (Barnes 2009).

We can also see that the media often sees its job to translate the one into the other: to make the formal definitions of intoxication understood in the *practical terms* of drunkenness. An article in *The New York Times*, for example, explains that 'the legal definition of drunkenness would be when 0.08 percent of a person's bloodstream is alcohol', which is equivalent to 'a 170-pound man with an empty stomach… having four drinks in an hour' (McKinley Jr 2001). This translation from intoxication to drunkenness works in reverse as well, as shown elsewhere in *The New York Times*: 'By 8 p.m., Mr. Gray had consumed 12 to 18 beers. His blood alcohol level an hour later was estimated by the prosecution's expert witness at 0.23 percent, more than double the legal threshold for intoxication' (Newman 2002). Such definitions rely on, of course, a prior understanding of what constitutes 'a drink', and that the formal definition of a 'drink' or a 'unit' is rarely equivalent to one serving of a drink. But this definition also varies. According to *The New York Times*, a drink is '12 grams of pure alcohol, the amount found in a 12-ounce beer, a 5-ounce glass of wine or a shot of 80-proof distilled liquor' (Brody 2002). In contrast, according to Melbourne's *Herald Sun*, 'a standard drink contains 10g of alcohol' (Burstin 2003; Critchley 2008).

The majority of definitions of intoxication used in media stories and commentary are provided in relation to the legal blood alcohol levels for driving. What is immediately evident in the discussion of the formal definitions of intoxication in this setting is how malleable these definitions are. The American news media in particular encourages debate as to what can be considered a 'safe' blood alcohol level for driving, and whether the Federal Government should require states to lower the blood alcohol level from 0.10 per cent to 0.08 per cent, or '0.08 grams of alcohol per 100 millilitres of blood' (Gold 2002). The press, for its part, see itself as playing an integral part in facilitating that debate (Pradarelli 2000; Jackman et al. 2000; Montgomery and LeDuc 2001; Elliott 2000b). In these debates we witness media-generated discussions about such things as the following:

- the lowering to 0.03 the level at which a driver "could be presumed to be impaired by alcohol" in Washington D. C. (Schulte 2005);
- the 0.02 blood alcohol level for drivers younger than 21 in Virginia (Markon 2007);
- the lowering of the legal blood alcohol content level to 0.05 in Victoria (*The Sunday Age* 2001).

When not being used in the formal context of policing, the news media regularly discusses intoxication as a metaphor for any kind of 'high'. Understandings of intoxication in this sense apply not only to licit and illicit drugs, but to any number of other social phenomena (Healy 2002; Kiley 2001; *The Guardian* 2004a). Describing the effects of drugs as 'intoxication' helps the press to draw a distinction between 'non-alcoholic intoxication', as William Safire calls it (2002) – which is what 'other people' do – and the more socially acceptable alcohol intoxication. The effects of drugs are one such object of discussion, and one in which the news media usually adopts a paternalistic attitude in its condemnation of drug culture (Nussbaum 2001; Strauss 2001; Leland 2001; Gray 2001; Liptak 2002; Tuller 2004; Moerk 2006). This is reflected in the litany of drug-related forms of intoxication, including: lithium intoxication (Boodman 2008), inhalant abuse (Vedantam 2005), petrol sniffing (Brown 2000), caffeine intoxication (Sontag 2002; Bee 2008), kava intoxication (Riding 2004), cannabis intoxication (Sieghart 2001; Blakemore and Iversen 2001; Dodd 2005; Stuttaford 2001; 2005; Bainbridge 2004; Whyte 2006), 'acute methadone intoxication' (Blumenthal 2006), LSD intoxication (Stone 2008), cocaine intoxication (Depalma 2007; Warner 2004; Whitlock 2000; Thompson and Ly 2000; Whitlock and Fallis 2001; Ruane and Duggan 2006), and carbon monoxide intoxication (Dao and Barringer 2006).

The second way in which media commentary uses the term 'intoxication' is entirely unrelated to alcohol, drinking, and drunkenness. There is a body of articles that employ intoxication as a metaphor for social phenomena, including the intoxication of fame (Kane 2001), affluence (Brooks 2002), and of the 'California dream' (Waldie 2001). Elsewhere, the press describes aesthetic beauty, including the beauty of nature, as 'an emotional state, somewhere between intoxication and death' (Jones 2004; see also Bostridge 2006; Wood 2006; Ozick 2006; Hamilton 2001; Bilger 2001). Intoxication is also used as a metaphor for political power (Jacques 2006; Sciolino 2003), and war and revenge (Brewer 2002). Aida Edemariam (2004) describes the 'certain madness', a 'frenzy' and 'paranoia' that defined America under the George W. Bush Administration as a kind of intoxication, while young supporters of the Mugabe regime are described as having 'eyes wild with intoxication' (Philp 2008; see also Wines 2003). In a similar way, John Crace (2008) suggests that terrorists are driven by the 'intoxication' of 'excitement and mayhem', while Mark Edmundson (2006) and Minette Marrin (2002; 2007) describe people as being enchanted by the 'collective intoxication' of figures such as Hitler. Finally, an Iraqi journalist describes his profession in the post-Saddam Hussein era as an indescribable 'intoxication' that 'you get from reporting the truths after so many decades of lies' (Abdul-Ahad 2005). The point to make here is that what are being described are altered states of individual and collective consciousness brought about by a variety of stimuli. But it is a description that is metaphorical and allegorical, and which draws on the sense many of us might share of being excited, stimulated, possibly out of control, not entirely rational. The connection of intoxication to these emotional, embodied states is not dependent on the understandings of various experts. Indeed, in this context such meanings are very much about individual and collective feelings and emotions.

When we come to the ways in which the news media treats, understands and comments on *drunkenness* we enter a space that appears to be highly subjective. As such, we end up with definitions of drunkenness such as that given in a *New Zealand Herald* editorial on binge drinking: a space which suggests that 'the best definition [of binge drinking] is drinking to drunkenness, that is, to a level where a youth would describe themselves as "wasted"' (*New Zealand Herald* 2008b). In the same way, Deborah Cameron (2007) defines drunkenness as being characterised by 'slurring and unsteadiness', which is problematic, because those same symptoms are characteristic of 'coma-inducing hypoglycaemia' – a medical emergency that can all too readily be mistaken for drunkenness. Even the supposedly *objective* legal definitions of intoxication end up relying heavily on subjective judgements. Virginian state law, for instance, defines intoxication as having drunk enough to 'observably affect' a person's 'manner, disposition, speech, muscular movement, general appearance or behavior' (Markon 2007). Alternatively, Claire Phipps (2004) offers a more precise definition of binge drinking – consuming six units of alcohol in one session – but that definition does not necessarily make it any easier to understand what binge drinking *feels like*. Tom Jackman (2002) gives a crude example of this when he describes a man as being 'very drunk' with a blood alcohol level of 0.35. Cathy Pryor (2008) describes the same difficulty with translating formal definitions of drunkenness into terms that make sense to the non-expert, writing:

> Drinking is so ingrained in Britain it seems many people… are similarly unwilling to rein it in, even for the sake of their health and even though recent figures estimate that 15,000 Britons a year die from drink-related diseases. Getting the message across is also complicated by public confusion over how such limits – 14 units a week for women, 21 for men – can really apply. Don't other health and lifestyle factors come into play?

While media commentary and stories may draw on a 'broad spectrum' of expert and non-expert knowledge on alcohol abuse – from physicians who 'testify to the horrific damage being done to the national liver', to police, 'who vainly try to keep order on the streets at closing time', to bar staff and to drunks themselves – *The Guardian* (2006) singles out epidemiology as offering a unique perspective on the problem of defining drunkenness. Distanced from the day-to-day consequences of alcohol abuse which physicians, police and bar staff have to deal with, it is claimed that epidemiologists offer 'a peculiar kind of clarity' that is 'valuable if we want to make real sense of our nation's love affair with the bottle'. The question that *The Guardian* poses is: 'Is Britain in the grip of a booze epidemic?' However, in this story it is suggested that epidemiology can give no concrete answer to that question, because while it grounds its research in scientific methodologies – blood tests, cognitive tests, and testing of the heart and other physical functions – the research still relies on the self-reported questionnaire responses of the drinkers themselves. Thus, even the most objective and 'expert' definitions of drunkenness are, in this account, obscured by the subjective appraisals of the drinker him or herself.

This reliance on the testimony of the lay person colours the news media's attempts to define drunkenness overall. After all, the lay person reading the newspaper is less interested in the formal definition of intoxication, and more in how drunkenness affects them and those they care about. So we see attempts by the media to translate, mediate even, the expert definition into a lay definition. McKinley Jr (2001), who we referenced, in part, earlier, illustrates this point well:

> The new standard would mean that the legal definition of drunkenness would be when 0.08 percent of a person's bloodstream is alcohol. In practical terms, a 170-pound man with an empty stomach could have four drinks in an hour before being drunk. Under the current law, the same man could have five drinks.

Translation, though, can be a complex, ambiguous and uncertain enterprise. For example, Dr Mark Wright, a liver expert from Southampton general hospital, argues that mediations between expert and lay understandings can often lead to confusion:

> "Even if people think they're sticking to those limits, they're often drinking two or three times that because they've got no idea how much alcohol is in the drinks they're drinking", he says. "There are

large swathes of the population that drink half a bottle of wine a night: they're not addicted, but they're persistently drinking far too much". (Pryor 2008)

A second tactic used in some media accounts for translating expert and legal definitions of drunkenness into lay terms is to cite the number of lives that will be saved by adopting changes to the ways in which various alcohol-related issues are governed and regulated. In one example:

> Proponents of the lower standard [0.08] estimate about 500 people die each year in accidents caused by people with blood-alcohol contents between 0.08 percent and 0.10 percent. About 40 of those deaths occur in New York State each year, these advocates say. "It would save 40 New Yorkers a year," said Marge Lee, a spokeswoman for the New York chapter of Mothers Against Drunk Driving. "Just off the top of my head I can name three families in Long Island whose kids were killed by point-oh-eight drivers". (McKinley Jr 2001)

One of the points of disjuncture between the expert and lay definitions – and perhaps one of the reasons why the lay are preferred to the expert – is that the expert definition serves to impose limits on, and therefore condemn, the drinker, whereas the lay definition often celebrates drinking. In a story in *The Guardian*, for instance, it is suggested that one of the reasons British slang has so many synonyms for getting drunk is that they represent 'a proud sense of achievement of the advanced stages of inebriation'. The British take 'a utilitarian approach to alcohol: what's the point of consuming it unless we end up rat-arsed?' (*The Guardian* 2004b). Comparing British slang to the Inuit's 80 different words for snow, which 'forms the limit of the Inuit's horizon', so too:

> does drunkenness saturate the fabric of British life... It's as if the condition of drunkenness for which we are striving lies beyond language – as indeed it often proves – and no word can hope to encapsulate the comprehensive dysfunction that is the proper result of "a good session". (*The Guardian*, 2004b)

The cultural phenomena of drunkenness and binge drinking produces its own, non-expert, lay language that is taken up and used by the media in framing its conversations about the roles played by 'booze' or 'hooch', or 'brew', in producing these states (Yardley 2008). Much media commentary in Australia is particularly keen to use the term 'booze' to describe Australians' drinking habits, rather than the more formal 'alcohol', which is reserved for discussions of intoxication. In doing so media reports circulate and shape the complex and contradictory ways in which we understand drunkenness. Australia is variously described as having a 'cultural love affair with booze' (Stark 2007), as a 'booze-soaked society' (Farrelly 2007), and as a country full of 'booze artists' (Summers 2008). On one hand the national capital Canberra, is described as being 'fuelled by booze and ambition', while former Prime Ministers John Curtin and Bob Hawke are celebrated for having 'fought a valiant battle with booze' (Middendorp 2004; Grattan 2003b; Strickland 2003; Totaro and Coultan 2004). Recently *The Age* was highly critical of the then–leader of the Australian Democrats Andrew Bartlett for letting his 'reprehensible' drunkenness jeopardise the future of the Democrats (Grattan 2003a). And, as we will see, 'booze' is also implicated in social disorder, drinkers' health problems, and youth gang crime – especially in Melbourne (Middendorp 2004; Mitchell 2008; Simper 2007).

In this sense it is not surprising to see the difficulty the *New Zealand Herald* has in separating drunkenness out from binge drinking, since, in a broader cultural context the two blur into one another. *The Age* does a better job of separating out the two, giving a formal definition of binge drinking as 'five or more drinks in one sitting for women and seven or more for men' (Farouque 2007). Such a definition is inadequate, however, since it describes only the lower limit of binge drinking and does little to illustrate the *scale* of binge drinking. As Anne Summers (2008) writes, 'if four glasses of wine enjoyed by adults over dinner is now going to be labelled binge drinking, we will need a whole new vocabulary to describe kids throwing down 24 vodka shots on a night out on the town'.

At this time, as we head into a more expert-oriented discussion in the following chapter, we can suggest that in Australia, New Zealand, the US and Britain, the news media is much more comfortable talking about drunkenness, which it considers to be a cultural activity, or something people do; and much less comfortable discussing intoxication, which it understands and uses as a formal, legal, or policy term it can only discuss in abstract ways. As a consequence, the most common method the news media employs to discuss drunkenness is constructing narratives that address the causes, problems, and solutions to problem drinking. However, while the media frames and facilitates much of this debate – even to the extent of setting the agenda in some settings in relation to particular issues – there are a number of problems with the way the press discusses drunkenness. These include:

- that the news media tends to *reinforce stereotypes* about the drinking behaviour of certain marginalised groups within society, in particular Indigenous people and youth, and;
- while the news media is quick to demand a government response to the problems it identifies in society, it is equally quick in its criticism of any responses the government comes up with.

So, while the media coverage of intoxication and drunkenness plays a significant role in informing, influencing and shaping the ways its audiences understand the problems of intoxication and drunkenness, the news media may be less helpful in facilitating a debate about the possible ways that these issues can be understood – socially, culturally, economically, politically and morally – and responded to. The nature of the news media, and its possibilities for explaining and covering these issues, offers no clear way through, let alone out of, the uncertainty, ambiguity and conflict in relation to these issues.

Chapter 2

The psychological, biological and medical dimensions of intoxication and drunkenness

Other respiratory effects [of acute alcohol intoxication] *include decreased airway sensitivity to foreign bodies, decreased ciliary clearance and aspiration, and increased risk of bacterial infection with consequent bronchitis and pneumonia. Gastrointestinal effects include nausea, vomiting, diarrhoea, abdominal pain secondary to gastritis, peptic ulcer, and pancreatitis. Prolonged vomiting can lead to hyponatremia. Acute alcohol intoxication can cause a dysfunction of oesophageal, gastric, and duodenal motility and an increase in duodenal type III (propulsive) waves in the ileum; this increased transit of intestinal contents may contribute to diarrhoea. Acute alcohol intoxication can induce acute alcoholic hepatitis, usually in subjects with chronic alcohol abuse and/or in patients affected by alcoholic cirrhosis. Most often the diagnosis is suggested by a history of excessive alcohol abuse in patients with features of hepatic decompensation. Symptoms usually include nausea, vomiting, and abdominal pain. Less frequently, fever, shivering, and jaundice can occur. Zieve syndrome has also occasionally been reported; this consists of hemolytic anemia, jaundice, and hypertriglyceridemia. Finally, acute alcohol intoxication can be found in patients affected by such psychiatric disorders as affective disorders and antisocial personality; suicide or suicidal gestures are also highly associated with alcohol intoxication...* (Vonghia et al. 2008; 'Acute alcohol intoxication', 563)

Introduction

In this chapter we present a discussion of the ways in which psychological, biological and medical expertise struggle over definitions of intoxication and drunkenness. In these struggles we see different forms of expertise attempting to develop more sophisticated ways to identify, define, measure and quantify states of intoxication and drunkenness. These attempts are characterised by an emphasis on what might be called objective, quantifiable, generalisable, 'scientific' measures, and the applications of these in various medical and psychological contexts in which the physical and mental health and safety dimensions of intoxication and drunkenness are of primary interest. What we hope becomes apparent in the discussion that follows is that in spite of an emphasis on calculation, measurement and scientific objectivity, these psychological, biological and medical discussions do not indeed remove ambiguity, uncertainty and imprecision from their debates.

In the first instance we explore the problematic, shifting and contested terrain in which definitions of intoxication, drunkenness and, in the recent past, binge drinking circulate. We then set out to establish the general and particular health and psychological concerns that attach to the problems of intoxication and drunkenness. In this context there are only minor disagreements about some of the physical and mental health and well-being and safety issues associated with states of intoxication and drunkenness. If there is a strong degree of agreement at this level, it tends to disappear when discussion turns to: attempts to calculate and measure levels of intoxication and drunkenness; who is most able to make these calculations; and what measures are most suited to this task. In concluding this chapter we examine the debates about whether individual self-reporting of feelings or experiences of intoxication and drunkenness, or attempts to calculate whether one is intoxicated or not, have much of a role to play in these 'scientific' discussions and debates. In this sense the individual and the subjective are seen as more problematic than the generalised and the objective.

Intoxication, drunkenness and bingeing: Same, different, interchangeable?

Intoxication and drunkenness are terms that are used in different ways by different health, medical and psychological professionals and researchers, in changing contexts and for varying affect. In this section we consider some of the most common definitions of intoxication and drunkenness from the perspectives of various experts and specialists in health, medicine and psychology. As we explain below, these terms are often conflated or used interchangeably. In dictionary definitions, intoxication is frequently associated with a kind of poisoning, a biological state. Here, intoxication is defined through direct reference to a state of drunkenness. Likewise, the entry for drunkenness explains that it is related to, or characterised by, intoxication. As such, these circular definitions do not take us far. Often when one of these terms is being used it refers to something quite specific.

That is, drunkenness can be seen as broadly characterised by outward behaviour relating to the consumption of a certain amount of alcohol. However, intoxication, while it can have the same connotation is sometimes used differently, for example, when referring to something measurable. Therefore, in the following sections, we note that intoxication is used more often in some areas and drunkenness in others. Our interest here is not to claim that any particular use of these terms is right or wrong but to illustrate the different ways in which these terms are used and understood by different researchers in the same or closely related disciplines.

Intoxication is described by some researchers as 'a condition that follows the administration of alcohol and results in disturbances in the level of consciousness, cognition, perception, judgement, affect, or behaviour, or other psycho-physiological function and responses' (Farke and Anderson 2007, 334; see also Babor and Caetano 2005). Here, intoxication is seen as a state that is distinguished from simply drinking alcohol. For example, Johnson et al. (2005, 1139) define 'alcohol telescoping' as 'the rate of self reported movement from regular alcohol consumption to the onset of regular heavy drinking' and examine it through the use of two questions. The first being 'the number of years the client used alcohol regularly in lifetime', and the second, 'the number of years the client used alcohol to intoxication regularly in lifetime'. The authors argue that comparing responses to these questions makes it 'possible to construct a telescoping score that reflects the relative speed, in number of years, for an individual to transition from regular use of alcohol to intoxication' (Johnson et al. 2005, 1143). Important here is the distinction made between 'regular use' and 'intoxication'.

Intoxication has also been defined as acute consumption, alongside alcohol abuse and dependence, hazardous/harmful use, and 'alcohol use disorder' (Neumann and Spies 2003). It also often appears in lists of the possible adverse consequences of consuming alcohol. For example, one study explains, that these 'acute consequences' of alcohol consumption include 'intoxication, injuries and accidents, as well as long-term or chronic consequences, such as liver disease, cancer and alcohol dependence' (Plant 2008, 155). While we might expect that the terms intoxication, drunkenness and binge drinking have distinct meanings and definitions, they are also often used interchangeably. In this sense, even though our primary interest is not with definitions of binge drinking it is important to illustrate how this term informs understandings of intoxication and drunkenness. Binge drinking is an ill-defined concept for researchers, policy makers and the general public. It has been noted that 'different definitions of binge drinking have been used in the literature, such that heavy drinking, drinking to intoxication, and occasional heavy intake are terms used interchangeably' (Yang et al. 2007, 186). Hammersley and Ditton (2005, 498), for example, reported that 7 per cent of 291 participants in the UK conflated binge drinking with 'drinking to drunkenness or intoxication'. In another study binge drinking was described as 'a drinking occasion leading to intoxication of the drinking person' (Van Wersch and Walker 2009, 126).

While intoxication and drunkenness are not always distinguished, it has been argued that intoxication is different to binge drinking (Farke and Anderson 2007, 334). There are two main definitions of binge drinking in the health research literature. It is often used to denote a pattern of drinking that occurs over time. Its more common application however, is as a 'single drinking session leading to intoxication, often measured as having consumed more than X number of drinks in one occasion' or, 'a single episode of acute intoxication' (Herring et al. 2008b, 477).

Participants in a recent study conducted by McMahon et al. (2007, 300) interpreted binge drinking not only in terms of a specified amount of alcohol but also by intent. Here, they found a range of motivations as to why an individual would engage in episodes of heavy drinking, such as, 'dependence, tension relief and celebration'. In this study, drinking to intoxication was a defining feature of binge drinking. The authors claim that the importance of intoxication was evident in a number of the definitions of binge drinking, 'drinking beyond personal limits, drinking to get drunk and drinking until physically unable to continue'. While it is not spelled out, the notion of intoxication is implicit in each of these definitions.

Common measures of binge drinking rely primarily on the amount of alcohol consumed. Some researchers in North America, parts of Europe and Australia use the 5+/4+ metric as an indicator of binge drinking, where five or more drinks for males and four or more for females across a two hour time period is considered binge drinking (Wechsler and Kuo 2000). The National Institute on Alcohol Abuse and Alcoholism (US) defines a binge as 'a pattern of drinking alcohol that brings blood alcohol concentration (BAC) to 0.08 gram percent or above' (National Institute on Alcohol Abuse and Alcoholism 2004). Other researchers, mostly in the UK, rely on an 8+/6+ measure. The 8+/6+ metric refers to 8 units/6 units of pure alcohol consumed within a two hour period (1 unit = 10 ml or 8 g of pure alcohol/ethanol; see Hammersley and Ditton 2005). Notwithstanding the relative merits of such guidelines, the lack of a standardised definition of binge drinking makes comparisons across studies difficult (Gill et al. 2007).

There are other problems with these sorts of definitions of binge drinking. Herring et al. (2008a, 498) explain that, 'it is probably not helpful to lump together those who have drunk anything from eight (men) or six (women) units with those who have drunk considerably more and are extremely intoxicated'. Nonetheless, intoxication is not defined here, and what makes the amount of drinks coupled to binge drinking enough to induce extreme intoxication is unclear. Again, the distinction between binge drinking and extreme intoxication remains ambiguous.

Lange and Voas (2001, 311–315) argue that, 'especially for men, the traditional 5+ drinks definition of binge drinking... is too low to reflect accurately the drinking events that produce excessive intoxication'. They argue that the current, 'use of this term [binge] to describe drinking events that do not produce illegal BACs [in relation to drink driving limits] or significant impairment may affect the credibility of responsible-drinking campaigns'. They also suggest that the concept of binge drinking 'implies excessive drunkenness' but that current definitions of binge drinking rely on such low BACs that they 'may not be capturing the "excessive-drunkenness" quality of the term'.

Some researchers argue that binge drinking should be considered 'a characteristic of the individual, not of the occasion when drinking occurred' (Wechsler 2000). Wechsler (2000) suggests that binge drinking is not 'intended to determine if [drinkers] are legally intoxicated at the time'. Instead, he proposes that it is more useful as a gauge for tracking the risk of potential problem-drinkers. Similarly, it is argued that the utility of such a controversial measure for researchers lies in its 'use as a measure of alcohol-related harm, which recognizes that much of the short-term harm associated with alcohol... arises from single episodes of drunkenness, rather than drinking more than the recommended weekly levels or individual daily drinking (Herring et al. 2008a, 482). However, as Herring et al. (2008a, 483) claim, 'within the general definition of binge drinking as single drinking session leading to intoxication there is no consensus as to what level of intake constitutes binge drinking'.

Measham (2008, 210) also argues that, 'varying definitions and measurements of "binge" drinking have led to problems of comparative research with a narrow focus on total units consumed unrelated to the duration of consumption, leading to the technical possibility of a sober binge drinker!' A further issue here is the problem of using the 5+/4+ measure as shorthand for intoxication when many young people who drink at this level do not exhibit signs of intoxication, or do not present unacceptable BAC measurements (Perkins et al. 2001). In a study with over 1000 college students in the US,

Thombs et al. (2003, 323) found that 66.3 per cent of those meeting the 5+/4+ criterion for the night had BAC < 100 mg/dl. They concluded that while a particular BAC measure might indicate moderate drinking, if an individual has consumed more than the 5+/4+ threshold they would be classified as having engaged in heavy episodic drinking 'at a relatively low BAC'.

A final observation here about the use and meanings of the term binge drinking and the marked lack of agreement about what it is and what should be done about it. In some contexts there is the perception that binge drinking is undertaken by a minority of individuals who undermine the responsible drinking practices of the majority of the population. The issue in these sorts of cultural, social and political contexts is understood in ways that might seek to downplay the extent and consequences of bingeing – or indeed, to highlight these and claim it as being a pressing concern. For example, Measham and Brain (2005, 272), 'question the [UK] government's claim that "binge" drinkers are a small and antisocial minority of people drinking in city centres who should not be allowed to derail the planned government policy of liberalisation of licensing hours for the sensible majority'. Suggesting that rates of consumption of alcohol are much higher than what is defined as a binge (using the 8/6 measure), Measham and Brain (2005) argue that binge drinking is not a minority issue, and instead, that this kind of consumption pattern is indicative of a new culture of intoxication. As our discussion indicates, anyone looking for some scientific, objective certainty with which to engage such claims will be unlikely to find it.

The physical and mental health consequences of intoxication and drunkenness

Having surveyed some of the difficulties associated with the slippery definitions of intoxication, drunkenness and binge drinking, we move to a discussion of some of the ways in which these definitions frame a range of physical and mental health and safety concerns.

The aim in what follows is to identify and map some of the ground covered by these concerns. Our list is extensive, but not exhaustive; illustrative, but not detailed. A useful starting point for this purpose can be found in the ways in which the American Psychiatric Association's (2000) *Diagnostic and Statistical Manual of Mental Disorders* (DSM-IV) defines intoxication:[1]

---

1 The influence of the DSM on constructing categories and types of conditions, pathologies, ideas of normal and abnormal behaviours is much debated in the behavioural and social sciences. An examination of these debates is beyond the scope of this discussion.

The essential feature of Alcohol Intoxication is the presence of clinically significant maladaptive behavioral or psychological changes (e.g., inappropriate sexual or aggressive behavior, mood lability, impaired judgment, impaired social or occupational functioning) that develop during, or shortly after, the ingestion of alcohol (Criteria A and B). These changes are accompanied by evidence of slurred speech, incoordination, unsteady gait, nystagmus, impairment in attention or memory, or stupor or coma (Criterion C). The symptoms must not be due to a general medical condition and are not better accounted for by another mental disorder (Criterion D). The resulting picture is similar to what is observed during Benzodiazepine or Barbiturate Intoxication. The levels of incoordination can interfere with driving abilities and with performing usual activities to the point of causing accidents. Evidence of alcohol use can be obtained by smelling alcohol on the individual's breath, eliciting a history from the individual or another observer, and, when needed, having the individual undertake breath, blood, or urine toxicology analyses.

The DSM (IV) definition is to be consulted as a clinical reference, and is frequently referred to in psychological research literature that is concerned with such things as the impact of intoxication on risk factors/behaviours associated with issues such as suicidal ideation. For instance, the effects of acute alcohol intoxication have been claimed to act as proximal risk factors for suicidal behaviour among alcoholics and non-alcoholics (Hufford 2001). In this instance it is suggested that intoxication affects levels and states of distress and aggression which may turn 'suicidal ideation into action through suicide specific alcohol expectancies'. Intoxication impairs cognitive processes which would otherwise allow the generation and implementation of alternative coping strategies (Hufford 2001, 797).

The effects of alcohol intoxication on emotional states are also of interest to psychological expertise. Hufford (2001) claims that some level of alcohol intake is thought by many people to be ameliorative to negative emotions and researchers believe this may be true under certain conditions. This model takes into account the 'biphasic' effect of alcohol, whereby it can act as both a stimulant and a depressant. Aggression has been shown to be affected by alcohol intake. Yet an individual's alcohol intake may also be influenced by feelings of aggression. Hufford (2001, 797) argues that the 'pharmacological effects of alcohol intoxication on attention is one mechanism that can increase the proximal risk of suicidal behaviour'. The effect of intoxication on attention is seen to work by restricting the range of cues perceived in a given situation, and by decreasing one's ability to meaningfully interpret these cues. That is, alcohol intoxication interrupts processes of inhibition conflict that are usually present when risky behaviours are contemplated.

Some psychological studies have been conducted to better understand the effect of alcohol intoxication on the ways in which men and women interpret signs of sexual advances. These studies are said to be important in understanding such things as so-called 'date rape' scenarios. Alcohol has been shown to disrupt higher-order cognitive processing, making intoxicated people more likely to focus on immediate superficial social cues, and therefore encouraging poor decision-making (Abbey et al. 2003). For example, one study showed that intoxicated men are more likely to interpret a man who committed acquaintance rape as less deviant and more typical than did non-drinking men (Abbey et al. 2003). Some psychologists are interested in the possible expectancy effects of a culture that equates alcohol use with sex and violence. That is, some researchers believe that individuals' expectancies about this link encourage this type of behaviour.

Abbey et al. (2003) outline and discuss three types of studies to examine this link. In one study participants are led to believe they are drinking alcohol but in fact they are not. In another, participants are asked to assess their pre-existing beliefs about alcohol use. Finally, sober participants are required to consider the behaviour of others who have been drinking. In a scenario presented to males in a laboratory, study participants who think they have consumed alcohol, as well as those who were given alcohol, took longer to suggest that a man should stop attempting to force a woman to have sex with him. In the same study both groups of men were also more likely to interpret the woman's behaviour as sexually aroused than the non-drinkers. The authors report mixed findings from placebo studies.

Another study involved 90 male and 90 female university students in the US who were randomly assigned to drink alcohol, a placebo beverage or a non-alcoholic beverage. They were then read a story of a man and a women who didn't know each other well drinking together at a party, consensually kissing and ending with the woman saying 'no' to the man's increasingly insistent sexual advances. The participants, who were randomly allocated to drink alcohol, were given 80-proof vodka calculated to achieve a peak BAC of .080 per cent (2.00 g/kg of body weight for men and 1.85 g/kg body weight for women). This amount was chosen because it is sufficient to impair a number of cognitive functions thus providing a definition of intoxication (Abbey et al. 2003, 675).

Results showed that people were more willing to consider the man in the scenario as acting appropriately if they had been allocated to drinking alcohol, approved of casual sex, or interpreted the female character as very sexually aroused. 'Participants were more likely to perceive the woman in the story as being very sexually aroused when they drank alcohol, when they had strong alcohol expectancies regarding sex and when they frequently drank alcohol on dates'. The findings 'support the hypothesis that sexual arousal may be a particularly salient cue on which intoxicated individuals are likely to focus their attention' (Abbey et al. 2003, 675).

A number of other psychological studies report on concerns with the disinhibitory effect of alcohol and risk taking behaviour related to certain criminal, sexual or violent practices: 'Alcohol produces a pharmacological effect that may be described as disinhibitory, or in other words, related to an increase in behaviours that, due to environmental context, otherwise normally occur at a low rate' (Lane et al. 2004, 74). The authors caution that 'despite a well-established epidemiological and clinical relationship between alcohol intoxication and maladaptive risky behaviour, results of laboratory studies seeking to demonstrate such a relationship have not been conclusive'. One laboratory study has shown that, 'otherwise normal subjects, when intoxicated, showed risk-taking patterns remarkably similar to subjects with a history of maladaptive risky behaviour' (Lane et al. 2004, 74)

Intoxication can affect cognitive function and interfere with performance on neuropsychological tasks including memory, learning and coordination (Calhoun et al. 2005, 285–288). However, Calhoun et al. propose that there is still much work to be done in mapping acute alcohol use with brain function. Using functional MRI technology the researchers used virtual-reality driving simulations to 'introduce the participant to a simulated environment rather than a series of tasks, thus allowing for a more realistic experience'. The authors claimed that their study 'revealed both global and local effects of alcohol', and that they were able to consider the 'relationships between behaviour, brain function, and alcohol blood levels'.

A number of health researchers in Australia draw on the National Health and Medical Research Council (NHMRC) drinking guidelines to classify types of drinkers according to risk. These guidelines define short-term alcohol-associated risk in terms of 'an excessive volume consumed in a single day, and the associated risks are intoxication and impaired judgement leading to accidents, injury and death' (Reid et al. 2007, 437). Similarly, the 2004 Australian Institute of Health and Welfare Report (2004, 3) defines intoxication as one of three broad categories of problem that may result from excessive alcohol consumption. These problems are summarised in three categories:

- Alcohol dependence (loss of personal control, withdrawal symptoms, social disintegration, etc);

- Heavy regular use problems (cirrhosis of the liver, cognitive impairment, pancreas damage, heart and blood disorders, ulcers, etc); and

- Intoxication and acute alcohol-related problems (alcohol-related violence, risky behaviour, road trauma, injury, etc).

The Australian Bureau of Statistics (ABS) recently published a series of articles describing Australian social trends in relation to alcohol consumption. One, entitled 'Risk taking by young people', draws from the 2007 NHMRC guidelines to describe the effects of 'high risk drinking' in relation to intoxication in the following way: 'Short term risky/high risk drinking – often referred to as binge drinking – leads to immediate and severe intoxication' (ABS 2008). According to this report, the likelihood of falling over or being involved in an accident or some form of violence increases markedly with high-risk drinking. The report specifically identifies young people aged between 15–24 years as the group most likely to experience the negative consequences of intoxication: 'Of the many alcohol-related disorders present in subjects referred to emergency care departments, acute alcohol intoxication is the most frequent. This condition is present not only in adults but also in adolescents' (Vonghia et al. 2008, 562). Apparent increases in rates of adolescent hospital admission as a consequence of alcohol intoxication continue to be a significant concern for health professionals and researchers.

The Australian Institute of Health and Welfare Report (2004, 1) also reveals that intoxication provokes the sorts of high risk behaviours that can readily result in the loss of life:

> An estimated 31,132 Australians (23,431 or 75% males; 7,703 or 25% females) died from risky and high-risk alcohol use in a period of ten years between 1992 and 2001. The leading causes of death were alcohol liver disease followed by road crash injury, cancer and suicide. These types of deaths reflect a pattern of drinking to intoxication with more people dying from acute rather than chronic effects of alcohol.

In the medical literature the term intoxication is not only associated with physical symptoms but is also linked to injury, trauma and violence. Vonghia et al. (2008) draw on a study conducted by the Australian Institute of Family Studies in 2000 (see Appendix B) to reveal that 'conditions deriving from acute alcohol intoxication, such as trauma and violence, were responsible for 46% of potential life years lost, twice that from chronic alcohol-related conditions' (Vonghia et al. 2008, 563). These authors also draw on other studies to claim a relationship between intoxication and violent crimes such as homicide, assault, robbery and sexual offences.

The health consequences of intoxication and drunkenness are things that attract the interest, concern and, often, the moralising of certain sections of the news media. In such accounts a range of statistics are cited as evidence of the damage heavy drinkers are doing to their health (it is not possible to cover them all here). Moreover, the statistics vary from country to country. What is apparent in these settings is the role that the media plays in translating the concerns and findings of psychological, biological and medical research. This popularising of science and the results of scientific research is never direct or *unmediated*. What is often apparent in media commentary on the health problems that face heavy drinkers is the paternalistic and condescending attitude that is adopted towards certain marginalised groups and populations. The apparent concern in such commentary for the drinker is constantly tinged with a disbelief that people seem 'unwilling' to rein their drinking in, 'even for the sake of their health', which Cathy Pryor (2008) attributes to the drinker's 'confusion'. In one account Anita Chaudhuri (2003) summarises a number of the key concerns regarding the damage drinkers are inflicting on their health:

> Drinking many of your weekly alcohol units at one sitting is much more harmful than moderate daily intake, because the toxic effects of excess alcohol put a huge strain on the body's vital organs. The results of a Scottish study published in the *British Medical Journal* showed that there was an excess of deaths due to coronary heart disease on Mondays (3.1% above the daily average of deaths). The journal argued that these deaths were partly attributable to weekend binge drinking, which accounts for 40% of all drinking occasions by men and 22% by women in Britain. When you compare that to France, where binge drinking accounts for only 9% of all drinking occasions by men and 5% by women, it is clear that Collins has a point about Brits and bingeing. Alcohol Concern warns that apart from feeling terrible the morning after, there also are several long-term physiological consequences of binge drinking: high blood pressure, risk of liver cancer and cirrhosis, reduced fertility, weight

gain, blood-sugar problems, stomach inflammation and bleeding, and increased risk of having a stroke.

In another story Sally Squires (2000) sketches some of the more troubling effects of alcohol on brain neurochemistry:

> Some of the brain's messenger chemicals excite nerve cells; others dull or inhibit them. Among other activities, alcohol affects the most powerful of the inhibitory systems – those involving the neurotransmitter GABA – and that results in a general depression of many kinds of nerve response. Too much alcohol floods neurons and changes gene function of the cells, which in turn appears to alter receptors and results in intoxication, brain-cell death and, if repeated, dependence and alcoholism.

At the same time, somewhat in conflict with these understandings, there is a strong social perception that regulators and policy makers need to adopt a more flexible approach to understanding what constitutes 'safe drinking'. The need for flexibility was evident in the debates about what constitutes a 'safe enough' blood alcohol level for drivers. Here the question becomes: What is 'moderate' drinking? What does it mean to drink 'in moderation'? Writing in the *New York Times*, Brody (2002) claims that: 'Studies of tens of thousands of people here and abroad have found that regular moderate alcohol intake diminishes the risk of heart disease and possibly stroke, probably by raising blood levels of protective H.D.L. [high density lipoproteins] cholesterol and estrogenic substances'. Moderate alcohol consumption has also been linked to a reduced risk of dementia in people over 55. The key word here is moderation. For younger adults, moderate is defined as no more than two drinks a day for men and no more than one drink a day for women. But for healthy men and women over 65, the new definition of moderate offered by the National Institute on Alcohol Abuse and Alcoholism is no more than one drink a day and some experts suggest that older women would be wise to cut that amount in half. These definitions are, of course, contested. The Australian news media regularly reports on studies that claim that moderate alcohol consumption can have positive health benefits for the elderly. The *Herald Sun*, for example, published a number of stories about some of the positive health effects moderate drinking can have (Burstin 2003; see also Cameron 2007). *The Sunday Age* (2001) reported that while alcohol abuse contributed to the deaths of 3271 people under the age of 64 in 1998, moderate drinking *averted* the deaths of 5642 people over 64 in the same period. Finally, the *Herald Sun* highlights the debates concerning the definition of what constitutes drinking in moderation:

> Dr [Phillip] Norrie says drinking in moderation means a maximum of four standard drinks a day for a man and two for women... But [Geoff] Munro says these are maximum limits for safe drinking, not recommended daily doses. And people should aim for at least one or two alcohol-free days a week... Men should aim for a weekly maximum 28 standard drinks and women aim for 14 to prevent risk of alcohol-related health problems. (Burstin 2003)

Calculating, measuring and testing: Debates and dilemmas

Many alcohol researchers in the fields of medicine and public health are concerned with identifying people in need of intervention to prevent them doing long term harm to their health (Aalto and Seppä 2007). Reynaud et al. (2001) argue that any form of hospitalisation that occurs as a result of intoxication should be 'interpreted as a sign of likely harmful alcohol dependency' (Reynaud et al. 2001, 96). In their analysis these authors confirm our broad distinction that *drunkenness* refers to outward behaviour, and *intoxication* is a biological state that can be measured using a range of laboratory and field-based tests. Within these domains the harmful consequences of intoxication or drunkenness are identified through the use of various measurements, such as BAC (blood alcohol content) tests (Hammersley and Ditton 2005; Poulsen et al. 2007), BrAC (breath alcohol content) tests (Barquin et al. 2008; Voas et al. 2006), counting the number of drinks consumed (Hammersley and Ditton 2005), looking at the frequency of drunkenness (Midanik 2003; Schmid et al. 2003; Zaborskis et al. 2006), the number of drinks required to feel drunk (Midanik 2003; Kerr et al. 2006) and self-perceived drunkenness (Midanik 2003; Gustin and Simons 2008; Harrison and Fillmore 2005; Thombs et al. 2003). The variety of such tests is just one indication of the uncertainties and ambiguities associated with measuring levels of alcohol concentration in the body. Of more interest is the sense that a greater dilemma relates to defining the levels of alcohol concentration that indicate or define intoxication. Given these dilemmas, which we describe in more detail later, Table 1 provides one example that sets out to list a range of health, psychological and behavioural symptoms, and the corresponding BAC levels which might trigger these symptoms.

Table 1. Main clinical symptoms in acute alcohol intoxication according to blood alcohol concentration (BAC)

SYMPTOMS	BAC
Impairment in some tasks requiring skill	BAC<50 mg/dl
Increase in talkativeness	(10.9 mmol/l)
Relaxation	
Altered perception of the environment	BAC>100 mg/dl
Ataxia	(21.7 mmol/l)
Hyper-reflexia	
Impaired judgement	
Lack of coordination	
Mood, personality, and behavioural changes, nystagmus	
Prolonged reaction time	
Slurred speech	
Amnesia	BAC>200 mg/dl
Diplopia	(43.4 mmol/l)
Dysarthria	
Hypothermia	
Nausea	
Vomiting	
Respiratory depression	
Coma	BAC>400 mg/dl
Death	(86.8 mmol/l)

Source: (Vonghia et al. 2008)

This sort of calculation establishes a relationship between a variety of physiological, psychological and behavioural states – some of which are readily identifiable and observable – and a series of thresholds of alcohol concentration in the blood (BAC). At one level, especially in terms of symptoms, this sort of calculation establishes a relationship that is recognisable – even to the non-expert. However, there is much more ambiguity and debate about the levels of BAC at which these symptoms appear.

Blood alcohol content (BAC), as we have indicated, is a way of measuring intoxication in individuals. It represents the amount of ethanol in a given amount of blood and is represented by weight by volume. The most commonly used measurements are grams of ethanol per millilitre of blood (g/ml) used in the US, and milligrams of ethanol per millilitre of blood (mg/ml), used in much of Europe. For example, 0.05 g/ml=50 mg ml (ICAP 2002). While it is tempting to define intoxication and drunkenness by simply counting the number of drinks consumed in a given time frame, it can be argued that understanding these terms is more complicated than that approach allows. A more accurate measure of intoxication necessarily relies on measurement of alcohol in units such as grams or ounces: 'Without specifying the percentage of alcohol in the beer or wine, an accurate interpretation of a standard drink is impossible' (Brick 2006, 1285). However, counting drinks is a common way that researchers measure intoxication. In one study undertaken to determine the 'relative influence of environmental and demographic factors on the drinking behaviour of servers, intoxication frequency was defined by the respondents and measured as a raw score with 10 times per month or more the highest category' (Nusbaumer and Reiling 2002, 736).

The difficulty in defining intoxication is highlighted in the research of Hammersley and Ditton (2005, 497–498). Their interviewer-completed questionnaire study of 291 people aged 16–25 looked at the quantity and rate of alcohol consumption in licensed premises. In this study they define intoxication as follows: 'People drinking less than 1 unit per hour are unlikely to be intoxicated, 1–2 units per hour will probably produce moderate intoxication, with BAC increasing over time. Faster rates (2 or more units per hour) are even more likely to result in intoxication with significant behavioural consequences'. They go on to suggest that, 'men drank more than women, but after adjusting crudely for body size and the recommended upper limits of intake for men and women, men's and women's drinking did not differ'. The implication is, 'that women's intoxication levels... were equivalent to men's, but women are not literally drinking as much as men'. Intoxication is not, then, something that can be linked simply to the number of drinks consumed. Using BAC measures Hammersley and Ditton (2005, 495) concluded that drinking:

> eight units steadily over 4 hours at 2 units per hour would produce a peak BAC of approximately 60mg% in an average sized man, occurring just after the end of the drinking session. Drinking the same amount of alcohol at twice the speed would achieve a peak BAC of approximately 100mg% by 2.5 hours, at which level most drinkers will be intoxicated.

In different settings these apparently objective calculations and definitions create their own dilemmas. Intoxication and drunkenness are sometimes defined with reference to the legal limit of alcohol for driving (Hammersley and Ditton 2005). That is, one would be considered intoxicated if BAC was above the legal limit for driving. BAC does not readily translate to a certain number of drinks consumed. There are many factors that effect a person's BAC at measurement, such as length of time between drinks, amount and type of food consumed and the context of consumption (Brick 2006). For example, the so-called 'hip flask defence' referred to in Simic and Tasic (2007), or the 'cognac alibi' (Simic et al. 2004) is used after a crime (drink driving or road accidents) to indicate that a drink was taken after the fact (say, to calm one's nerves) and not before. This is a means to mount a defence that drinking alcohol was not the cause of the accident. Simic et al. (2004) explain the complications that arise for prosecutors who must draw upon the expertise of 'medico-legal experts' or forensic pathologists and toxicologists to establish blood alcohol levels after the fact. Simic et al.'s (2004, 367) response to these concerns was to develop a more complex and refined calculation of BAC:

> It consists of three inter-related phases in which it combines the obtained BAC values, with testimonies of the drunk driving suspect and also witnesses. A specific algorithm was designed for calculating absorption and elimination of consumed alcohol. All the above-mentioned elements and blood-ethanol values calculated according to Widmark's method were inserted into appropriate cells of MS Excel software in order to calculate BAC in the function of time. The result is a relevant analysis of the drunk driving suspect's BAC in 5-minute intervals, as well as a graphic representation in chart form. (Simic et al. 2004, 367)

It is possible to imagine that this sort of algorithm may be more complex, but that it does little to clarify the debate about the ways in which intoxication and drunkenness is to be identified or measured. Brick (2006) illustrates some of the complications that may arise in using BAC measures of intoxication. For example, 'researchers relying upon alcohol test results from a hospital laboratory often neglect to inquire or report whether the results are derived from whole blood, serum, or plasma samples' (Brick 2006, 1284). This difference matters because 'a hospital serum alcohol concentration will be higher than a whole BAC drawn from the same patient at the same time' (Brick 2006, 1284; see also see Miller et al. 1991 in Appendix B).

Brick's discussion identifies a problem with inconsistent reporting of the quantitative measurements of alcohol intake. Here it is clear that definitions of intoxication and drunkenness which rely on quantitative and objective measurements are not always standardised, nor as reliable and precise as their calculations may imply.

The procedures for determining BACs are labour-intensive, time-consuming, expensive and, because of these factors, not always available in all situations (Shin et al. 2008, 194). In the context of hospitalisation for symptoms that are suspected of being related to intoxication, the 'confirmation of the diagnosis can take as long as 48 [hours], which places the patient at risk for many complications, which include death' (Shin et al. 2008, 194–195). Again, the context and the particular needs and ends promote different ways to identify and measure intoxication. So, Shin et al. (2008, 201) have developed a laboratory test for intoxication, 'which use[s] extremely minute quantities of saliva, can be performed with easily obtainable and inexpensive reagents, and these tests can be completed within 30–40 min'.

Given the complexities and costs associated with calculating and measuring BAC, other methods have been developed to meet the needs to identify and determine intoxication. A common way of assessing intoxication levels in the field is by measuring breath alcohol concentration (BrAC). Passive alcohol sensors (PAS) draw in a mix of expired and environmental air in front of a person's face and have found to be strong predictors of alcohol concentration. Breath analysers have been used in many contexts to monitor drink driving (Voas et al. 2006). These devices enable law enforcement officials to quickly and easily gauge a driver's alcohol intoxication status with some level of confidence. Voas et al. (2006, 720) cite studies indicating that when police officers have less than one minute to evaluate a driver (before deciding to undertake more thorough drink driving checks) 'the officer misses approximately 50% of the drivers who are above the legal limit'. PAS, it is argued, allow officers to make more informed decisions about an individual's intoxication status.

In another study, Poulsen et al. (2007, 514) use a number of variables for measuring the effects of alcohol intoxication on motor performance: 'To obtain a blood alcohol concentration level (BAC) of 1.5 g/l (32.6 mmol/l) the amount of alcohol given was adjusted individually based on gender, age (A), height in metres (H), weight in kilograms (W), total body water (TBW), breath alcohol concentration (BrAC) and expected metabolism'. In this study, BrAC was measured by Digital Alcohol Detector CA2000 (an FDA approved 'breathalyser', available to purchase on the Internet for about US$50 dollars; see also Barquin et al. 2008).

These sorts of volume-based measures have been queried at the level of methodology because they fail to take into account the length of drinking session, time between drinks or other important attributes of the drinking encounter in non-laboratory settings (Hammersley and Ditton 2005; Wright 2006). In other words, as with the use of BAC to measure intoxication, volume-based measurements must be considered in light of other factors such as length of time spent drinking, time between drinks, food consumption (amount and type), body size and alcohol-content. It appears that in order to understand intoxication we must consider alcohol consumption in context. While measures such as the 5+/4+ or 8+/6+ might be useful indicators, they tell us little about the state or experience of intoxication and drunkenness in themselves. From a sociological perspective, there are other aspects that are harder to measure that help to define intoxication and subjective interpretations of drunkenness.

Subjective understandings of intoxication and drunkenness in scientific discourses

We conclude this chapter with a brief overview of the debates and discussions that attach to attempts to develop calculations based in more subjective reporting and accounts of levels of intoxication and drunkenness. Again, there is little consensus about the ability of individuals to do this with accuracy. Some researchers argue that individuals are not reliable in predicting or calculating their own levels of intoxication, that they may, in fact, be 'unaware that they are intoxicated' (Gustin and Simons 2008, 606). Yet other researchers have found scenarios in which participants are able to estimate their BAC levels with some accuracy (Thombs et al. 2003). Thombs et al. (2003), in their study of college students in the US, found that those with mid-ranging BACs ranging from 70–90 mg/dl exhibited the greatest accuracy in estimating their BAC; those with lower BACs tended to overestimate their level of intoxication, whereas those with higher BACs tended to underestimate it.

A study by De Visser and Smith (2007, 350–351) examined some of the more qualitative dimensions of the expectations and uncertainties associated with the possibilities of drinking to levels that might produce intoxication. Their account of interviews with 31 young men in London develops and deploys a vocabulary based on the ambivalences related to the expectancies, attitudes and motivations that shape the use and consumption of alcohol:

> Expectancies are perceptions of likely outcomes from drinking; attitudes are a product of expectancies and evaluations of these outcomes, and motives reflect a desire to act on attitudes and expectancies in order to achieve or avoid particular outcomes. To illustrate this distinction, an expectancy might be that "Alcohol enhances sociability"; the accompanying attitude might be that "Alcohol is good because it makes people more sociable", whereas the motive might be "I will drink to be more sociable". As predicted by theories of health behaviour, outcome expectancies and motives are important correlates of drinking behaviour.

De Visser and Smith (2007, 351) suggest that there is a danger of making the notion of expectancy static. They introduce the idea of the *drinker's dilemma* to suggest that the ways in which drinkers understand their drinking is, indeed, a shifting, mobile, uncertain space:

> Rather than simply having favourable or unfavourable expectancies and motives, most people are ambivalent about alcohol. Ambivalence is not surprising given the paradoxical effects of alcohol, which may produce positive or negative outcomes at different stages of a single drinking episode. This produces a "drinker's dilemma": although drinkers know that alcohol can have both positive and negative consequences, it is difficult for them to predict whether, and at what point, their drinking will lead to net positive or negative outcomes. Thus, outcomes may not be consistent with motives. For example, someone who drinks to be less inhibited but drinks too much may become antisocial, because they are less concerned about the effects of their behaviour.

Developing this idea of the drinker's dilemma, of the uncertainty and ambiguity that often accompanies drinking, De Visser and Smith (2007, 352) suggest that 'motives for drinking became reasons for not drinking as the volume consumed increased. For example, positively evaluated confidence accompanying mild intoxication could easily become negatively evaluated arrogance following excessive consumption'. Moreover, drinkers and non-drinkers 'gave the same range of motives for not drinking. This implies that drinkers and non-drinkers alike have plenty of motives for not drinking, but the addition of more (or more convincing) motives for drinking determines drinking behaviour'.

In their study Morzorati et al. (2002, 1300) developed a hypothesis which suggested that an individual's family history may influence the subjective interpretation of the effects of alcohol. They designed a study which enabled them to separate participants into groups which differed by family history of alcoholism. They used what is called a BrAC clamp, 'a method whereby a predetermined steadystate BrAC is achieved and maintained for a prolonged period of time' to evaluate self-reported subjective effects of alcohol in these two different groups. They argued that 'the BrAC clamp greatly minimizes the experimental variance in the achieved alcohol concentration and makes possible long intervals at a target BrAC that is nearly identical in all subjects'. Morzorati et al. (2002, 1301) argue that:

> The visual analog scales for *high* and *intoxicated* consisted of 100-mm lines used to rate current perceptions from "same" (score=100, how the subject felt before alcohol) to "extremely" (score= 200, the biggest effect alcohol has ever had). The subject placed a single vertical slash mark through the line, and the distance (mm) from the left edge was measured. Because the subjects knew there was no alcohol infusion at baseline, the *high* and *intoxicated* scores were generally 100 at baseline. (Morzorati et al. 2002, 1301)

Participants were found to feel more intoxicated after alcohol infusion than after the placebo, but the two groups, those with a family history of alcoholism (FHP) and those without (FHN) experienced this differently. For Morzorati et al. (2002, 1303):

> A differential family history of alcoholism was reflected in self-reported subjective perceptions of intoxication when BrAC was clamped at 60 mg%. From baseline to the start of the clamping interval, FHP [family history-positive] subjects reported significantly more intense feelings of intoxication compared with FHN [family history-negative] subjects. During maintenance of the clamp, the FHP subjects adapted to the effects of alcohol, and their perceptions of intoxication were no longer distinguishable from those of the FHN subjects. Thus, according to self-reported perceptions of intoxication, FHP subjects developed significant acute tolerance to alcohol, whereas the FHN subjects did not. The response differences between FHP and FHN subjects are not explained by drinking history, because the numbers of drinks and drinking days in the 4-week interval before the study were not different between the family history groups.

Another study asked participants to fill in the Subjective High Assessment Scale; rating the items of subjective feelings of intoxication as changes from baseline. Each SHAS question is scored on a 36-point Likert scale from 0 (no effect) to 36 (extreme effect) for items that reflect both more positive effects of alcohol (high, intoxication, a floating feeling, and so on) and potential negative effects (nauseated, feeling bad, feeling clumsy, and so on) (Schuckit et al. 2004, 1501).

In a number of studies evidence about self-reported drunkenness is determined through a question such as: 'Have you ever had so much alcohol that you were really drunk?' Respondents were provided with the following possible answers: 'No, never (0), Yes, once (1), Yes, 2–3 times (2), Yes, 4–10 times (3), Yes, more than 10 times (4)' (Schmid et al. 2003; Zaborskis et al. 2006). Self-reporting can take other forms than those described above. In their research Coleman and Cater (2004, 351) were interested in young people's experience of risky drinking and used a self-report survey to record 'young people's experience and frequency of being "very drunk" and the location where this drinking occurred'. They used a questionnaire which defines intoxication without reference to counting drinks. The questionnaire states: 'By very drunk we mean that you may not have remembered what you've been doing, or ended up by being sick, or falling over, or having a hangover, etc.' They argue that they use this definition of very drunk 'to reduce the complexity of defining and recalling "units" or "number of drinks" (particularly relevant for unsupervised locations)', and that it also 'accounts for individual differences in intoxication thresholds'. Their findings suggest that 'the increased experience of becoming very drunk is most notable between ages 14–15' and further, that:

> the progression from first experience of drunkenness to more regular drunkenness is relatively swift, illustrating the importance of delaying this first drunken experience as a means of harm reduction. Recording the transition to first drunkenness, alongside first ever alcohol consumption, has commonly been overlooked as an indicator of potential alcohol related harm. (Coleman and Cater 2004, 352)

They also indicate that, 'younger people aged 14–15, who reported experience of drunkenness, were more likely to report becoming very drunk unsupervised in outdoor, and potentially more harmful, locations' (Coleman and Cater 2004, 353). In a Danish study of intoxication, debut participants were asked two questions to assess their experience of intoxication: 'How old were you the first time you drank at least one drink?' and 'Have you ever been drunk two days in a row?' Response categories included: have never drunk alcohol; never been drunk; first intoxication at age 12 or younger; first intoxication at age 13; first intoxication at age 14; first intoxication at age 15–16 (Järvinen and Gundelach 2007).

In order to try to quantify subjective interpretations of intoxication some laboratory studies may administer a known dose of alcohol to participants who then predict their level of intoxication. Harrison and Fillmore (2005, 459–464) explain different ways that this has been measured, such as estimation of BAC; estimating the number of standard drinks participants predicted would bring on a state of intoxication; or a perceived ability to drive after a measured intake of alcohol. They argue that, 'the dominant finding of this research has been that people tend to be poor estimators of intoxication. In particular, individuals often underestimate their BAC and the amount of alcohol they consume'. Harrison and Fillmore therefore went beyond a measure of the individual's estimation of BAC to test the accuracy of individual self-report of specific behavioural measures of intoxication. 'The study found no relationships between drivers' estimated and actual levels of behavioral impairment... Thus, despite the opportunity to use specific performance experiences to estimate impairment, participants appeared unable to accurately evaluate their performance'. For Harrison and Fillmore 'self-evaluations of alcohol intoxication are influenced by a host of factors, including interoceptive cues, such as subjective and behavioral changes associated with alcohol use (e.g. sedation, slurred speech, impaired gait)'. Likewise, Moore et al. state that 'self-report data are not suitable to assess consumption in heavy drinkers' (Moore et al. 2007, 629).

It has been argued that these measures do not necessarily reflect the same understandings and definitions of intoxication from all respondents. Levitt et al. (2009: 499) argue that single self-report items (for example, 'To what extent were you drunk?') in assessing subjective intoxication levels is not adequate because different individuals do not define, perceive, or experience being 'drunk' in the same way.

Conclusion

Our purpose in this discussion has not been to question bio-medical and psychological expertise and its attempts to identify the array of possible physiological, psychological and behavioural consequences of intoxication and drunkenness. These often harmful and damaging consequences are manifest in an array of situations, relationships, health and well-being indicators and policy contexts. In many respects some of these consequences are beyond question. But, the ways in which intoxication and drunkenness might be identified, calculated and measured are far from being beyond question. It is the ambivalent, ambiguous and complex nature of these debates that has most concerned us in this chapter. We have begun to map some of these debates so that we can more firmly locate understandings of intoxication and drunkenness in a variety of social, cultural and political contexts. The following chapter continues this move.

Chapter 3

The social, cultural and symbolic dimensions of intoxication and drunkenness

The same volume of alcohol will have quite different behavioural, emotional, and cognitive consequences depending on whether it is taken on a solitary and melancholic evening at home, at a celebratory fortieth birthday party, on the terrace of a football match, or in the controlled setting of a psychological experiment. As sociologists have long demonstrated, these "effects" are never simply given in the drug: they are embedded in complex situations and the affects they generate require all manner of social and contextual support. (Rose 2007, 100, *The Politics of Life Itself*; see Appendix B)

Introduction

While public health, medical and psychological researchers tend to emphasise the objective and individual aspects of alcohol consumption, the cultural and symbolic discourses which surround the terms intoxication and drunkenness play a major role in the way they are understood and enacted in everyday life. As Sande (2002, 279) explains: 'Intoxication has a dualistic form both as a natural object and as symbolic intentions and functions in society'. Therefore any attempt to understand intoxication or drunkenness must approach these terms for both their 'objective', scientific meanings and their contextualised social and symbolic meanings.

A useful introduction to these dilemmas can be found in the ways in which media commentary approaches the roles that alcohol, drunkenness and debauchery play in artistic forms, practices and cultures, and in the lives of artists (see Mayes 2004; Welsh 2002). Discussions of artists' reflections on drunkenness occupy a prominent place in the American news media in particular. The general attitude towards drunkenness and intoxication in the arts is that intoxication is neither unnatural, nor deviant, as a *New York Times* review of Richard Davenport-Hines's book *The Pursuit of Oblivion: The History of Narcotics* makes clear (Kenneally 2002; see also Knightley

2001). In this respect, when we read of Dylan Thomas's '20-year orgy of drunkenness and lechery' (Salusinszky 2004), Richard Harris's '30-year cavort with "Rabelaisian drunkenness and boudoir folly"' (Macaulay 2000), or Peggy Guggenheim's 'drunkenness and promiscuity', and the 'angry wives and girlfriends' she left in her wake (Maslin 2002), art practices and the artistic life serve as a metaphor for the personal and social complexities and contradictions associated with drunkenness more generally.

The dichotomy of drunkenness as a lure and an escape underpins Rhodes's account of Patrick Hamilton's 'heroic drinking' which spurred his best novels, but which also became his downfall (Rhodes 2004). Likewise, Hadley Freeman (2007) describes the novels of Edward St Aubyn as being absorbed with the '"varying states of being trapped, and the false lures along the way", whether they are drugs, drink or false gods and beliefs'. Similar themes emerge in the films of Gillian Wearing and John Cassavetes. Wearing's *Drunk* (1997–1999) is a study of the way drunkenness gives the drinker a mask behind which he or she can hide (Smith 2002), while for Cassavetes, the 'breakdown and breakthrough' of drunkenness 'were sides of the same coin'. Cassavetes's films, writes John Sutherland (2007), 'connect with the problem that torments every problem drinker: is what emerges, in drunkenness, the real you? Or are you, as the phrase "the demon drink" implies, "not yourself" in your cups? Is the final "veritas" really located "in vino"? Or is drunkenness (too literally often) a dead end?'

The tensions between the transcendence and the depravity enabled by drunkenness are also reflected in the paintings of artists such as William Hogarth and Nicolas Poussin. On the one hand, Hogarth's paintings represent the dark side of drunkenness – the side that condemns and which is self-destructive – while Poussin's paintings celebrate the transcendence facilitated by alcohol. On Hogarth's eighteenth century paintings, Adrian Searle (2007) writes that:

> we recognise Hogarth's social types and situations and take them as our own, seeing crack fiends where he saw gin-sodden drunks, aids where he saw syphilis... The endemic drunkenness and violence, the cheapness and carelessness of life that we see in Hogarth's street scenes could be any town in the UK now on a Saturday night.

In contrast, Poussin's classical friezes 'come to wild and crazy life; they celebrate debauchery with a joyous panoply of sins: sexual congress of several varieties, dancing, drunkenness, wantonness, gluttony' (Weisgall 2002). Media commentary on these tensions can also be found in relation to other art forms, including music (Tindall 2008), photography (Cotter 2000), sculpture (Sirmans 2001), theatre (Brantley 2001), and television (Delaney 2007; Hastings 2008).

What this commentary introduces in this chapter is our concern with exploring the cultural, social and symbolic dimensions of intoxication and drunkenness. To explore some of these aspects we turn to, in the first instance, cross-cultural differences in measuring and understanding intoxication and drunkenness. Following this discussion, which also reviews media commentary on the (apparently) national cultural characteristics of drinking cultures, we examine social science research on the dichotomy between 'wet' and 'dry' drinking cultures, terms long used by researchers to characterise different drinking patterns found within Europe. The discussion of these cultural, social and symbolic dimensions of intoxication and drunkenness suggests, in quite powerful ways, that: 'Some basic words, such as "drinking" and "intoxication" are often heavily loaded culturally and are likely to be interpreted differently according to the culture and the individual' (Raitasalo et al. 2005, 360).

Measuring intoxication in different drinking cultures

It may come as a surprise to some readers that the 'hard' science evidence-base on intoxication outlined in the previous chapters varies according to cultural context. Intoxication, like the alcohol content of 'standard' drinks, is measured differently in different countries. For example, in a number of European contexts, 'alcohol concentrations are reported as "pro mille". Pro mille means parts per thousand and is abbreviated ‰. In the United States, Great Britain, and other countries, alcohol is expressed as parts per hundred (%)' (Brick 2006, 1283). Breath alcohol tests (BrAC) are calibrated differently as well:

> Outside the United States, breath-alcohol test results are usually reported in grams of alcohol per 210 L of air, whereas in most of the United States, breath testing instruments are calibrated to convert grams per volume of breath into milligrams of alcohol per 100 mL of blood (mg/dL) or grams per 100 mL (g%). (Brick 2006, 1283)

Furthermore, the alcohol level at which a person is considered to be legally impaired varies by country. The list in Table 2 provides an example of BAC (blood alcohol content) limits for the operation of a vehicle in different countries.

Table 2. Standard BAC limits by country

Country	Standard BAC (in mg/ml)	Country	Standard BAC (in mg/ml)
Albania	0.01	Lithuania	0.04
Argentina	0.05	Luxembourg	0.08
Armenia	0	Malta	0.08
Australia	0.05	Moldova	0.03
Austria	0.05	The Netherlands	0.05
Azerbaijan	0	New Zealand	0.08
Belarus	0.05	Norway	0.02
Belgium	0.05	Peru	0.05
Bosnia and Herzegovina	0.05	Poland	0.05
Bulgaria	0.05	Portugal	0.05
Canada	0.08	Romania	0
Croatia (Republic of)	0.05	Russia	'drunkenness'
Czech Republic	0	Singapore	0.08
Denmark	0.05	Slovak Republic	0
Estonia	0	Slovenia	0.05
Finland	0.05	South Africa	0.05
France	0.05	South Korea	0.05
Georgia	0.03	Spain	0.05
Germany	0.05	Sweden	0.02
Greece	0.05	Switzerland	0.08
Hungary	0	Thailand	0.05
Iceland	0.05	Turkey	0.05
Ireland	0.08	Turkmenistan	0.03
Israel	0.05	United Kingdom	0.08
Italy	0.05	United States	0.08
Kyrgystan	0	Zimbabwe	0.08
Latvia	0.05		

Source: (Standard BAC Limits by Country; ICAP 2002)

Signs of intoxication are considered to be both objective and subjective. That is, some can be measured and others are felt or known by the individual. Across these different settings some of the signs of drunkenness include 'facial flushing, slurred speech, unsteady gait, euphoria, increased activity, volubility, disorderly conduct, slowed reactions, impaired judgement and motor incoordination, insensibility, or stupefaction' (Farke and Anderson

2007, 334). These expressions of intoxication are largely physiological and considered to be more or less universal. However, the behavioural indicators of intoxication are thought to be 'strongly influenced by cultural and personal expectations about the effects of alcohol' (Farke and Anderson 2007, 334).

As we have indicated, intoxication and drunkenness can be, to an extent, objectively measured. Yet when social context is taken into account we find that the meanings that attach to the terms vary in time and place and between social groups (Abel and Plumridge 2004; Room 2001; Room and Makela 2000). In particular, research shows that there are different ways of understanding intoxication and drunkenness in different cultures. One study suggests that 'the definition, acceptability and experience of intoxication vary' even between similar countries, such as Denmark, Finland, Norway and Sweden (Mäkelä et al. 2001, 1575). Likewise, Link (2008, 362) argues that German drinkers drink low amounts of alcohol on a daily basis, and rarely become intoxicated. To take another example, the drinking culture in New Zealand has been said to be very similar to that in the UK, where there is a general tolerance of drunkenness, a lack of concern about physical and mental well-being in relation to alcohol, and a reluctance to limit alcohol (Measham 2006). World Health Organization (WHO) statistics show that the average rate of alcohol consumption per head of population varies considerably across countries and it is likely that levels of intoxication also vary (WHO 2004; see also Lyons and Willott 2008).

Subjective understandings of intoxication and drunkenness

In this section we examine the ways in which individuals themselves define intoxication and drunkenness. Many policy and governmental reports on the use of alcohol in the community frame drunkenness and intoxication in a negative light. Some researchers however, argue that we should address the notion of pleasure and consider how drunkenness is linked in many ways to positive experiences (Midanik 2003; Measham 2008). The use of alcohol as a social lubricant, a way to forget one's problems and peer-related pressures which encourage people to drink for social acceptance all may act as positive influences on people's drinking choices (Measham 2008, 212). Despite the dangers of hospitalisation or violence associated with intoxication, many people enjoy getting drunk.

In one US study, Midanik (2003) examined how drunkenness is defined both quantitatively and qualitatively by asking participants to describe what 'feeling drunk' meant to them. Participants' definitions of drunkenness were categorised into six different themes: 1) Physiological Symptoms, 2) Mobility (Driving/Walking), 3) Positive Outcomes, 4) Control Issues, 5) Speech, and 6) Cognition (Midanik 2003, 1293). Physiological symptoms include dizziness, nausea, vomiting, and light-headedness. Drunkenness is defined in relation to a loss of control and the lack of the ability to walk or drive. In other words some responded by defining drunkenness as 'what activities they could not do in terms of movement' (Midanik 2003, 1297). Control, which is linked to both cognitive and physical function, impacts on people's perceptions of whether or not they considered themselves drunk. Speech problems, such as slurring or mumbling, are indicators of drunkenness. Another way speech can indicate drunkenness for respondents is in the way in which they describe the disinhibiting effect of alcohol consumption. When drunk they speak about things which they later say they would not otherwise have revealed. Drunkenness can also be defined as something that is pleasurable, providing positive outcomes such as stress-relief, relaxation, having fun, being social. Another indicator of drunkenness is the 'inability to think like one normally does' (Midanik 2003, 1297).

Some researchers have explored the ways in which individuals define such terms as *alcoholic*, *heavy drinker*, and *drunkard*, which are social identities related to intoxication (Abrahamson 2003). Indeed, the terms *alcoholic*, *heavy drinker*, and *drunkard* were distinguished in the Swedish study, in part, by the 'quantity, frequency and degree of intoxicated behaviour' (Abrahamson, 2003, 820). An alcoholic is described by one participant as someone who is 'unable to control consumption, drinks until intoxicated even when alone', or as another participant stated, an alcoholic is someone who is 'constantly intoxicated, doesn't have a job' (Abrahamson 2003, 826). Despite the use of measurements based on the volume of alcohol consumed for constructing policy and public health recommendations, Abrahamson (2003) found that none of the participants in his study of young adults in Sweden described or defined drunkenness in terms of the quantity of alcohol consumed.

Kerr et al. (2006, 1429–1436) explain that individual definitions of drunkenness from their US-based research include behavioural and physical consequences of alcohol use that survey measures – involving number of drinks consumed – cannot capture. However, while they also suggest that individuals may define drunkenness based on 'what they consider to be impairment of some type', their study is focused more on 'the meaning of drunkenness and the social, demographic and regulatory forces that appear to influence it'. The participants in this study also described drunkenness in terms that referred to impaired ability to walk or drive, physical symptoms, lack of control, and impaired cognition. Comparing research data between 1979 and 2000, Kerr et al. found that individuals reported needing fewer drinks to get drunk. The authors link this trend to 'more moderate expectations regarding intoxication'. Though the number of drinks declined, the number of respondents reporting being 'drunk in the past year' increased 'to include more moderate drinkers'. The authors argue that this is evidence of a 'shifting definition of drunkenness'. Despite possible cultural shifts, the authors claim that there is a 'wide variability of alcohol intake reported to be required to reach the subjective drunkenness threshold'. They discuss cultural understandings of alcohol trends and shifts in the definition of drunkenness over time, finding that as per capita alcohol consumption fell between 1979 and 1995, the 'number of drinks needed to feel drunk' fell 'substantially' over time. While the trend was for respondents to claim that it took fewer and fewer drinks to reach drunkenness, there was a rise in alcohol use between 1995 and 2000. Kerr et al. (2006) explain these trends as a 'cultural lag' in the social construction of 'what it means to be drunk'. They conclude that this perception of drunkenness related to fewer alcoholic drinks is a positive one: 'the clear reduction in the level of intoxication considered to imply drunkenness' has positive public health implications.

As with expert understandings, some lay people define intoxication on a continuum. In a US study undertaken by Green et al. (2007, 269) the authors illustrate participants' beliefs about moderate drinking in the following way:

> Hmm... It is so subjective. [Pause] I guess I'd have to say a moderate drinker would be somebody who goes out occasionally on the weekends and gets intoxicated to the point where it does not interfere with their life for the rest of the weekend. So they don't get intoxicated to the point Friday night that Saturday they're completely hung over; so that they're still productive Saturday.

While intoxication could be described here as being found along a continuum of alcohol consumption, Green et al. (2007) interpret this participant's description of moderate drinking in another way. They argue that participants understood moderate drinking as the absence of the attributes of drunkenness, as defined in Midanik (2003). In this interpretation, definitions of drinking become black and white; that is, either it is harmful, and attributes of drunkenness, such as the physiological effects, cognitive, speech or other issues around control, are present, or, they are not and it is then interpreted as safe or non-risky drinking. According to some researchers, this black and white way of understanding moderate drinking encourages participants not to consider 'the increased risk associated with higher consumption that does not result in short-term negative consequences or drunkenness' (Hammersley and Ditton 2005, 498).

In their research Mäkelä et al. (2001, 1577–1583) posed the following question to get a subjective definition from participants across Denmark, Finland and Norway: 'During the past 12 months, approximately how often did you drink so much beer, wine or spirits that you felt intoxicated?' This measure seeks to quantify intoxication *frequency* but does not ask participants to define intoxication. Instead, this study measured 'intoxication drinking' by 'recording the number of days in the week prior to the interview when the respondent had drunk six or more drinks during one day'. A drink, here, was defined as 1.5 cl of pure alcohol. The authors claim that this means the participants then 'reported having drunk at least nine centiliters of pure alcohol in a day' and they define this as 'intoxication drinking'. In other words, this article defines what they call 'subjective' intoxication quantitatively. By comparing the answers to these two measures (frequency of drinking 6+ and the subjective measure of the frequency of intoxication) Mäkelä et al. (2001) suggest that they are gauging whether participants felt that six or fewer drinks were enough to feel intoxicated.

In this cross-cultural study, the authors found that 'the Danes reported drinking 6+ more often than they reported intoxication, while Finns reported intoxication more often than they reported drinking 6+' allowing them to conclude that 'on average, in Finland clearly less than six drinks sufficed for the subjective feeling of intoxication, whereas in Denmark six drinks were not enough, and in Norway just slightly less than six drinks were required' to induce a feeling of intoxication (Mäkelä et al. 2001, 1587). Two of the reasons given for this discrepancy between the measures were, that Danes drink more, and more frequently, giving them a higher tolerance. And second, some people in all these countries require more than six drinks to feel intoxicated. Mäkelä et al.'s (2001, 1587) argument that 'the way people define the word intoxication or picture the concept in their minds has a great impact on the results' is relevant here. It was also suggested that being intoxicated may be less socially-acceptable in some countries, such as Denmark, where respondents were less likely to label themselves as intoxicated. Interestingly, the authors say that 'they have no data on *attitudes toward drunkenness*' (our emphasis), and use the terms intoxication and drunkenness interchangeably: 'In cases where intoxication is expected, people may act as if they are more drunk than they actually are. In other words, acceptability of drunkenness affects drunken comportment and reporting behaviour'.

In summary, both scientific measures and lay understandings of intoxication and drunkenness vary according to cultural context. Research primarily from the US and Nordic countries, has found that lay understandings of drunkenness tend to focus on observable behaviour and short-term consequences rather than fixed definitions, objective measures and long-term consequences.

Drinking cultures and the popular imagination

We want to introduce a more detailed discussion of the cultural, social and symbolic dimensions of intoxication and drunkenness by examining the ways in which the news media – as both mirror and shaper of the popular imagination – highlights social anxieties about local drinking cultures. In a review of some of this commentary we are presented with a heady mix of racial stereotypes, selected research findings and drinking anecdotes about which cultures are civilised drinkers and which are problematic. Anglo cultures, particularly the British, their former colonies and northern Europeans are presented as problematic bingers and drunkards. By way of contrast the French or 'the Europeans' are viewed as civilised drinkers who are sometimes presented as being corrupted by changing global patterns, and the Swedes and Nordic countries are viewed as sensible managers of alcohol. Cross-cultural comparisons are used to shine a light on the host culture by either justifying its drinking culture, criticising it or both.

Frequently the news media assumes that a country's attitude towards alcohol reflects that country's attitude to life in general. This, of course, makes it a lot easier for the media to distinguish between different countries since a discussion of the drinking cultures of each country stands in for the culture as a whole. This was certainly the view of Frank Kelly Rich, the author of *The Modern Drunkard*, whose advice on 'How to Drink With Foreigners' includes: 'The Belgians, for example, like to pound wine at football games, while the English prefer to pound Belgians. In Wales, on the other hand, they refer to intoxication as being "flogged", while in Iran they like to think of it as a good reason to "be flogged"' (cited in Smith 2005).

By focusing on how drinking cultures differ between countries the foreigner serves two functions in much media commentary. On the one hand, she/he is the negative other – the Scot, the Australian, and the Russian – whose 'uncivilised' drinking allows a country to see that its own drinking habits are not so bad after all. Alternatively, she/he is the positive other – the 'European' – whose 'civilised' drinking puts a country's own drinking habits to shame, and who offers an alternative perspective on how drinking and drunkenness can be managed differently.

The case of Ireland highlights how the drinking culture of a foreign country can serve these two functions simultaneously. On the one hand, Angelique Chrisafis details the level of intoxication amongst young Irish men, who 'drink to excess on 60% of their nights out', she writes, and are 'three times more likely than the European average to get into a drunken fight' (Chrisafis 2004; see also Quinn 2001). At the same time, Chrisafis argues that Ireland has tried to counter the 1950s 'racist stereotype of the drunken emigrant drowning his sorrows in a north London pub' (see also Hamilton 2003). In another context one account claims that the Irish should be commended for overcoming their penchant for 'debt, drunkenness and despair' (Waters 2004; see also Burns 2001) in being declared the best place in the world to live by *The Economist* (in a study in which the US ranked 13th and Britain 29th).

Often, then, media commentary references the drinking habits of the foreign culture in order to both condone and condemn their own country's drinking culture. This is particularly true of the British press, which seems particularly sensitive to problems with the way Britons drink. Writing in *The Times*, Joan McAlpine (2008) argues that Britain must take lessons in how to drink from countries with 'similar cultural roots'. The comparisons here are with the Americans, who consume eight litres of pure alcohol per head per year, compared to 10 in Britain and 14 in France. She argues that 'the one French success' Britain should try to emulate is 'not their tradition of opening all hours or giving the 10-year-olds burgundy diluted with water. The lessons from both France and America are clear. Whether it is forced on us by the law or simply fear of illness, we have to say "no" more often. It's really that simple' (McAlpine 2008).

At different times, and in different spaces, the Scots, Australians and Russians embody the foreigner with uncivilised drinking habits. Nick Thorpe (2004) describes the attitude of Scottish drinkers as 'prohibition in reverse' when they refuse to allow him to not drink an extra pint, while one account in the *New Zealand Herald* (2003a) describes Edinburgh as 'home to snivel-nosed urchins, ladies of bawdy repute and grave-robbers'. Further, that 'it was the scene nightly of drunkenness, hefty opiate abuse and dead-eyed copulation, a murky netherworld devoted to hedonism and treachery'. More pragmatically, Angus Macleod (2005) argues that the Scottish 'booze culture' is having significant damaging impacts on the Scottish people, suggesting that more than 40,000 Scots were admitted to hospital with alcohol-related medical conditions in 2004–2005. This apparently represents a 21 per cent increase from 2000 (see also Hjul 2006; Mahoney 2001). The problem, writes Macleod (2005), is that Scotland has a drinking culture 'similar to other parts of northern Europe... a culture of heavy drinking, pure and simple', and while it is possible to increase people's understanding of the damage that excessive drinking can do, there is little one can do 'in terms of improving levels of personal responsibility'. In *The Times* Macaskill and McKendry (2007) report that:

> A United Nations study claimed [Scotland] was the most violent country in the developed world with more than 2,000 people being attacked every week and three times more likely to be victims of violent assault than those in America. Another study, published by the University of California, claimed that Scotland had a higher violent death rate than America, Israel, Uzbekistan, Chile and Uruguay.

A story in the *New Zealand Herald* (2006b) describes Sydney in much the same terms, citing how 'the faint stirrings of the nation's social conscience', emerged only 'when floggings for "insubordination" and drunkenness were limited to 50 lashes in response to concerns about brutality in the new colony'. As part of its coverage of the 2000 Sydney Olympics, *The Wall Street Journal* described the city as 'reveling in vice', a 'licentiousness' that Tony Horwitz (2008) traced 'to 1788, when the "First Fleet" arrived here with 736 convicts, mostly petty thieves'. Contemporary Melbourne 'after dark', moreover, is described as having 'a distinct Gotham City feel about it', marked by the Friday night 'routine' of 'violence and intoxication' (Anderson 2006).

Another account in *The Washington Post* considers the influence that vodka has played in Russian history, claiming that 'to say that alcohol has played an important role in the history of Russia would be an understatement' (Baker 2001b). On a number of occasions stories in *The New York Times* have depicted the *Russian* in terms of a moral vacuity in which *he* resorts to 'criminality, drunkenness, indifference and inactivity' (Figes 2002; see also Binyon 2002; Williams 2000; Finn 2005; Higgins 2000; Chazan et al. 2002), and Moscow is depicted as plagued by alcohol-fuelled racism (Mydans 2003). This representation draws on historical examples – the 'Cossack world of brutality, drunkenness, syphilitic disfigurement, cunning, valor and unintentional comedy' (Bernstein 2001) – as well as modern counterparts in Boris Yeltsin (Service 2000) and the mercenary soldier fighting in Chechnya:

The kontraktniki, as they are called, are not the professional career soldiers that typify Western armies. They are more like mercenaries. They are older than the conscripts and better trained when it comes to using weapons. In Chechnya, they are said to make up about a third of all Russian troops. They have also been linked to many of the cases of looting, drunkenness and attacks against civilians, which is not surprising since they are generally rowdy men, excited by violence and serving for relatively brief periods and only for pay. (Gordon 2000)

For Gordon (2000) British drinking habits - 'the discussions, the games, the drunkenness, the foibles of the landlord, the conviviality, the unpredictable gathering of diverse people' – appear positively harmless by way of comparison. However, the 'dark' side of British and Australian drinking frequently emerges in comparison to the 'civilised' drinking habits of other cultures. Here *European* drinking represents the possibility of a more 'civilised' drinking culture. Bachelard (2008) highlights the difference between Melbourne's drinking culture, and the European civility to which it aspires in an article examining the causes of alcohol-related violence in Melbourne's CBD during the years at the start of the twenty-first century:

> In Melbourne the main concern seems to be about the very large bars, such as CQ in Queen Street, which has a licence for 6170 patrons. This is hardly the European ambience that Premier John Cain envisaged when he made Victoria's licensing laws the most liberal in the country in the late 1980s.

The contrast here, writes Kate Legge (2008), is between 'the Paris end of Collins Street, where the European ideal of restaurants and bars that Melbourne celebrates' exists, and 'the King Street scourge at the other end of town'. Of course, what the press considers to be a 'civilised' drinking culture is relative, for while Melbourne strives towards a 'European ideal' in its drinking, Sydneysiders strive for the more 'thriving, adventurous scene in Melbourne, Perth, Brisbane, London or Wellington' (Farrelly 2007).

New Zealand papers also often lament the drinking culture that they inherited from the British. One story in the *New Zealand Herald* (2003b) claims that the history of the country's liquor laws 'more than anything else represents a microcosm of New Zealand social history as a whole'. The temperance campaigner Rev. W. J. Williams said, 'the white man and the whisky bottle came to New Zealand together'. These white men included

European explorers, followed by whalers and sealers in the eighteenth century and then the 'mostly working-class British, brought a binge-drinking pub culture' that New Zealand is still living with today. From very early on in its drinking history, it was recognised that alcohol played an ambivalent role in New Zealand society. Since the first brewery was set up in 1835, New Zealanders have 'tended towards an all-or-nothing approach – drink until you fall over or don't drink at all'. For nineteenth century New Zealanders, alcohol was both a 'faithful companion' and 'responsible for "nine-tenths of the evils of society"' (*New Zealand Herald* 2003b). Thus, despite its ubiquity, Dr Mike MacAvoy argues that New Zealanders 'have always had an uneasy, ambivalent relationship with alcohol', a 'love/hate relationship – "enjoyable for many, but ruining the lives of others"' (*New Zealand Herald* 2003b).

Often European drinking cultures are admired but at other times the Australian news media displays ambivalence towards supposed 'civilised' drinking cultures, such as that of Spain. On the one hand, a story in *The Australian* (Bennett 2008) celebrates Spain as 'the only country... where the doctors prescribe red wine to pregnant women (it's good for the baby)', where 'public drunkenness is institutionalised', and 'where *botellon*, or "mass boozing in public places", is central to the national culture'. On the other hand, celebrating such a drinking culture is hardly imaginable for the Australian *Herald Sun*, which is keen to highlight the dangers that drinking during pregnancy poses to the foetus (Burstin 2003). There are, it seems, both advantages and disadvantages to such 'civilised' drinking cultures.

The same contradictions are evident in the way the British media discusses drinking in France. On the one hand, the French are celebrated for their 'sophisticated' and 'continental-style' – that is, non-British – drinking. For instance, in a period in which it is claimed that the British have increased their per-capita drinking consumption by 50 per cent, the French reduced theirs by the same amount (*The Guardian* 2006; see also O'Reilly 2003). Polly Toynbee (2005) attributes the persistence of Britain's problems with drunkenness to that 'extreme end' of British culture 'that finds any reference to drink coyly funny, the wink-wink, nudge-nudge, don't mind if I do, ooh but I shouldn't attitude that imbues drink with the wearisome naughtiness of beer mat-collecting and poker-work booze jokes hung up behind the bar'. What is common to these examples is an attitude that glorifies drunkenness and intoxication, an attitude that condemns male and female drinkers alike by making drinking 'macho... the symbol of bonding mateyness where bingeing becomes de rigueur' (see also *New Zealand Herald* 2006a;

Macintyre 2005). The alternative to glorifying binge drinking in this way, writes Toynbee (2005), is to be found 'across the channel', with the French and the Germans, who, while once drinking more than the British, are now drinking less. For the French and Germans, she writes, 'drunkenness isn't cool'.

But even these sorts of accounts exist in tension, even contradiction, which seem to suggest quite contrary views. In a story from 2008 *The Guardian* is particularly concerned by studies that show that French young people are becoming more like British young people, rather than the other way around:

> So what has gone wrong? What has prompted France's youth to turn from sensible tipplers to full-on booze abusers? Etienne Apaire, who heads up an inter-ministerial body aimed at combating both drug and alcohol addiction, has told French media that he believes the phenomenon is simply part of a 'globalisation of behaviour' evident in all 27 EU member states, in which teenagers increasingly seek 'instant intoxication' as an end in itself. (Henley 2008)

In another account *The Guardian* (2004b) cites Belgium as an example of a European drinking culture in order to highlight the problems with British drinking. In order to gauge how drunk Britons really are, the anonymous reporter visited both Nottingham (the 'home of binge-drinking') and her sister city, Ghent, in Belgium. Both cities are of similar size (approximately 250,000 people live in both) and both feature 'historic centres with lots of bars'. But the incidence of violence is markedly lower in Ghent than in Nottingham:

> In Ghent, the police told me, they dealt with a violent incident on average once every fortnight. In Nottingham, I couldn't get close to the police to ask them: they were too busy breaking up fights and arresting people. In Ghent, some of the bars remained opened until 8am in the morning and you could buy beer in McDonald's. In Nottingham, there were teams of bouncers on every bar and at chucking-out time (11pm or midnight for bars, 2am for clubs), gangs of intimidating young men roamed streets that were devoid of public transport and conveniences.

The difference between the British drunk and the Belgian, the reporter concludes, is that the Belgian is a 'contented drunk – to be drunk is the goal, and he is not looking for anything more than that'. For the Nottingham drunk, in contrast, getting drunk is the means to 'something more, be it another drink, a bus, a taxi, somewhere to relieve themselves or a fight' (*The Guardian* 2004b; see also Morris 2001). And it is the sense that British drinkers are looking for something more than drinking that is the cause of much of the social disorder that media commentary claims is associated with drinking in Britain. In the same way, Andrew Martin (2004) argues that one of the reasons mass-produced lagers are so popular with American drinkers is because 'they provide no distraction on the way to intoxication', while *The Australian* sums up the logic of heavy drinking as: 'If being drunk is a sign of a good time, then being very drunk must be a sign of a better time' (Hutchinson 2003; see also Milburn 2002). According to the WHO, this attitude of 'drinking to get drunk' is now the norm for young people around the world (cited in Farouque 2007).

Giles Whittell (2004), writing for *The Times*, expresses considerable self-loathing in his description of the 'exuberant reality of industrialised British drunkenness':

> We drink. We pee. We drink. We dance. We drink. We eat. We vomit. No one else does this for fun. It doesn't seem to occur to people in Paris, Berlin, New York or Istanbul that it might be worth the effort, but it does to us, over and over again, often several times in a single 48-hour recreational cycle. We are as unrivalled for the energy we put into getting drunk as for the fun we get out of it, and of course we take the ritual with us when we go abroad. We take it to the Balearics, where they tolerate the smell of our sick because they like the colour of our money. We take it to Faliraki, where there was no police station until we started mooning the local virgins. And this month we have taken it to Portugal for the football.

Some media commentary suggests that such drinking cultures can be changed. Simon Jenkins (2007), writing in *The Guardian* argues, for instance, that the 'so-called social habits' of British teenagers – unruliness, drunkenness, drug-addiction, pregnancy and imprisonment – 'can be influenced by government policy'. Jenkins argues that there is a clear correlation between the ease with which people can access drugs, and the personal and social disorder that results from their consumption. So, just as 'consumption of cigarettes fell as higher duties were imposed', so should we expect to see an *increase* in drink-related crime if proposals by the British government to introduce 24-hour drinking licenses go ahead. Indeed, as Neilan (2000) suggests in *The New York Times*, the problem with the current law in Britain that pubs must stop selling alcohol at 11 pm is that it encourages drinkers to drink as much as possible in as short a time as possible. As a result, closing time sees large numbers of highly intoxicated people spilling out onto the streets *en masse*. This can lead, argued the former Home Secretary, Jack Straw, to 'increased drunkenness, with people "hitting the streets – and sometimes each other – at the same time"'.

British drinking is also condemned in comparison to the example that is set in Sweden. In some media accounts Sweden represents not only the idyllic space that has escaped the scourges of drinking and drunkenness encountered elsewhere in Europe, it also represents possible solutions to those problems. Sweden has adopted the 'Scandinavian' approach to alcohol regulation, which involves strict State monopoly over the production, distribution and sale of alcohol, which experts claim are 'effective in reducing drinking' (Daley 2001). This approach has also ensured that Sweden has one of the lowest rates of drunkenness in the European Union (EU). Yet, rather than seeking to emulate the Swedish model, the EU is trying to force Sweden to change its anti-alcohol policies to bring them into line with EU rules of fair competition (Boyes 2004). This is, according to Daley (2001), an opportunity wasted by Britain, which could have learned from the example set by Sweden. Sweden is nevertheless hoping that 'they can influence the rest of the European Union to see alcohol as a health problem', especially in the southern countries, which are 'seeing a rise in binge drinking among the youth'. Maria Renstrom, an expert on alcohol policy with the (Swedish) Ministry of Health and Social Affairs is quoted claiming that: 'We are getting some of their drinking and they are getting some of ours… So maybe we will be able to find common ground'.

In the meantime, however, Swedish officials have fashioned a new anti-alcohol plan that focuses on education, including programs for pregnant women, tough drunk driving laws, tougher regulations governing serving drinks to minors and a ban on liquor advertising (Daley 2001). In many, if not all of these cases, media commentary tends to emphasise the social costs of drinking, drunkenness and, in the case of Sweden, anti-alcohol policies. The primary concerns with much of this commentary are the impact that drinking has on young people, on addicts, and on crime – and therefore on how governments should respond to these problems. What Daley (2001) has highlighted here is the way that the narrative the media constructs about drinking and drunkenness centres on two key themes: the *consequences* of drinking – the personal and social disorder caused by alcohol abuse – and the *solutions* to drinking.

Comparing 'wet' and 'dry' drinking cultures

Cross-cultural differences in drinking and intoxication have been given much consideration by social scientists, particularly in the European context. Researchers have developed a way of understanding drinking patterns using a geographical division between northern European drinking styles (Britain and North America are often put into this category) and southern European drinking. Some studies have shown that:

> Societies in which alcohol is traditionally an accepted and morally neutral element of everyday life, such as southern European cultures of Italy, Spain, France and Greece, have lower rates of drunkenness among young people than societies with a more ambiguous, uneasy relationship with alcohol, such as Scandinavia, Britain and North America. (Elgar et al. 2005, 249)

This divide between different types of drinking cultures has been characterised as 'wet' versus 'dry':

> At the "dry" end would be the traditional pattern in the Nordic countries, where drinking is largely segregated from everyday life routines into specific drinking contexts and where intoxication is the central concern when drinking. This kind of cultural environment requires careful consideration for the distinction between the boundary of drinking and non-drinking contexts, as well as the boundary between intoxication and non-intoxication. At the "wet" end is the Mediterranean drinking culture, where alcoholic beverages have permeated into everyday life in a multitude of ways, and social survival requires command of a very variable cultural code of the proper use of appropriate drinks in appropriate contexts. (Raitasalo et al. 2005, 370)

By way of example, Raitasalo et al. (2005, 361) suggest that:

> In Finland, people mostly drink at weekends and festive occasions and drinking often aims at intoxication, whereas in Italy, daily drinking is a widespread practice and people are rarely intoxicated. Germany and the Netherlands are situated in between these two extremes. In these countries there is more variation in respect to time and place of drinking compared with Finland and Italy, whilst in drinking to intoxication there is more variation in these countries compared with Italy, though less compared with Finland.

While these differences are often referred to, there are also researchers who find the wet/dry dichotomy increasingly problematic as drinking habits and cultures have changed over time. For instance, Room and Makela (2000, 478) argue: 'consumption levels have been converging in Europe, with per capita consumption falling in wine cultures and rising in northern Europe. The labels "dry" and "wet" make less sense as the per capita levels converge'. Traditionally, this model has been used to describe alcohol drinking in European countries. However, as the 'frame of reference expands beyond Europe, it also becomes clear that the label "dry" has been applied to rather divergent cultural framings of drinking'. The dilemmas associated with this method of framing different cultural contexts for drinking are further developed by Room and Makela (2000, 478), when they suggest that:

> A society in which almost no one drinks within the national borders can be described as dry. But what about a society in which drinking is confined for many to a few fiestas each year and in which the public discourse around alcohol is negative and moralistic? Or a society in which consumption has risen in a few decades from very low levels to levels that rival the levels of the wine cultures, but which seems to have retained a tradition of sporadic extreme drunkenness? These descriptions approximate the positions of Saudi Arabia, Mexico and South Korea, respectively; although each has features that fit the dry archetype, it is questionable how useful it is to treat them all as a single type.

Nordlund (2008, 87) suggests that it is difficult to use the terms intoxication and non-intoxication across cultural settings as they will be defined very differently by different groups. However, 'there might be a common understanding of the meaning of "strongly intoxicated" since there is an upper limit to how intoxicated a person can be without losing consciousness'. While still acknowledging that this limit can vary between people, 'when someone is approaching this limit', she argues, 'we can certainly state that this is regarded as "strongly intoxicated" in all cultures' (see for example; Cameron et al. 2000 who propose a methodology for comparing terms cross-culturally). Nordlund (2008, 87) goes further to claim that there are two 'fixed endpoints' to 'the interval of intoxication': sober and strongly intoxicated, which is defined as 'on the limit of unconsciousness'. These points are understood to be 'independent of culture (a pure biological fact)'.

Wolska et al. (2004, 67–69) illustrate cross-cultural and gendered differences to understanding and talking about intoxication in their small, qualitative study with Polish–Australian immigrants. Male participants, and some female, spoke of women who drank alcohol as 'having "loose morals, being unfit mothers and bad wives…"' In other words, 'a drinking woman became stigmatized, a disgrace to the family, and a "black sheep" in the eyes of the community'. Interestingly, Polish women immigrants to Australia appeared to be shy talking about their own and other women's behaviour when intoxicated, often describing themselves as light drinkers. However, women were observed drinking 'heavily' at parties (an ill-defined, '8 large drinks') then acting 'as if they had had nothing to drink but water throughout the whole night'. This finding is in contrast to how their male counterparts were perceived. These men 'appeared intoxicated after a few drinks…' Young girls spoke of their alcohol use in similar ways to their mothers. One said, 'I have a couple of mixed drinks before we go out and later I might have five to six or more… no, I never get drunk'. Self-reported drunkenness is, then, a product of not only the amount of alcohol drunk but also the socio-cultural expectations around drunkenness and appropriate gendered behaviour.

Another study by Dean (2002, 755) discusses the way in which weekend evening drinking in a public bar in the isolated Western Isles (Hebridean islands) off the west coast of Scotland differs from the mainland. Initially, the scene resembles that of a comparable night on the mainland. However:

> Intentions cause the outcome to be both more gregarious and more drunken than elsewhere. Islanders intend to participate in collective drunkenness, and through that to enter a shared disinhibited celebration of friendship and shared identity. The event resembles a private party, such as a Western wedding reception or a 21st birthday celebration, more than an evening in a bar. The relative isolation of the Western Isles may explain these drinking patterns. Most people have known each other for most, if not all, of their lives. Many are related in some way. Thus an atmosphere exists of great familiarity and relative security, which is seldom reproduced in less-closed communities. In consequence, the loss of inhibitions due to drinking occurs largely away from the gaze of strangers, and drinking is both rapid and extensive.

Only particular kinds of communities can promote this kind of relationship, which is one of *collective drunkenness* between patrons in a bar. This contrasts with the ways in which drunkenness and intoxication are defined through some of the issues related to the night-time economy of the UK and Australia.

There have been a number of large scale surveys in Europe to better understand how drinking habits differ between countries. These studies tend to report drinking patterns and levels of consumption. One example is the European Comparative Alcohol Study (ECAS) which involved national surveys carried out in six countries: Finland, Sweden, Germany, Great Britain, France and Italy. It is comprised of survey data collected in May 2000, in these six EU member states, with about 1000 respondents (aged 18–64) that were randomly selected in each country (Room and Bullock 2002, 627; see also Leifman 2002a; 2000b). While there were reported methodological issues with this survey – as is common to large scale surveys of this kind – what we are interested in concerns the different ways in which the ideas of intoxication and drunkenness may be defined and understood in different cultures. These ideas do not stand separate from levels of consumption but our main focus here is related to definitions and understandings of intoxication and drunkenness. Thus the ECAS study provides a useful insight into these.

Clear differences emerged in the frequency of drinking (found to be highest in France and Italy, lowest in Finland and Sweden, and increasing with age in France and Italy in particular, but also in Germany); and the quantity of alcohol consumed (the average consumed quantity per drinking occasion is highest in Finland, Sweden and the UK, and lowest in France and Italy, with the youngest in age showing the highest quantity per drinking occasion in most countries). While not explicitly defined, 'intoxication-oriented drinking' was found to be 'most common in Finland, Sweden and the UK, and in all countries except Italy the youngest report the highest frequency of intoxication' (Leifman 2002a, 501). This report uses intoxication and 'heavy drinking occasions' interchangeably and claims that younger drinkers are more likely to drink to intoxication. Leifman explains, 'young French and Germans, as well as the youngest in Britain, Sweden and Finland, show a higher frequency of intoxication than their elders' (Leifman 2002a, 545 –546). Anxiety about 'intoxication oriented' behaviour of young people in Finland has been heightened as the alcohol control system has been relaxed (Törrönen 2003, 284).

To get a better idea about the implications of intoxication, about the ways in which individuals interpret the social role of intoxication, 'five items about expectations about alcohol's role in violence, and the potential excuse-value of intoxication' were included in this survey. As Room and Bullock (2002, 619) report:

> The results were not in the expected direction. Finnish respondents were more likely than others to value not showing any effects after drinking. Italian, French and British respondents were the most likely

to believe that getting drunk leads to violence. Italian, German and British respondents were most likely to believe that friends should forgive and forget after drunken anger, and Italians and British were the most likely to excuse behavior because of drunkenness.

The ECAS data was analysed using the theoretical framework of *wet* and *dry* drinking cultures. The role of alcohol-related violence has been hypothesised to have different relationships in each: 'A hypothesis that drinking plays a stronger causal role in violence in "dryer" cultures than in "wetter" cultures has long been latent in the literature' (Room and Bullock 2002, 622). Room and Bullock (2002, 642–643) examined the link between wet and dry drinking cultures and violence and found that the wet/dry distinction is not clear cut. They asked: 'Can alcohol expectancies and attributions explain western Europe's north-south gradient in alcohol's role in violence?' In their discussion they find no easy answer to this broad question:

> On none of the five items that we examined in this paper was there a clear north-south gradient. Agreement with the idea that "anyone might become violent after drinking too much" was quite strong in all six samples, but strongest in Italy and weakest in Finland – against the direction that would fit with the findings of a greater role of alcohol in violence in northern Europe. Italian respondents, again, were the most likely to agree that a drunken person is not as responsible for his actions as a sober one – with the greatest contrast here being provided by those from another "wine culture", France. In agreement with this, the French respondents are also least likely to agree that behavior while drunk should not count between friends afterwards – this time joined by the Finnish respondents. While agreement was not high on the idea that "it doesn't matter how much you drink as long as you don't show the effects", there was more agreement on this from Finland, Italy and the UK than elsewhere – again, not a north-south split.

It seems that drinking cultures are dynamic and in an era of globalisation not as fixed as previously imagined. For Room and Bullock (2002, 644–645) this dynamism means that:

> We may need to start again to develop an understanding of how drinking norms and social control of drinking work in southern European cultures. From the present study and others, there are several challenges to the picture of southern European drinking that is often presented in English-language and Scandinavian sources, which, as

Olsson (1990 [see Appendix B]) has pointed out, often has elements of a projected fantasy. It is often said that people in wine cultures learn to drink in a controlled way at an early age, at the family dinner table, and that because of this they don't get drunk. But the results from the ESPAD surveys and from Leifman (2002a) cast doubt on this. Although southern Europeans drink more frequently in between the heavier drinking occasions than northern Europeans, there does not seem to be a systematic north-south split in terms of prevalences of fairly regular heavy drinking. Social control around drinking in wine cultures is also usually thought of as internalized, in terms of self-control. Yet in the present data sets it is the Finns and the Swedes (along with respondents from the UK) who are most likely to report regretting things they've said or done while drinking (Ramstedt, 2002 [see Appendix B]), and it is the Italians who are most likely to have tried to influence others to drink less (Hemstrom, 2002 [see Appendix B]).

In light of these ambiguous, and shifting, understandings of intoxication and drunkenness Room and Bullock (2002, 645) caution against ready, self-evident conclusions about cultural similarities and differences among wet/dry lives:

> Underlying many hypotheses about cultural differences in drinking is a half-hidden assumption that handling drinking and problematic drinking is more effortless and unself-conscious in some societies than in others – and particularly, in the wine cultures. The data set we have been analyzing calls this assumption into question. Heavy drinking occasions occur in southern Europe as well as in northern Europe, and minimizing the harm from them does not seem to be something that happens without attention or effort.

In the next section we turn to smaller scale studies to examine different understandings of drunkenness and intoxication in different social locations.

Local drinking cultures and the moral holiday

Smaller scale studies by anthropologists and sociologists and the relatively new field of tourism studies have also considered the different understandings and meanings of intoxication and drunkenness between cultural groups in different settings. This research has tended to focus on the ways in which different groups stage intoxication over the life course or at festival or holiday times. For example, in a study of Italian men aged 40 to 45 and 65 to 70 Scarscelli (2007, 314) used individual interviews to examine the drinking trajectories of these men. Scarscelli (2007, 314) identified three models of alcohol consumption patterns over one's life. They were characterised as follows:

> the use of alcohol gradually increases and remains a constant in the subject's life until the adult phase is reached, when it decreases; alcohol consumption rises gradually until reaching a peak that characterizes a phase of elevated consumption, after which it decreases; alcohol consumption varies considerably over the years – a pattern which is characterized by different phases.

Further, Sarscelli (2007, 324–327) argues that: 'The intoxicating use of alcohol, which was little integrated into daily life, was abandoned by the majority of the younger group members, as life changes eventually impacted their drinking patterns. Eventually, they would adopt more integrated drinking habits that were very similar to those of their parents'. Scarscelli analyses her data through a sociological framework, reading the intoxication patterns of older men with an eye to the importance of context:

> Different systems of norms guiding the use and abuse of alcohol co-existed within our society. Consumption styles could be judged by referring to different criteria: the "intoxicating" use of alcoholic beverages (away from mealtimes and aimed at changing one's conscious state) was more easily tolerated when occurring in particular circumstances by those adopting new consumption models. Instead, such use was stigmatized by those embracing traditional models; an "addicted" use of alcohol (that of an alcoholic or "drunkard") was most probably stigmatized by both the groups. The stories of our panel of interviewees confirmed the existence of both controlled and uncontrolled excessive behavior. From a sociological point of view, only the second could be considered a problem, being a drinking behavior that did not conform to those social rituals controlling alcohol consumption in specific social and cultural contexts.

Shifting our focus a little we encounter research that focuses on the use of intoxication as an excuse for a 'moral holiday'. In one study Sexton (2001) considers the role of intoxication through ethnographic research of the rural Cajun *Courir du Mardi Gras* (Mardi Gras run) in south Louisiana. While intoxication is considered the cause of the rowdy behaviour which characterises this event, Sexton (2001, 28) argues that alcohol consumption does not have a causative role, but instead works in conjunction with 'the anonymity of masking' associated with the event:

Intoxication, or the appearance of intoxication, which may involve minimal alcohol consumption, confers a degree of immunity for the foolish conduct that defines Mardi Gras. It also serves as a ready excuse for unacceptable behavior. Drunkenness in this context is thus better viewed as a culturally constructed form of ritualized inebriation although there is the potential for actual over-consumption to the point of physical impairment.

Using this type of framework to understand intoxication, it then becomes possible to imagine ways of understanding common outcomes of excessive drinking, such as violence, in alternative ways to typical medical and public health interpretations. For example, when Sexton (2001, 28) encounters violence and unruly behaviour it is interpreted in the broader context of Mardi Gras and the relationships of participants to each other, not simply individualistically, where number of drinks or blood alcohol content impact upon an individual's behaviour: 'When violence and play reach an unacceptable level they are more accurately attributable to longstanding personal conflicts, loss of temper, overzealous play on the part of participants, and spectators' negative reactions to Mardi Gras antics'. The complexity of violent acts and behaviours, and their problematic association with levels of intoxication are evident in Sexton's (2001, 31–32) definition of violence in the context of Mardi Gras:

> A range of behaviors including vandalism and inadvertent property damage, serious arguments and threats, injuries, fighting, and minor scuffles. Violence includes acceptable or marginal Mardi Gras play such as roughhousing among Mardi Gras, wrestling between Mardi Gras and captains (which is responsible for many of the injuries that occur), teasing young children until they cry, roughing up adolescent boys who tease the Mardi Gras, and overzealous pursuit of chickens that results in damage to shrubbery, flower beds, and fences.

Sexton (2001, 28) locates and positions this ethnography in French Louisiana, where alcohol consumption 'contrasts with adjacent areas where Anglo–Protestant ethics traditionally frowned on alcohol consumption. Alcohol in south Louisiana is available at drive-through Daiquiri shops, liquor stores, convenience stores, and gas stations. Beer is sold at Catholic Church fairs and community fundraisers'. While alcohol is an important part of social relations, excessive drunkenness and a lack of attention to responsibilities is, still, frowned upon. Sexton (2001, 29–30) uses the

Mardi Gras as a context in which to explore this 'duality in the Cajun cultural ethos':

> On Mardi Gras morning participants begin to gather at 7 a.m. at a farm in the heart of Tee Mamou operated by the captain's extended family. They cluster in small groups consuming beer, wine, whiskey, and homemade concoctions such as cherries soaked in whiskey and oranges injected with Vodka. About 8 a.m. the captain calls the group to order and announces various rules regarding, for example, drinking in moderation, respecting people and property, not fighting with captains, and obeying the captain's commands. The captain frequently goes to great lengths to articulate concerns about responsible drinking, for example, telling the group one year that "If you are here just to throw a big drunk then you might as well go home".

Sexton (2001, 33) concludes, then, that despite raucous behaviour exhibited by Mardi Gras participants, the role of alcohol and intoxication is not found to be causative: 'For those who do not understand the event, and even for many who possess some knowledge of Mardi Gras, such non-normative behaviour seems understandable only within a framework of intoxication'. However, many of these 'acts are learned behaviour that is part of the Mardi Gras performance that requires one to play the beggar and clown rather than a direct consequence of drunkenness'. Without denying the impact that excessive alcohol consumption has on participants who do drink to intoxication, Sexton highlights the importance of role playing in this ritual event.

The recent emergence of a new field in cultural studies broadly labelled tourism studies also examines the connections between intoxication and cultural contexts. In this field researchers such as Bell (2008, 296) use the term 'alcotourism' to identify a field of research that 'aims to take seriously the study of alcohol, drinking and drunkenness as situated cultural experiences and practices'. Bell explains that this sub-discipline finds impetus in 'its desire to understand and participate in local drinking cultures, and its broader fascination with locally embedded meanings and uses of alcohol'. Bell (2008, 296) draws from Wilson (2005; see Appendix B) to note, for instance, 'regular and repetitive drinking is not necessarily perceived as drunkenness or alcoholism, and such behaviours may not be a sign of a breakdown in culture, but rather may be evidence of a strong and supportive cultural framework'. Bell argues that this view provides 'an important reminder to attend to the local in research on drinking places and practices, and a caution against universalizing taken-for-granted understandings about drink and its effects'.

In this milieu then, alcohol, and particularly intoxication can be interpreted as 'a liminal experience, a time-limited escape from "normal life", a chance to let go, to be someone else, do something new... including the "letting go" that comes with intoxication' (Bell 2008, 293). While it is argued that travel is becoming increasingly 'banal' there are still, Bell argues (2008, 293), many accounts of travel where this letting go aspect of alcohol use looms large. Not only is this experienced by individuals on holiday, but, Bell argues, it is in fact packaged for easy consumption. 'Various forms of "party tourism" package this letting go, providing an ambivalently sanctioned liminal zone, understood as necessarily restorative: the holiday is a needed break that helps the tourist "recharge" and therefore re-enter society relaxed and refreshed'. Essentially, Bell argues that intoxicated holidays are not a free for all, but rather that they follow their own logic and are governed by a unique set of rules. Regulation of intoxication and drunkenness is finely balanced in the alcotourism context. Drawing from the work of Nicholls (2006), Bell (2008, 293) suggests that:

> Drinking remains a deeply problematic social practice in that, especially in the context of deregulation, it rests on a fine balance between rights (or freedoms) and responsibilities. This idea, enshrined in notions such as "sensible" or "responsible" drinking, is inherently troublesome, Nicholls rightly notes, since "intoxication is an antonym of control".

The tension between marketing a party-atmosphere and regulating this context of liminal space is central to alcotourism. However, Bell (2008, 293) argues, 'alcotourism practices should not be straightforwardly aligned with debates about alcohol regulation or deregulation, since the many meanings and uses of drinking on holiday require a more nuanced analytical framework'. This framework has yet to be developed, though in doing so, holiday intoxication and drunkenness are likely to be distinguished from everyday life at home.

A new culture of intoxication and the night-time economy

Human geography is not a discipline often associated with public debates about alcohol and its consequences (Jayne et al. 2008, 249) but geographers offer an important perspective on the social context of alcohol consumption, particularly in their work on the operation of the night-time economy in contemporary cities in the industrialised democracies. Sociologists and public health researchers have also contributed substantially to research on the social dynamics of the night-time economy.

The 'night-time economy' refers to the rapid development of inner cities, the creation of night-time entertainment precincts and substantial increase in the number of pubs, clubs and restaurants in many late twentieth, early twenty-first century post-industrial cities. The development of the night-time economy throws up contradictions for Western governments in their dual concerns of enhancing economic development and maintaining public health and safety (Hayward and Hobbs 2007). Local councils have encouraged the development of night-time entertainment precincts to enhance local business and employment opportunities. However, difficulties have arisen in managing problems of intoxication that go with these developments. The night-time economy is defined as a space of contradictions. On the one hand young people are encouraged to use inner city spaces to consume – thus enabling increased development and business opportunities. On the other hand increased surveillance, policing, and other forms of social control increase debate around the problematic nature of young people's use of that space. Young consumers are blamed for 'binge drinking' instead of government policies (Measham and Brain 2005; Hayward and Hobbs 2007; Lindsay 2009). The use of city space for young people's drinking and entertainment has been called a 'subversion of space'. However, Hayward and Hobbs (2007, 438–439) argue against this interpretation. Instead, in their view, drunkenness and violence is 'a pathologizing rendition of the transgressive dynamics of the night time economy that utilizes the spectacle of public drunkenness as a cautionary, yet seductive tale' (see also Tonkiss 2004; Appendix B). Lindsay (2009) discusses the dynamics of the night-time economy in Australia and argues that young people 'stage intoxication' in these settings.

Jayne et al. (2006, 452) argue that understanding urban drinking rituals is an important way of theorising the city as well as drinking practices within the city. At the same time they argue that we need to contextualise this activity in a global network of corporate, individual and cultural practices:

> This includes, for example, studies of how supranational, national, regional and local drinking practices (and related issues) are played out in specific urban spaces and places. A key element of such a project is to develop a more nuanced understanding of the social relations and cultural practices associated with the emergence of particular kinds of historic and contemporary urban drinking spaces.

The nuanced understanding that Jayne et al. (2006) call for involves understanding the city and its economies as interrelated, not deterministic.

According to Jayne et al. (2008, 249) 'alcohol studies have been overwhelmingly dominated by a focus on medical issues and a pathologizing of alcohol as a social problem, or as a legislative, crime or policy issue'. However, as we have argued throughout this discussion, intoxication and drunkenness are inevitably social practices and they can be more usefully understood in their social context. Drawing from Mary Douglas (1987; see Appendix B), Jayne et al. (2008, 249) argue for more engagement with the 'everyday social relations and cultural practices bound up with drinking'. They describe a study by Kneale (1987; see Appendix B), which examines data from the 1930s and 1940s in the UK and which discusses the central social and cultural role that drunkenness played in that time and space. The study by Kneale describes 'how experiences of drunkenness were learnt through socialization' and, highlighting the sociality of drunkenness, 'Kneale argues that drinkers did not consider that they were involved in a transgressive practice, but rather that drinking was simultaneously about being part of the community and also about being a good customer'. Relationships and community developed in spaces such as this: 'Pubs were considered by their patrons to be spaces for relatively intimate social relations, and encapsulated within this are associations of drunkenness with... trust and reciprocity that encouraged a relaxation of inhibitions' (cited in Jayne et al. 2006, 456).

Measham and Brain (2005, 268) argue that the current debates around binge drinking in the UK are not simply a 'repackaging' of older debates around alcohol use but they are in fact reflective of a new 'culture of intoxication'. This new culture, so they claim, has been ushered in by recent social changes including such things as the following: the normalisation of illicit drug use; the transformation of the alcohol industry to respond and compete with psychoactive drugs; the recommodification of alcohol and sessional consumption, including the changing types of drinks and the way that they are marketed as lifestyle markers; the increase in the strength of alcohol-based drinks; and the changing styles of venues, such as from traditional pub culture to vertical drinking in bars and clubs. It is claimed that such developments have all influenced this new culture of intoxication.

Measham (2006, 258) argues that 'moderation and restraint are culturally at odds with a contemporary emphasis on economic deregulation and excessive consumption' and that 'an emergent culture of intoxication has been facilitated by supply-side initiatives'. She claims that 'a new culture of intoxication is emerging that features a determined drunkenness by young adults as part of a broader cultural context of risk-taking and hedonistic consumption-oriented lifestyles bounded by occasion and location' (Measham 2006, 263). Lindsay (2006, 30) also argues that in Australia 'there is evidence that the "decade of dance" is over' and the use of party drugs, such as ecstasy, is 'declining and young people are turning back to determined drunkenness as their preferred mode of intoxication'.

McCreanor et al. (2008, 945) suggest that there is a danger that the notion of *determined drunkenness* 'can be cast as a property of young people themselves' as opposed to a possible 'critical reading of the concept to raise the question "determined by whom?", to foreground the roles played by alcohol marketing in achieving these outcomes'. For these authors 'marketing belongs among the "causes of causes", a key social determinant powerfully shaping the discursive and material conditions that produce health promoting or health demoting behaviours at a population level'. Of course, the literature points not only to alcohol marketing but also licensing regulation. In this context Eldridge and Roberts (2008, 365) comment on the Licensing Act of 2003, effective in England and Wales, allowing licensed premises to operate for 'up to 24 hours per day'. By their interpretation, the purposes of the new act, which updates the former act of 1964, more specifically provide:

> Greater "freedom and choice" for the consumer and, in turn, generate a more civilised attitude towards alcohol consumption. In contrast to the former regime, where patrons would be forced to "drink up" before the standard 11 pm closure, the 2003 Act would allow for a more measured and "European" style of leisurely consumption.

However, others, such as Nicholls (2006, 146) have interpreted the 2003 Licensing Act as representing 'the micro-management of harm reduction'. In other words, legislation such as this is seen to shift the responsibility for managing intoxication away from the government:

> While upholding the right to trade and consume, it devolves responsibility for managing the effects of intoxication to the lowest level: local authorities can target specific retailers and can create "alcohol disorder zones"; retailers are responsible for managing the drinking on their premises and for promoting "sensible drinking"; consumers will be subject to both public health campaigns and ground-level measures such as on-the-spot fines.

The contradictory nature of the night-time economy can be understood as stemming from legislation such as this, in which:

The government insists that it is "encouraging individuals to exercise choice based on improved knowledge and awareness" (Home Office, 2005: 4 [see Appendix B]), but the great paradox of "drinking responsibly" is precisely that intoxication is an antonym of control... The "freedom" of intoxication, such as it is, is a freedom from regulation, discipline and order. The expectation that consumers will exercise their freedom to drink in a "competitive and vibrant marketplace" for alcohol (Home Office, 2005: 14), while both micro-managing their consumption and resisting intoxication, is a clear instance of disciplinary practice. (Nicholls 2006, 147)

In this sort of argument contradictions are seen to arise when people are required to act as informed, rational consumers while participating in consumption in a competitive marketplace.

Eldridge and Roberts (2008, 366) 'question the manner in which consumers are commonly represented as either civilised "social drinkers" or "binge-drinking urban savages"'. In their research they conducted focus groups with 160 people in five locations around England, each of which had or has established an emerging evening economy including bars, clubs, restaurants and other leisure zones. Three major themes emerged from the study: 'the central role of alcohol in the evening economy, the need to look at drinking practices in context, and the desire for more "comfortable" venues at night'. In this research the contradictory nature of the night-time economy is made evident. That is, Eldridge and Roberts argue that while: 'Concerns about health and city-centre violence, as raised by both tabloid and broadsheet newspapers, are, of course, important' they also find that the mundane nature of 'drunkenness and the everyday experiences of the city at night are often far more nebulous than such reports imply'. Their findings present a Britain in which the consumption of alcohol is central and therefore, they argue that 'it is crucial to acknowledge the sometimes ambiguous behaviours and practices that inform alcohol consumption, and the ways in which cities are often experienced as a composite of complex and sometimes competing emotions, behaviours, motivations and experiences'.

In other words, the ways in which media commentary in Britain characterises intoxication and drunken behaviour, as we outlined earlier in the chapter, is often superficial, simplified and not responsive to the multiple ways in which individuals use alcohol in their lives. As Eldridge and Roberts (2008, 369) suggest:

A night out, for one participant, could just as easily entail heavy drinking in a loud, youth-orientated venue, as it could having a quiet drink with friends at her "local" or in a restaurant. Her desire, as she phrased it, to "be stupid" some nights did not preclude her desire to "be sensible" on others, which often entailed visiting the theatre or ballet with her mother. For another participant, though she was reluctant to venture out due to a fear of violence, she lamented the closure of a "£10 all-you-can-drink" venue. These venues have been singled out for irresponsible promotions, and yet, for her, they had been an enjoyable and comfortable place to socialise with friends.

These participants bring attention to a simplification often found in media commentary that characterises people as either *intoxicated, urban savages* and/or as *social drinkers*, 'wrongly assuming' that revellers cannot be both. The researchers explain that this dichotomy which 'frames current conceptions of late-night Britain is not altogether inaccurate – there are problem drinkers, and town and city centres at night can be sites of alcohol-related violence'. However, the 'figure of the "binge" versus "social" drinker as imagined by tabloid headlines assumes a consistency in drinking practice and a stable drinking identity that is not entirely accurate' (Eldridge and Roberts 2008, 369).

The context we have discussed in this section is the contemporary, often cosmopolitan city, which, as David Bell (2006; see Appendix B) notes, 'generally includes the provision of "drinkatainment", based around drinking attractions (and other contemporary landmarks, including theatres and restaurants) such as themed bars and pubs ranging from staged authenticity provided by Irish theme pubs to Soviet-styled vodka bars' (cited in Jayne et al. 2006, 457). The night-time economy is a contradictory social space: 'simultaneously conflictual and segregated, commodified and sanitized, saturated by both emotion (enhanced through alcohol, drugs, dance, sex, encounter) and rational elements (planning, surveillance and policing) – and that such tensions are not always easy to understand and reconcile' (Jayne et al. 2006, 459). Jayne et al. (2006, 464) therefore argue for accounts and forms of understanding that can engage with the ambiguity of the night-time economy, and which enable a new way of understanding drunkenness linked to active citizenship. Such accounts, they suggest, could:

> be considered in terms of the connectivities and belonging generated in public space, and as being grounded in pleasure, enjoyment and the "riskyness" of heterogeneous groups of people mixing in city spaces in

ways that perhaps would not be acceptable, to them or city authorities, if the mediating factor of the consumption of alcohol in bars, pubs and other establishments did not enable drinkers to claim to be active citizens.

In summary the night-time economies developing in globalised cities around the world are an important new context for alcohol consumption and intoxication and drunkenness. In the next section we examine other key settings.

Settings for intoxication and drunkenness

In this section we extend on our discussion of the night-time economy to examine the different social, cultural and symbolic dimensions of intoxication and drunkenness in drinking settings such as neighbourhoods, bars, pubs and clubs and university accommodations (fraternity houses in the US), and with friends in public spaces and domestic settings.

Ahern et al.'s (2008, 1046) epidemiological study involving 4000 respondents in New York City illustrates the importance of neighbourhood context in relation to drinking habits. Without explicitly defining drunkenness their study explores the relationship between local norms related to drinking alcohol and drunkenness and finds them to be distinct. That is, 'even when an individual believed that it was acceptable to get drunk regularly, if there were stronger norms against drunkenness in the neighborhood, that individual was less likely to binge drink'. These findings were independent of family, friend and individual norms, highlighting the important influence that immediate social context, such as one's neighbourhood, can have on patterns of drunkenness.

Some studies show that the location of alcohol consumption relates to incidence of intoxication. Kypri et al. (2007, 2592) found that 'pubs/bars/clubs were the locations with the highest odds of drinking to intoxication'. Lindsay (2006, 42) also found that drinking practices vary across locations. For example, she explains:

> Niche venues tended to sell boutique alcohol products including imported beers and top-shelf spirits. Good quality wine and spirits were available from the bar and some of the niche venues did not have beer on tap but only sold bottled beer in individual serves. Patrons were drinking excessively at niche venues but drunkenness was rarely evident; perhaps it was not socially acceptable to appear intoxicated in these venues.

By contrast visible intoxication was more accepted in mainstream commercial venues such as large dance clubs that catered to younger patrons, students and non-professional workers (Lindsay 2006).

Some social science research touches on the issue of place in relation to intoxication. For example, the level of risk associated with young people's alcohol use is seen to be related to the location or context of the drinking. In one study it was claimed that high risk drinking 'occurred in a variety of public or "hidden" outdoor locations where it was more likely to result in intoxication' (Newburn and Shiner 2001, 25). In this research it was also suggested that 'supervised drinking, particularly drinking within the home, is relatively unlikely to lead to drunkenness' (Newburn and Shiner 2001, 73).

However, other research suggests, for example, that private parties in domestic settings are key contexts for intoxication. Abrahamson (2004, 8) argues that 'drinking to the point of intoxication is generally a collective experience, especially among the young'. In their research Demant and Ostergaard (2007, 526–529) examined the ways in which intoxication is both an individual and collective event and has an influence on the 'ambience' of a house party. This focus group study asked not only about the individual's level of drinking but also how the individual rated her quantity of drinking against the other drinkers to gauge the 'relational drinking style' of the participants. They concluded that having a 'drinking style that is similar to the others' is then interpreted as drinking collectively'. Examining the space in which drinking occurs, Demant and Ostergaard propose that 'it is the collective feeling of intoxication, not just the function of drinking, which is decisive in transforming the room into a party space'. Their main conclusion, that 'it is more difficult for adolescents to see themselves as drinking collectively if they do not consume rather large amounts of alcohol… suggests that the collective experience "of drinking like the others" is associated with getting intoxicated together'. Young people must monitor themselves and drink an amount determined solely by each other's behaviour that is acceptable in the group. In this way, 'the feeling of getting intoxicated becomes a collective and not an individual experience'. As one of the participants explains: 'It's not cool to be the first one to run around and say uh uh [acting silly]'. Demant and Ostergaard suggest that each group has its own drinking style and each individual must be aware of what that is. Unlike health and medical researchers, for young people (and arguably other individuals as well), 'what matters is not the specific number of alcohol units consumed – as long as it is relatively high'.

For Demant and Ostergaard (2007, 533) defining a collective state of experience of intoxication appears essential for young people to carve out their space: 'Getting intoxicated collectively is essential to these adolescents' way of partying, but mainly because it is the way to zone the place into "our space" and reassures the proxemics of the network. Intoxication, then, is an effective way to mark that the space is now captured and controlled by the teenagers themselves'. They suggest that the space created by young people drinking alcohol is perceived very differently by young people than it is by adults. For example, they argue that:

> From the outside it may look like serious drinking pressure. However, from the point of view of the adolescents it looks different. According to the adolescents, getting intoxicated together is a mutual way of reassuring attraction to one another. When they drink in similar manners and offer each other drinks, every single one of the participants shows that they are committed to the party and appreciate the company of friends. Thus, drinking alcohol is the central aesthetic communication that unites the partygoers at a specific party. Refusing to drink, especially if one is offered something, then becomes a rejection of the aesthetic that creates the sociality in the group.

Intoxication, it appears, can serve many purposes for young people. If this is so it is a context in which counting drinks to define intoxication would make very little sense.

Much media commentary, however, does not consider the social importance of intoxication when it discusses the impact of alcohol on education. One long-term consequence of heavy drinking represented in media accounts is a diminished capacity to attain academic achievement. A drinker is marginalised from opportunities in education due not only to the long-term damage done to a drinker's brain (see Farouque 2007), but also because many elite American universities tolerate 'aggressive drunkenness' in their striving for sporting success, even if it comes at the expense of academic success. So, as Jane Brody (2008) argues:

> of all the advice parents give to children heading off to college, warnings about alcohol – and especially about abusing alcohol – may be the most important. At most colleges, whether and how much students drink can make an enormous difference, not just in how well they do in school, but even whether they live or die.

The reality of college life, according to Goldenberg (2006), is a situation in which education is forced to the margins for the sake of sporting success (see also Wilson and Glater 2006a; Wilson and Glater 2006b; Brody 2008). For example, at Duke University in the US, success in sport and in education is largely incompatible and when the bad behaviour of students who will bring the university the former is tolerated – as it increasingly is – their opportunities for educational achievement necessarily suffer:

> Some critics see a growing tension between Duke's twin ambitions of achieving national prominence in academia and sport. Although a strong college football or basketball team puts a university on the national map – and can be extremely lucrative – some professors fear the effects of big-money sports on the academic side. In their drive to build a championship team, universities spend millions on top-flight coaches and players. And they will tolerate a lot to keep them: poor academic performance, prolonged absences, aggressive drunkenness and, it seems, criminal acts. Simply put, sports stars are gods on the campus, and get away with things that other students cannot. (Goldenberg 2006)

The university or college as a space for drinking to levels that cause intoxication and drunkenness has been the object of much research. In one US-based ethnographic study with 21 participants drawn from college-based fraternity houses Workman (2001, 433–436) found that euphemisms for drunkenness – such as *blitzed*, *trashed* and *loaded* – were used to frame drinking stories. Adventure and risk-taking along with resisting authority were seen 'as both positive and respectable, and danger is seen as an unquestioned virtue' in this context. Workman's analysis explored drunkenness as a performance, where the drunken actors performed for those who are limiting their alcohol intake, or staying sober. These activities lead to 'stupid stories' which serve 'an important function for the culture in framing drunkenness as a form of recreational play'. Workman argued that 'most stories revolved around a streaking activity that combined bravery (risk of embarrassment) with drunkenness (careless abandon)'. Here, then, drunkenness is itself defined as a state of 'careless abandon'. Turning to the construction of sexuality within drunkenness, Workman (2001, 440–441) suggested that 'many of the constructions of sexuality mirror other textual cues such as alcohol product advertising'. Taking a cue from many of the 'product advertisements, sexuality is seen as a gendered activity that views women as a source of pleasure and alcohol as an aphrodisiac'. Importantly, Workman finds that drunkenness itself underpins the experience of being at university and in particular being in a fraternity. 'The social practice [of drunkenness] also represents the college experience; drunkenness is seen as a key confirmation of having been at the university'.

The ways in which alcohol use changes over time was also highlighted by Workman (2001, 441): 'There is a clear sense among members of the fraternities that the need for drunkenness changes over the course of an academic experience, moving from extreme to moderate as the newness and adventure begins to fade and as the student develops competence in consumption'. Essentially, Workman's study illustrates the social and cultural discourses that influence drinking practices within fraternities and that those students found drunkenness important for many reasons. These context/setting specific reasons outweighed the negative consequences advertised by public health campaigns. In fact, most participants were unwilling to contemplate these messages:

> Drinking spaces, commercial messages, and other cultural artifacts support the view that drunkenness has positive social functions. Particularly for men, the interpretation of alcohol consumption being connected to sexual conquest from advertising is almost cliché. Much like the habitus of the fraternity drinker, the commercial message avoids the tragic tale, opting instead to tell stories that show only positive consequences or to frame negative consequences as ultimately entertaining. The message from the public health institution, then, is truly in the minority to the many messages that equate consumption (and particularly overconsumption) as ultimately positive and functional. (Workman 2001, 443)

Given that students tend not to be affected by negative campaigning found in many public health campaigns, Workman (2001, 443–444) suggests that 'Our task may be to find other approaches than identifying the negative consequences of high-risk drinking, but to promote the positive consequences of low-risk or moderate consumption'. In conclusion, Workman explains the limits of public health discourse which focuses on the number of drinks consumed. The 'ultimate goal' of drinkers such as those studied by Workman, 'is drunkenness, particularly ritual drunkenness'. Workman further argues that it is in addressing the 'dysfunctional meanings of drunkenness' which would provide benefit, not counting of drinks. He suggests targeting 'areas of meaning construction' such as 'the connection of drunkenness to sexuality and sexual subjectivity (especially from the standpoint of participating women) to the detachment of negative consequences when relating stories in all mediums'.

Conclusion

The social and symbolic dimensions of alcohol consumption are important for understanding drunkenness and intoxication. There is ample evidence that definitions of intoxication and drunkenness vary according to cultural context, geographic location and drinking settings. In both the popular imagination and social science literature there is considerable anxiety and ambivalence about cultures that value intoxication and drunkenness. In much media commentary simplistic cultural stereotypes are drawn such as the bingeing British and Australians, the easygoing southern Europeans and sensible Nordic cultures to criticise public behaviour and imagine alternative cultural arrangements. These are partly supported by the social science literature – southern European drinking has been typified as moderate drinking of wine with meals whereas British and northern European drinking was typified as 'binging' or drinking beer or spirits to achieve rapid intoxication. However, recent research also questions these cultural differences and with the development of globalisation the distinction between 'wet' and 'dry' cultures is becoming less useful and more nuanced metaphors are necessary.

Intoxication and drunkenness are often social practices rather than simply individual practices and getting drunk with others is valued in some social groups and settings. Drinking settings strongly linked with drunkenness and intoxication include the night-time economy in post-industrial cities but also university fraternities and private parties. The new culture of intoxication identified in the UK literature describes the phenomenon of large numbers of young people drinking rapidly to intoxication as a means to pleasure, escape and loss of control. Pleasure and escape from everyday life are also key elements of contemporary 'alcotourism'. In the following chapter we explore the ways in which intoxication is practiced by particular social groups and the way 'problem' groups and settings are defined and managed.

Chapter 4

Young people, men and women and Indigenous Australians: Different understandings of intoxication and drunkenness

Introduction

In this chapter we examine the various understandings and meanings of intoxication and drunkenness as these relate to different populations. In this discussion we draw on the ways in which media commentary represents the problem of intoxication and drunkenness in relation to young people, Indigenous communities in Australia, and men and women. These accounts are located alongside, and in contrast to, the ways in which the psychological, scientific and sociological research literature understands intoxication and drunkenness in relation to these populations.

Our discussion suggests that the population that attracts the greater focus in all of these accounts is young people. Media commentary tends to be sensationalised and reinforces stereotypes but even here there are differences in reporting, with some journalists taking a more balanced view. There are some attempts in this reporting to define intoxication and drunkenness but on the whole, the meanings of these terms are often taken for granted and meaning is to be inferred by the context of the reporting. What is clear, however, is that there are different norms around intoxication and drunkenness amongst different groups, and that these norms are strongly mediated by both geography and culture. The story that emerges from the media commentary that we examine here is about how people drink; therefore, what drunkenness 'is' consists largely of stories about the drinking cultures of different groups *within* a society. So, in this case, we encounter stories about Indigenous people, young people and women, and the problems that stem from 'their' drinking. This commentary often paints broad pictures of the drinking cultures of these groups as a way of contrasting the dominant drinking culture with those 'problem drinkers' on the margins of society.

The research literature also, often sees certain populations as posing particular problems in terms of intoxication and drunkenness. What our discussion suggests, however, is that there are a number of attempts to explore, discuss and understand these issues in ways that can account for the symbolic, social and cultural meanings that drinking, intoxication and drunkenness may have for individuals in these groups. This research points to the shifting, and often contested, meanings that individuals attach to drinking, intoxication and drunkenness.

Young people and the problem of intoxication and drunkenness: Media commentary and the popular imagination

The dominant theme in media commentary on the drinking cultures of young people – drinking cultures often characterised in terms of *binge drinking* – is that it poses a problem that demands government intervention. This theme of youth binge drinking, however, also considers the role that parents play in facilitating young people's drinking, and the crime that is perceived to result from binge drinking. The characterisation of young people's binge drinking is not, however, consistent. Much of the news media seems content to reproduce the stereotype of the binge drinking youth, such as those who attend spring break in the United States (Warren 2007), and university 'O-Week' (Roginski 2006), or schoolies week in Australia. For the Melbourne *Herald Sun*, schoolies is a 'holiday from hell for many, with sexual assault, stabbings, hundreds of fines and arrests, drug and alcohol binges, sexually transmitted infections and even death' (Ford 2008; see also Halliday 2007; Haywood 2005; Wilson 2002). These sorts of characterisations are considered unhelpful by some, and they earned the media a rebuke from Professor Rod Morgan, the British Government's chief advisor on youth crime, who 'pleaded with politicians and the media to stop calling children "yobs". [He] said young people were getting mixed messages: on the one hand, they were the country's future; on the other, they were thugs in hoods' (Button 2005). Young drinkers themselves also want to resist being reduced to such stereotypes in the media, with one girl telling *The Age*: 'I don't like it when adults depict teenagers as if they don't have any idea of the world, that we're not responsible about drinking or drugs or our own personal health. I have my own limits. I know when to stop' (Farouque 2007).

Indeed, some newspapers do attempt to question the link between youth and problem drinking. For instance, in a report on the Victorian State Government's new alcohol policies, which it claims are driven by 'alarming trends' in 'the increase in extremely drunk young people turning up at hospitals to be treated for accidents or acute intoxication', *The Sunday Age* (Bachelard 2008) points out that the figures that led the Government to this conclusion are complex, and that 'anecdotal evidence' from police suggests that alcohol-related assaults were falling. And so while much commentary does not doubt that there is a problem with young people binge drinking, many others seek to highlight when the figures do not coincide with official claims about youth drinking.

Moreover, although they are rare, the media also runs stories that depict youth in a more flattering light. Claire Halliday (2007) notes that while schoolies week is notorious for the binge drinking of school leavers, 'the majority of young people are more behaved than belligerent', and that 'most of them make good choices and have their own safety strategies in place'. Likewise, Jessica Shepherd (2008) is critical of the media's portrayal of students as hard-drinking hedonists, which she argues is no longer appropriate at a time when 'sober is becoming cool'. Shepherd's research is based on figures drawn from the National Health Service (NHS), rather than from the British media's usual source, the Home Office. These findings contrast with the dominant depiction of youth drinkers in the press. She suggests that for many university students, 'it's becoming more socially acceptable not to drink huge amounts – or at all'. The NHS figures would appear to confirm this view. According to the figures that are referenced the number of teetotallers aged between 16 and 24 is rising; the proportion of both men and women who are (binge) drinking more than 21 units and 14 units of alcohol per week respectively fell markedly between 2000 and 2005; and the number of teetotallers aged between 11 and 17 rose from 36 per cent to 46 per cent in the decade from 1996 to 2006 (Shepherd 2008). The same rise in teetotal youth has been observed in Melbourne (Bachelard 2008), contradicting the media 'rhetoric [that] suggests that the problem [of binge drinking] is suddenly escalating'. However, *The Age* also notes that an international study has shown that 'young Australians are outstripping their American counterparts in drinking' (Farouque 2007). This is evidence of what Shepherd calls a 'polarisation' in youth drinking cultures. On the one hand there are a group that might be called the 'abstainers' who are very often overlooked by the press. The media more often focuses on 'heavy drinkers' who drink more often, and 'consume stronger brands of beer, cider, lager and spirits' (Shepherd 2008). *The Australian* identifies this same polarisation in the drinking habits of individual drinkers, writing that young drinkers often have 'a relatively teetotal working week, followed by one or more binge sessions on the weekend when... "all hell breaks loose"' (Nogrady 2008).

Ultimately, Shepherd (2008) takes an optimistic view of youth drinking, suggesting that 'the 2000s could be characterised as the calm after the storm, in terms of young people's drinking. By and large, the millennium has seen the turning of the tide in terms of the practices and preferences of intoxication'. The same trend has been observed by the *Otago Daily Times* (2004b) in a story that argues that university students in Dunedin, New Zealand, are not stupid, 'but they act stupid sometimes. The result of intoxication is that their common sense goes out the window and they do unnecessarily stupid acts'.

Another story in the *New Zealand Herald* (2003b) seeks to position the issue of young people's intoxication and drunkenness as a historical problem, and one which is shaped by generational relations between parents and children/young people:

> The images of alcohol we see most often are still the extremes – the good times of beer commercials or the shocking drink-driving ads. Ambivalence remains. And with our new liberalism comes new problems... The fallout of that has been that alcohol is more readily available and well within the reach of young people who have more mobility and disposable income.

The article continues: 'More than half the alcohol underage drinkers consume comes directly from their parents... Teenagers today, mimicking their parents – and, unknowingly, the pioneers of 150 years ago – still see binge-drinking as a badge of adulthood and a cure for boredom'. This commentary appears to draw on familiar discourses of 'rites of passage' and bored and disaffected youth.

Discussions of young people and alcohol are almost universally framed in terms of a paternalistic concern for young people who, it is presumed, cannot take care of themselves. But, as David Bruce (2003) writes in the *Otago Daily Times*, the reason for a crackdown on young drinkers by politicians has less to do with any inherent concern for the health and safety of young people, and more to do with their 'disgust' at the 'state of the main street the morning after the night before'.

Young people are often depicted by the press as living risky lives, and binge drinking is but one part of that risky lifestyle, along with, writes

Nicci Gerrard (2004), 'drugs, sex, deafening music, outbreaks of violence'. Writing in *The Guardian*, Emine Saner (2006) provides a typical narrative of the problems that face young people who binge drink. According to this narrative, the consequences progress from the mere embarrassment of 'doing things you wish you hadn't', to dependency, to the risk of causing long-term damage to the brain, to coma, and finally to death. Yet, other sections of the media suggest that deaths from alcohol poisoning are rare – in 2002, nine teenagers died in Britain – but alcohol plays a significant part in teenage deaths due to accidents, violence and suicide. Thirteen teenagers a day are hospitalised as a result of drinking – either for alcohol poisoning or from injuring themselves when drunk. In this story it is claimed that by the age of 13, more teenagers drink than those who do not and that the amount consumed has doubled since 1990.

While this narrative is repeated often in the media, different aspects of it are emphasised in different stories in different spaces. Thus, when there was a sudden jump in 'alcohol-related admissions to hospital for children aged 10 to 14' in New Zealand, the *New Zealand Herald* (2007c) used it as a basis for calling for government intervention – 'to reform our boozing behaviour' – by raising the legal drinking age to 20. But the paper remains sceptical as to whether any government-led campaign can work if it does not address the drinking habits of adults, whose 'tolerance and acceptability of drunkenness as a social norm' it blames for fostering drunkenness amongst young people. Writing in the *New Zealand Herald*, Doesburg (2004) admits that for many adults, getting drunk is 'a rite of passage', with many adult New Zealanders engaging in something akin to binge drinking. Indeed, Doesburg suggests that 'some of the worst stories of drunkenness... have come from today's middle aged parents about their own youthful exploits' (see also Lisante 2001). Accounts in *The New York Times* (Kilgannon 2002) and *The Age* (Farouque 2007) agree that 'it is hard to address drinking among children and not among parents' since 'parents set the example at home, and a well-stocked liquor cabinet is a message, a temptation and an easy source'. Likewise, Doesburg (2004) writes that for most New Zealanders, 'there's a general belief that it is okay to be drunk'. He explains '85 per cent of us drink alcohol, half of us think drunkenness is socially acceptable, and an estimated more than a quarter of a million were aiming to end up in that state when they last drank'.

In many of these stories there is often a scepticism related to relying on parents to discipline their teenage children since many commentators often regard parental indifference as contributing to teenagers' binge drinking in the first place. As one New York social worker suggests: 'many teens in these towns have permissive parents, so they have to try harder and go further to shock them – what better way to rebel and separate from your parents than showing up drunk at homecoming?' (Kilgannon 2002). One story in *The Age* (Farouque 2007) also argues that permissive parents are largely responsible for the binge drinking of their children. It is claimed that this sort of permissiveness results in incidents such as the drunken brawl involving an estimated 100 to 150 students from a secondary school in the affluent eastern suburbs of Sydney (Hutchinson 2003). In New Zealand a story in the *Otago Daily Times* (2006c) argued that one of the problems with trying to regulate young people's drinking is that it can inadvertently turn intoxication into a 'badge of defiance', giving young people an incentive to drink excessively. Writing in *The Sydney Morning Herald* Kang (2006) argues that the problems of youth drinking can only be addressed if we 'stop celebrating drunkenness and hangovers as though they are trophies to be won to gain social status'. The same concerns are raised by Ellen Moorhouse, the president of a US-based not-for-profit organisation that seeks to reduce alcohol and drug abuse: 'There is more of a tendency among some affluent parents to say, "My child works hard all week, so as long as they get straight A's, why can't they blow off some steam too on the weekends?"' In this story the narrative suggested that some parents' concept of severe punishment amounts to taking away their child's mobile phone or depriving them of some other luxury item, and that some parents' main concern after hearing that their child has been caught drinking is that it might affect their college acceptances (Kilgannon 2002).

In contrast to the scepticism that accompanies discussions in the media about the capacity for government intervention to reform the drinking habits of young people, a story in *The New York Times* broadly supports programs set up by young people to help other young people who find themselves in trouble because of alcohol. This account details the damage young people do to themselves as a result of drinking, such as the incident when a star high school football player died at an after-school beer party 'after getting punched and hitting his head on a patio'; or when 200 students showed up to their homecoming dance drunk, many of whom 'wound up passing out or vomiting into trash cans' (Kilgannon 2002). And like their counterparts in Britain and New Zealand, young Americans readily admit that 'alcohol – often binge drinking – dominates their social life... They say young people are experimenting with alcohol at younger ages, and the overall goal of many teenage drinkers is to get "totally wasted", or falling-down drunk' (Kilgannon 2002). This story claims that any 'intervention' must be led by young people themselves, not from adults and governments whose paternalistic view of youth drinking is a barrier to understanding their drinking culture. The journalist cites the example of *Safe Rides*, an organisation based in Westchester, New York, a community 'plagued by underage drinking and the dangers, image-tarnishing and reckonings' it causes. *Safe Rides* is 'a high school volunteer group that offers rides home to their classmates who have spent the evening drinking' (Kilgannon 2002). In another story *The Washington Post* also cites favourably the example of Duke University, where groups of student paramedics patrol large parties on campus, 'on the lookout for anyone drunk enough to need medical attention or a trip to the emergency room' (Okie 2002; see also Gruley 2003; Stowe 2005; Lewin 2005). Writing in *The Washington Post*, Steinberg (2002) does acknowledge that relying on students to regulate the behaviour of other students is not ideal, since 'older students are reluctant to write up their 18-year-old brethren for alcohol violations'. Nevertheless, having students police other students is still regarded as a better option than relying on government, police forces and parents to intervene into young people's lives.

In these narratives, age is the defining characteristic of the problems and meanings associated with intoxication and drunkenness. It is *young* people's drunkenness that needs to be understood. However, much commentary also touches on issues such as social class, ethnicity, geography and gender as influences on young people's intoxication and drunkenness. While patterns of alcohol use and abuse 'cut across economic lines' – while 'bingeing is classless', as Mary Riddell writes (2003) – sometimes it is suggested that 'affluence is a factor in underage drinking' for the simple reason that teenagers from wealthy families 'have more access to money and liquor is as close as the refrigerator, the liquor cabinet or the rec room bar'. Likewise, teenagers from wealthy families 'have the money to get a fake ID and to go to the clubs'. The 17-year-old president of *Safe Rides* sums up the situation by stating simply: 'The kids have plenty of money and time and nothing to do, so they drink' (Kilgannon 2002). Riddell (2003) concludes that 'from Sir Toby Belch, via Euan Blair, to Prince Harry and his polo-trash friends, getting hammered is the province of the affluent'. However, while there is plenty of evidence in the media to support this view about the ways in which affluence shapes young people's drunkenness, there is also more than enough evidence to suggest that the less affluent are able to access alcohol and get 'hammered' as well, something that Riddell acknowledges but then does not discuss.

Folsom Lake College Library

Young people and drunkenness: Different stories in different countries

The European School Survey Project on Alcohol and other Drugs (ESPAD) is an ongoing survey which started in 1995 and is conducted every four years. According to a number of analyses ESPAD has found 'considerable inter-country variation... in drinking patterns... For example, in Cyprus, only 6% of drinking episodes were reported to result in intoxication, whereas in Iceland, the figure was 88%, and the overall mean (SD) was 39% (22%)' (Kypri et al. 2005, 447). The 1999 report argues that 'children in the UK... have the highest rates of drunkenness, binge drinking and alcohol consumption in Europe' (cited in Weinberg and Wyatt 2006, 774). In this report, as Weinberg and Wyatt (2006, 774) indicate, intoxication and drunkenness are measured as different terms, although these terms are not explicitly defined. For example, the report explains, 'On average, half of the ESPAD students have been intoxicated at least once during their lifetime, to the point of staggering when walking, having slurred speech or throwing up'. This particular claim is followed by a somewhat contradictory claim that: 'Another way of measuring drunkenness has been to ask how often the students had been consuming five drinks or more per occasion. This measure of "heavy episodic drinking" shows to some extent a different pattern than the question about intoxication'. It appears as if these terms have not been clearly defined, but used for different questions in the questionnaire. How they are being defined by the participants themselves is also unclear.

Demant and Järvinen (2006, 589) also draw on the ESPAD surveys (and other sources) to cite the commonly claimed finding that 'Danish teenagers hold the European record for drinking alcohol. They drink more, very often and with a clearer focus on drunkenness than young people in most other European countries'. The authors look closely at this claim to find that for young people, alcohol consumption in linked to popularity, that is, 'the teenagers who reported the highest alcohol consumption were regarded by their peers as the most prestigious ones to hang out with'.

Järvinen and Gundelach (2007, 56) conducted a study in Denmark with quantitative and qualitative components. The quantitative data is from a survey with a representative, random sample of 2000 teenagers aged 15–16 (all respondents were born in 1989), with a 72 per cent response rate. They describe their qualitative methods as follows:

> The qualitative data is of 28 focus group interviews with teenagers in the eighth and ninth grades in different parts of Denmark. The teenagers

were interviewed twice. First, 14 groups of classmates or friends were interviewed in focus groups when the participants were 14–15 years old. One year later, the same youths were re-interviewed in order to gather information about the development of their drinking habits, and attitudes towards alcohol. Some of the groups consisted of girls, others of boys, and others again were gender-mixed. In all, 117 teenagers participated in the focus group interviews: 63 girls and 54 boys.

In their study Järvinen and Gundelach (2007, 60) claimed that Danish teenagers had 'an intoxication debut at age 14–15' followed by a social life incorporating 'partying now and then'. The authors suggest that for these participants 'it is "natural" to drink alcohol when you are 14–15 years old, while 12 year olds who are heavy drinkers are frowned upon in many interviews (even by those who had their own drunkenness debut when they were 12)'. Since drinking alcohol as a teenager is so 'natural', 'non-drinking and avoidance of drunkenness is obviously not an easy lifestyle choice for Danish 15–16 year olds'. Drinking goes together with friendship networks, popularity and 'maturity': 'If you do not follow the culturally prescribed pattern of drinking to intoxication at this age, you may find yourself excluded from a very important arena of teenage life, the arena of parties, friendships and alcohol-related status negotiations' (Järvinen and Gundelach 2007, 68; see also Bogren 2006).

The effects of alcohol use on young people are considered in a Norwegian survey conducted in 1997, and reported in Hoel et al. (2004, 362–366). This study examined the psychological effects of intoxication and drunkenness habits on young people. The data was based on a cross-sectional survey of 828 tertiary school students (46 per cent of the students were female; 54 per cent were male). The majority of the students were aged 15–17 and were drawn from three vocational and one academic school in Førde. The questions asked covered health, psychosocial environment, demographics, attitudes and lifestyle matters, were mainly multiple choice, and were based on a WHO cross-national survey *Health Behaviour in School-aged Children* (HBSC). This survey found that: 'Excessive drinking, characterized by a high frequency of intoxication, is already established by age 15–17 among both genders'; and, that 'alcohol use and intoxication are established elements of mid-teenage behaviour for both sexes'. This study also found that 'emotional and psychosomatic problems increase the greater the level of alcohol consumption'. This research suggests that alcohol consumption is significantly related to several aspects of social integration although 'moderate to heavy consumers report greater problems in their relations with school and parents, especially in early adolescence'. The authors suggest that 'more than any other age group, young people report the positive effects of alcohol'. In addition, 'Drunkenness may be the release necessary for the shy teenager to perform socially and thus increase the number of positive and important relationships'.

In Finland, 'drunkenness-oriented drinking' and drinking patterns leading to drunkenness have been found to be widespread among young adolescents, especially in comparison to their counterparts in other European countries (Lintonen and Konu 2004). This study on the misperceptions of the social norms of drunkenness suggested that adolescents in Finland do indeed assume others have a heavier drinking practice, leading to drunkenness (though drunkenness here is undefined).

Cultural differences in alcohol use are also discussed by Schmid et al. (2003, 651) who argue that frequency of alcohol use and the use of spirits influence drunkenness. They explain that 'across countries one may expect a considerable variation in the number of occasions in which drunkenness occurs... and a high variation in the extent to which drunkenness is determined by a specific beverage'. Their research asks the question: 'Does the number of adolescent drunkenness occasions differ between countries?' Focusing on 15-year-olds in 22 countries they examine the relationship between 'alcohol consumption characteristics and drunkenness in male and female students separately'. They suggest that alcohol use and drunkenness among young people varies between countries, with results which are consistent with other large inter-cultural surveys, such as the ESPAD. Geographic location, for example, was related to drunkenness: 'Southern European countries showed moderate associations [between alcohol use and drunkenness], whereas strong associations were found in Scandinavia, the Baltic countries and Russia'. In addition, types of drinks seemed to influence drunkenness: 'The frequency of alcohol intake and the extent to which intake is from spirits relate to drunkenness. It is more likely for students to have been drunk when the frequency of alcohol intake was high and when the alcohol intake was largely in the form of spirits' (Schmid et al. 2003, 659).

Understandings of intoxication and drunkenness among different groups of young people

In this section we explore the meanings, definitions and understandings of intoxication and drunkenness for different populations of young people. These terms are understood differently both for different age groups as well as different social and cultural groups. Following on from our earlier discussion we start by exploring young people's ideas about intoxication and drunkenness, and also how researchers and experts conceptualise young people's drinking. We examine young people's intoxication and drunkenness in the context of socio-economic status, types of drinks on the market, as well as the role of advertising.

As we have already seen, the research literature on young people and alcohol use is primarily concerned with the health and well-being consequences (short and longer term) of what is often referred to as young people's binge drinking (Miller et al. 2007; Schmid et al. 2003). Much of the research literature related to young people's use of alcohol often does not define its use of the term 'intoxication' but uses it in relation to the term 'acute' and with reference to young people's vulnerability, and the hazardous consequences of intoxication (Miles et al. 2001). Likewise, many researchers find that 'the consumption of large quantities of alcohol in a short time' results in intoxication which poses 'an immediate risk to health and safety' (Polizzotto et al. 2007, 469). Lintonen and Rimpelä (2001, 145), for example, suggest that 'the two main methods for measuring drunkenness in adolescent population surveys are related to the concepts of *being drunk* and *binge drinking*'. As they indicate, the 'first method relies on the subjective perceptions of the state of drunkenness', while the 'second deduces that ingestion of a certain amount of ethanol, usually corresponding to five "standard drinks"… within a short period of time results in drunkenness'.

Sociological perspectives on young people and intoxication and drunkenness, such as those of Lintonen et al. (2000, 261–269), consider alcohol consumption in the context of broader social changes. These authors report on the effects of societal level changes on the increased drunkenness of 14-year-olds in Finland based on biannual nationally representative survey data. In this study, drunkenness was measured with the question: 'How often do you use alcohol to the extent that you become really drunk?' Respondents were asked to pick from the following: 'once a week or more often', 'once or twice a month', 'less frequently' or 'never'. Their study's findings suggest a relationship between social factors such as income availability, or level of disposable income and drunkenness.

In another study Weinberg and Wyatt (2006, 774–775) conducted observational research over a period of 18 months in the emergency department of the Royal Cornwall Hospital in Truro, Cornwall (UK), which investigated young people who presented with acute alcohol intoxication. Acute intoxication was measured by blood alcohol levels (BALs):

Sixty two children (31 boys) presented with acute alcohol intoxication proved by BALs. All patients were admitted to hospital. The mean age was 14.5 years (standard deviation (SD) 1.54). Twenty (32%) children were aged <14 years. No significant difference was seen between BAL among boys and girls (p=0.76). Forty five (73%) children were brought to the emergency department by the ambulance services, the remainder by their parents or guardians. The most common type of alcohol consumed was spirits, in the form of whisky, gin, vodka and tequila (50%). Other types included cider (8%), wine (4%) and beer (3%), with 35% not specified or unknown. The mean BAL was 203 mg/dl (SD 80.7; range 27.6–418.6). As a point of reference, 56 (90%) children had BAL above the UK legal driving limit of 80 mg/dl.

Alcohol intoxication is sometimes defined as a loss of consciousness. One Australian study found that people at high risk of this effect of intoxication are tertiary students who play drinking games. The study found that '75% of respondent tertiary students had participated in a drinking game at some time. Nearly all of these (89%) reported being present when someone had lost consciousness from alcohol intoxication, and had often been left alone to "sleep it off"' (Australian Institute of Health and Welfare, 2004, 5).

In a UK study Best et al. (2006, 1427–1432) examined what they identified as 'excessive drinking' in 2078 young people aged 14–16 in London. In their research, 'excessive drinking' was defined as 'drinking at a level of consumption that could be expected to produce intoxication with significant impairment of thinking, judgement and behaviour'. They operationalised this definition when consumption was 'more than 10 standard units [where a unit is 8 g] of alcohol on any drinking occasion'. One in three young people reported at least one episode of excessive drinking, with one in ten having done so more than five times. Best et al. (2006) link excessive drinking to intoxication, which, while not defined, is linked to impaired cognition, judgment and behaviour. Further, excessive alcohol consumption by young people is seen to be linked to a 'broader pattern of substance misuse behaviours', 'delinquent acts' such as theft and shoplifting, fighting, truancy, driving while intoxicated, and 'coexisting mental health problems'.

While these sorts of research data and findings reveal important trends in the consequences of young people's alcohol consumption, there is a disconnection from how young people themselves have been found to interpret and use information such as this. In their study of drinking games, Polizzotto et al. (2007, 474) found that young players associated intoxication with risks of injury, argument or violence, but instead of dissuading them from becoming intoxicated, 'many of the participants were proud of their extreme intoxication and regarded many negative outcomes, such as losing consciousness or vomiting, as "badges of honour"'.

Psychological research has also indicated that not only do social and cultural expectancies influence drunken comportment, but personality plays a large role in individual responses to consumption (Westmaas et al. 2007). For example, a survey completed by 239 students in the US claimed that individuals with impulsive personalities are more likely to become more *emotionally labile* when intoxicated. Using personality attributes, Westmass et al. (2007) claim that they can predict positive and/or negative outcomes for intoxication. They identified/named three main groups of intoxicated behaviours: intoxicated sociability, anti-social behaviour and emotional lability. Unsurprisingly, research indicates that college-aged students rate sociability of intoxication high on the scale of reported behavioural outcomes. That is, flirting, dancing, telling jokes and laughter were most often reported as outcomes of intoxication. Demant (2009, 37) covers similar ground in a study that examined the relationship between alcohol use and flirtation for young people in Denmark: 'In all 37 focus group interviews from the study, both boys and girls discussed intoxication in relation to being able to think of each other sexually at parties and engage in romantic or sexual relations'.

A number of researchers have considered the connection between income inequality, and young people's health outcomes in the context of other sociological factors. Wells et al. (2009, 5), for example, claim that: 'It is no longer a marginal phenomenon to be found among subcultures of poor or troubled youth'; rather, 'determined drunkenness seems to be a mainstream phenomenon, occurring in all social classes, in larger cities as well as in the countryside, among girls as well as boys'.

The interest in possible relationships between socio-economic status and young people's alcohol use also informed research conducted by Elgar et al. (2005, 245–247) who studied the contextual effects of income inequality on drinking behaviour among 11-, 13- and 15-year-olds in 34 industrialised countries. The study used self-report data that was collected from 162,305 adolescents in the 2001–2002 WHO's HBSC study. Like other studies, this one used a single item in the questionnaire to measure drunkenness:

> How often do you drink anything alcoholic, such as beer, wine or spirits?' (1 = never, 2 = less than once a week, 3 = once a week, 4 = 2–4 days a week, 5 = 5–6 days a week, 6 = once a day, 7 = more than once a

day). Episodes of drunkenness were measured with the item 'Have you ever had so much alcohol that you were really drunk?' (1 = never, 2 = once, 3 = 2–3 times, 4 = 4–10 times, 5 = more than 10 times).

Elgar et al.'s (2005) analysis suggested that income inequality was associated with drunkenness only for the 11-year-olds and not the older adolescents.

Using the same data set Richter et al. (2006, 9) reported similar results:

> Socio-economic circumstances of the family had only a limited effect on repeated drunkenness in adolescence. For girls only in one out of 28 countries a significant association between family affluence and repeated drunkenness was observed, while boys from low and/ or medium affluent families in nine countries faced a lower risk of drunkenness than boys from more affluent families. Regarding parental occupation, significant differences in episodes of drunkenness were found in nine countries for boys and in six countries for girls. Compared to family affluence, which was positively related to risk of drunkenness, a decreasing occupational status predicted an increasing risk of drunkenness. This pattern was identified within a number of countries, most noticeably for boys.

The authors concluded that socio-economic status was only of limited influence 'for the development of excessive alcohol use in early adolescence' and that parental occupation may play a larger role (Richter et al. 2006, 9).

The possible relationships between social class, ethnic background and young people's alcohol use was the object of interest in research undertaken by Stewart and Power (2003, 582) in the US. In their study the authors measured frequency/quantity; motivation or reasons for consumption; situational factors such as when, where, with whom they drank and how the alcohol was obtained; and the consequences of drinking: 'Frequency and quantity of drinking were assessed with eight questions about the frequency of drinking in the past year and month, frequency of intoxication, typical quantity of consumption, and frequency of consumption of large quantities. Students responded to the questions on 6- to 10-point Likert-type scales'. Two of their claims/findings are of interest here. In the first instance Stewart and Power (2003, 578) argue that:

> Both European American adolescents and adolescents from higher social classes... report high levels of drinking frequency. Because European Americans are more likely than members of ethnic minorities to come from higher social class backgrounds, the often-reported higher levels

of drinking among European American adolescents may be due to their social class.

In addition Stewart and Power (2003, 592) suggest that:

> ethnicity was a much more powerful predictor of adolescent drinking patterns than was social class, and that most of the ethnic differences in adolescent drinking were not simply the result of ethnic differences in the frequency and quantity of alcohol consumption. That is, in the analyses where the independent effects of ethnicity and social class were examined, many more ethnic than social class differences were found (i.e., 22 significant differences for ethnicity versus 5 for social class).

Significantly, Stewart and Power (2003, 592) conclude that 'social class and ethnicity are not causal factors in themselves – they are simply marker or "social address" variables that are correlated with a wide range of underlying variables, including adolescent opportunities, beliefs, attitudes, and values'. Intoxication and drunkenness are only casually referred to in this research. However, this study is instructive in its theoretical approach to class and ethnicity, in that causal links are not attempted. Rather, these sorts of variables are examined in ways that aim to better map or understand the social, cultural and economic landscape which shapes the ways that young people engage with and use alcohol.

These sorts of relationships were also examined in a Danish study that drew on data from a multi-item survey completed by 4824 respondents. Andersen et al. (2007, 22–30) tried to identify what they called *Family Socio-Economic Position* (SEP). They identified and measured this concept via two items that related parent's occupations that were 'coded according to the standards of the Danish National Institute of Social Research into six groups as follows: social class I (high) to V (low) and a group VI covering parents who were living from social welfare benefits'. They asked participants, students aged 11, 13, and 15 (though the analysis in the paper referenced here used the data from only 15-year-olds): 'Have you ever been really drunk?' with possible response choices as follows: no, never; yes, once; yes, 2–3 times; yes, 4–10 times; yes, more than 10 times'. Of the 1453 students of 15 years, 681 girls and 621 boys answered the questions about alcohol use and were included in the analyses. The authors argued that there were differences in risk factors for drunkenness between socio-economic groups but that 'different aspects of poor well-being at school were important for drunkenness in the different socio-economic groups'. More specifically, they suggest that:

experiencing low influence on their school environment was the most important predictor among both boys and girls with higher socio-economic positions. This was also the strongest predictor among girls from the intermediate socio-economic groups, but low satisfaction with school had the strongest impact on drunkenness among boys from the intermediate socio-economic groups. Among students from poorer social circumstances low parental engagement in school related matters had the strongest impact on drunkenness.

This research suggests that while there are important differences in young people's alcohol use that are related to socio-economic status, personal well-being as measured by student engagement at school, and positive interpersonal relationships with parents appear to be important factors in moderating young people's alcohol use.

In another study Demant (2009), a sociologist working with young people in Denmark, developed an innovative approach to the conduct of alcohol studies with young people. The aim was to move beyond social interpretations of alcohol as a symbol or marker that is attached to particular people, and try to come to an understanding of what intoxication means for young people. Using a social constructivist approach, Demant (2009) conducted 37 focus group interviews and, in this account, reported one young woman interviewed over three years. Demant (2009, 29) suggests that researchers are only privy to the explanations of experiences that young people want to share which creates problems for researchers. Specifically, 'it is difficult to clarify which aspects within a given practice are to be understood as social and which it would be sensible to address as the workings of alcohol'. However, Demant seeks to avoid the difficulties of some social constructionists for whom the social 'tends to be a collective matter, which acts behind the backs of the agents'. The implications for studies on young people and alcohol are that: 'concepts like drinking pressure, excuse value and peer pressure often have a tone of this kind of "invisible agency", which ascribes power to a collective that works behind the backs of drinking teenagers'. A quote from Susanne, one of his participants, expresses the importance of alcohol to her identity: '*If you are too sober, then it won't work. Then it is not fun at all... I would not dare to talk to anyone if I wasn't drunk. Then I would just stand in a corner or something. It becomes easier to talk to others*' (Demant 2009, 35). Demant (2009, 35–36) interprets alcohol use not in symbolic terms, 'but as something that is important to becoming part of the relations at the disco'. In his analysis, Demant apportions a degree of conscious choice to young people's drunkenness: 'The girls drink in order to make their state of drunkenness as perfect as possible. They therefore make themselves available to the effect of alcohol to a certain limit and, in this way, invite alcohol to take over some of their control'. The girls here are accommodating their drinking to the party space. They are 'training to be affected in the right way according to the specific party space. Alcohol creates a bodily effect, which the girls make themselves available to, and at the same time are surrounded by' (see also Demant and Ostergaard 2007).

In another study Bogren (2006, 520–528) works with this concept of control by defining a loss of control as 'becom[ing] intoxicated'. For young Swedish people who do not drink, 'drinking is implicitly linked to drunkenness, in that when drinking is mentioned, so are what is commonly understood as the consequences of *drunkenness* (e.g., memory loss the next day)'. Bogren discusses drunkenness in terms of physicality. In this study young people also describe this aspect of drunkenness, including 'vomiting, becoming unconscious ("passing out"), having one's stomach pumped, hangovers and memory loss'. By way of cross cultural comparison, Bogren explains that Spanish young people also describe the physicality of drunkenness. In contrast, Finnish youth describe it as 'a change in mood that facilitated communication' (Bogren 2006, 528). In this way young people express some of the positive aspects of drunkenness (for example, increased communication), and do not simply refer to negative physical consequences (see also Midanik 2003; Sulkunen 2002).

In some research young people are reported as not considering drunkenness to be harmful. Despite the fact that where this finding was reported drunkenness was not explicitly defined, the researchers nonetheless found this casual attitude toward alcohol to be concerning (Graham et al. 2006). Not only do some young people consider drunkenness not to be harmful, it has often, also, been considered to confer positive social attributes to some young people, reinforcing their positive associations with achieving drunkenness with their peers. Demant and Järvinen (2006, 590) explain their data from a large qualitative study in which 28 focus group interviews were conducted with boys and girls from the 8th and 9th forms in different Danish lower secondary schools as follows: 'The aim of this article [which considers data from two focus group interviews with six and eight girls respectively, aged 14- and 15-years-old] is to demonstrate how the struggle for social recognition – with alcohol as the central marker – transpires in two groups of teenagers'. In their account the authors claim to illustrate:

how alcohol experience and positive attitudes towards drinking are used to symbolize maturity – the teenagers who drink the most construct themselves as "socially older" than the others. The function of alcohol in this struggle for recognition is so strong that the teenagers who drink very little or not at all are put under considerable pressure. With alcohol as the central marker of maturity – and the parents of the teenagers who drink are described as supporters of this view – teenagers who do not drink come out as potential losers in the status negotiations of the groups.

Many young people who drink alcohol when they socialise also participate in pre-drinking, where they drink with friends (usually at someone's home) before going out to socialise with others: 'Intoxication is also a primary motive for pre-drinking. For example, one participant in a Pennsylvania study reported: "No matter what the quantity, if it gets the job done, the intent is to get wasted"' (Wells et al. 2009, 5). Drawing from both Measham and Brain (2005) and Järvinen and Room (2007; see Appendix B), Wells et al. (2009, 5) argue that: 'Pre-drinking may be symptomatic of a "new culture of intoxication" apparent in European and other countries whereby young people drink and use other drugs with the strategic and hedonistic goal of achieving drunkenness and other altered states of consciousness'. In another study with young people in Switzerland, Steinhausen et al. (2008) also claimed an association between drinking and wanting to feel drunk or *high*. For these young people drunkenness was associated with an altered state of consciousness.

While arguing that there is no consensus definition of the term binge drinking, Guise and Gill (2007) examined young people's own ways of understanding the term. Guise and Gill (2007, 896) explain that student drinking habits in the UK are structured around priorities such as studying and that 'binge drinking was also structured; the aim was controlled intoxication to reduce inhibition and have fun'. Similar arguments are made by Measham (2006, 261) who suggests that:

> empirical research suggests that young people intentionally manage their levels of desired and actual intoxication by using strategies that incorporate aspects of perceived risk, accessing well-informed and credible sources, such as online scientific journals, health sources, and the popular dissemination and discussion of these on websites, in chat rooms, and by mobile phones (e.g., Moore, 2004 [see Appendix B]; Moore & Miles, 2004 [see Appendix B]).

In their research Lintonen and Rimpelä (2001, 146–150) used data from a cross-sectional mailed survey, The Adolescent Health and Lifestyle Survey, in Finland in 1999, to explore young people's understandings of alcohol use and to correlate these perceptions of drunkenness with BAC levels. The survey asked young people (n=7751) about their 'subjective perceptions of drunkenness... from the most recent drinking occasion'. The young people were asked: 'In your opinion, the last time you drank alcohol, were you: "completely sober", "slightly drunk", "really drunk", "so drunk that I passed out"?' They were also asked to explain what and how much they drank: 'Think back on your last drinking occasion and describe in your own words as accurately as you can what you drank and how much? (If you shared drinks with other people please try to tell us how much you personally drank)'. This research suggested a high correlation between subjective perceptions of drunkenness and BAC, suggesting that young people, aged 14–18, are capable of assessing their level of drunkenness. This study concluded that: 'The perception of being really drunk, on average, related to the consumption of around 100 g of pure ethanol, or a six-pack of beer'.

The roles that intoxication and drunkenness may play in an individual's life can change throughout the life course. We trace some aspects of this trajectory here. In their research Harnett et al. (2000) created a typology of different types of drinking by young people in which recreational drinking was defined as *hedonistic* and involving *excess*. Summarising Harnett et al., Newburn and Shiner (2001, 11) describe how intoxication was understood in this context: 'Intoxication and losing control were considered to be "fun" and featured in most of the recreation of most of the young men over 17 or 18 – either by intention or as a by product of "enjoy[ing] a drink"'. Consistent with these other studies Kypri et al. (2005, 448) found that alcohol use and intoxication frequency decreases with age. The authors used a web-based drinking diary to collect data on university students' alcohol use and intoxication levels and 'to present a descriptive epidemiology of intoxication in a university community':

> Drinking measures used in the analyses presented in this study included a 7-day retrospective diary, in which the number of standard drinks (defined as 10 g ethanol) consumed on each day and the duration of the drinking session were recorded. Respondents were also asked to indicate how many of the drinking episodes resulted in them becoming 'intoxicated/drunk/impaired'. Pictures of standard drinks were provided on the web pages as a guide. Elsewhere in the questionnaire,

respondents were asked to enter their weight in kilograms or pounds for the purpose of computing an EBAC [estimated blood alcohol content].

In defence of their choice to use the EBAC as a measure of intoxication, Kypri et al. (2005, 449–450) argue that: 'Compared with subjective reporting of intoxication and the standard binge criteria, an EBAC threshold of 0.08 g per cent produced a more conservative estimate of the incidence of intoxication'. Whether participants lived in university residence halls or shared housing was found to make a difference in drinking patterns and practices, particularly for women. For example, students in residence halls drank more heavily per drinking occasion than those in share houses.

As we have indicated a number of times self-reporting of perceived drunkenness to assess intoxication has been used in a number of studies. For example, Monshouwer et al. (2003, 156–160) looked at the age of onset of first alcohol use and first intoxication for young Dutch people, where the measurements were based on the following questions: 'How old were you when you drank at least one glass of alcohol for the first time?', and 'How old were you when you got drunk for the first time?' Results indicated that the earlier a person starts drinking, the more likelihood of intoxication. They suggest that early onset of alcohol use is linked to socio-demographic characteristics. The authors also claim that the: 'Onset of alcohol use is part of a behaviour pattern, also involving other "problem behaviours" like truancy and other substance use'. Here, Monshouwer et al. link alcohol use to intoxication to 'problem behaviours' indicating that drinking alcohol is a problem, although, as has been argued in other studies (see for example; Measham 2008), many young people do not interpret alcohol use in this way.

Parents of young people have been shown to associate both short and long-term risk with adolescent use of alcohol. However, in one study most parents described more concern with the potential, immediate short-term risk of drunkenness, such as 'injuries (including assault), accidents, aspiration of vomit, unconsciousness, drowning, sequelae of unsafe sex, drink spiking, loss of control and death' (Graham et al. 2006, 8). According to Graham et al. (2006, 8–10), parents have difficulty responding to adolescent alcohol use and drunkenness and worry about their exposure to alcohol-related dangers while intoxicated. However, they argue that 'it is not clear for these parents... what is "normal" and what is "problematic" alcohol use'. While these parents, and the researchers, are able to define some of the risks they believe are associated with drunkenness and intoxication, they are not explicit in their definitions of these terms. Some parents have been shown to believe that 'adolescents hide their own and their friends' intoxication'.

Young people and drinking as a rite of passage

Much of the research literature and media commentary suggests that young people's intoxication and drunkenness should be understood as a public nuisance and/or a public health issue requiring intervention. However, another way of examining this issue is to think about young people's drinking as a rite of passage. In this sense it is argued that young people go through a number of drinking phases during the journey to adulthood, and that drinking practices take on different symbolic meanings at different times (Demant and Ostergaard 2007; Kloep et al. 2001; Clemens et al. 2007).

In their research Beccaria and Sande (2003, 100–101) are concerned with the ways in which 'global youth culture impacts on local traditions of "rite of passage" and intoxication', and the tensions between traditional ways of drinking and the reflexively modern creation of 'social identity as a "life project"'. They argue that the contemporary practice of young people's drinking games provides an example of a new form of ritual, or rite of passage to adulthood. Intoxication is understood as having both physiological effects and also 'symbolic intentions and functions in society... [which are] embedded in different cultures and religions'. Alcohol use can be understood as 'offering an opportunity to communicate meanings among members within a society and culture'.

Beccaria and Sande (2003, 101–107) go on to argue that the process of intoxication can be understood literally as a rite of passage, whereby young people pass through the three phases of a ritual: the separation phase, the liminal phase and the aggregation phase. With intoxication, the intoxicated person is first separated 'from personal identity, social structure and social categories and turned into a liminal phase of playing and games', then: 'in the process of transformation and transition outside the normal order of the society' and finally, 'in the aggregation phase the novices are "timed into" the social structure with new identity and status'. Drawing on Turner (1969) they argue that this ritual process is 'a game in which individuals discover and develop common cultural codes, meaning and values'. In Norway, for example, the official, or traditional rite of passage described by Beccaria and Sande is religious confirmation, where a small amount of red wine is consumed. This rite is contrasted to the modern (so-called, although it dates back to the seventeenth century), secular 'use of alcohol and ensuing drunkenness, [which] occurs between the ages of 16 and 18, in the celebration commonly known as russefeiring which is performed by school leavers in their final year'. Beccaria and Sande situate *russefeiring* by describing how the 'Norwegian term "russ" is taken from Latin: (cornua deprositurus, which translates as "taking off the horns")'. For these authors:

> This term and social practice originates from an old academic ceremony in Germany and Denmark dating back to the 17th century or earlier. The name of the tradition today denotes both the connection to the old academic ceremony and to the Norwegian word for intoxication "rus", which means "the party of".

Comparing and contrasting Italy and Norway's youth drinking culture and transitions into adulthood, Beccaria and Sande (2003, 110–113) find that 'in both countries, young people experience close friendship and local belongingness during the process of intoxication and transition'. Despite the ways in which rites of passage are enacted in both Italy and Norway for young people, Beccaria and Sande argue that, today, a rite of passage is not blindly followed but instead actively constructed and performed as a celebration and transformation of life and identity into the public arena. Further, 'the ritual process provides the individual young person in transition with opportunities to initiate and celebrate individual skills in the making of social, symbolic and cultural capital'. However there are different expectations which each culture brings to the performance of alcohol intoxication:

> Young Italians experiment with long and strong intoxication without losing public self-control (or at least not always). The individual goal is to be strongly intoxicated without losing public social control while together with other people. Norwegians are also experimental. The code among young Norwegians involves heavy drinking with a symbolic performance of drunkenness and individual lack of control over the intoxicated body. Public intoxicated action is a sign of personal identity. In Italy, heavy drinking is exhibited in performance as normal as possible and under control. Intoxicated manifestation of the body is a sign of lack of personal identity. Cultural codes are still different with regard to the interpretation of intoxication of the brain and body in northern and southern Europe.

In their research Demant and Ostergaard (2007) also use the concept of a rite of passage in their examination of a 'house party' attended by 14–16 year old Danish students. However, they suggest that the concept of a ritual or a single rite of passage is not really accurate for understanding the role of alcohol and intoxication in young people's lives. Alcohol is instead, they argue, a central organising aspect of their social lives and, the role it plays is more sustaining than a rite of passage implies.

Consumerism, marketing, advertising and young people

In this final section on young people, intoxication and drunkenness we provide a brief sketch of the ways in which the marketing of alcohol, and the images and meanings associated with varying drinking practices and beverages, are claimed to impact on meanings and understandings of intoxication and drunkenness.

McCreanor et al. (2008, 941–944), for example, consider the sociological context for young people's drinking habits in New Zealand and argue that: 'The discursive resources available and normative in this social climate support arguments and understandings that alcohol is not for low or moderate consumption but is seen as intended for producing intoxication'. They recruited '24 groups (12 Maori, 12 Pakeha) of between three and six friends with the intention of interviewing them at approximately eight-month intervals'. Participants were drawn from three age groups: '14–15 years, 15–16 years and 16–17 years'. There were four groups each of females and four groups of males (eight groups) and 'a further four groups that were mixed by gender'. In all, 70 interviews were recorded. In addition they conducted '29 data sessions of a "one-off" nature with other groups of friends in whatever combinations of age, gender and ethnicity occurred within an opportunistic sample'. The aim was to understand how participants experienced socialising and drinking in a range of actual youth events such as Big Day Out (a music festival), New Year celebrations, school balls/afterballs, birthday parties, weekend drinking and the like.

In their research McCreanor et al. (2008, 939–944) report on the incorporation of 'pro-alcohol discourses within broader youth accounts of social life that resonate with contemporaneous marketing messages and emphasise the pleasures and compulsions (but not the harms) of alcohol intoxication'. The authors claim that their research shows 'direct associations between branded products and the will to intoxication'. They quote Ed (17 years old, Pakeha, mixed group) as saying: *'I was just like "yes Smirnoff Blue, Smirnoff Blue, I'm going to get so wasted tonight". I was in the taxi and I was like passing it back to see if anyone wanted it, and everyone was "no screw that shit", and I had it straight. I was just like going, "oh you guys are just pussies"'.*

McCreanor et al. (2008, 939–944) claim that these findings provide support for Measham and Brain's (2005) notion of a 'culture of intoxication'. Their data demonstrates that 'the synergistic, cumulative effects of environmental exposure of young people to alcohol marketing creates and maintains expectations and norms for practices of drinking to intoxication'. As Tony (17 years old, Pakeha, male group), one of their participants explains: *'Yeah well I've got to get drunk don't I? Because that's the trend. It's just you know if everybody else is drinking you don't want to not drink. I mean I could if I wanted to, I say that of course but then'*. McCreanor et al. (2008, 944) suggest that: 'Tony is reflecting on the "carrot and stick" character of the intoxigenic environment in which peer pressure is applied to the abstainer and peer esteem awaits the accomplished drinker'. In this way of thinking young people grow to 'trust and value industry-given knowledge and messages presented in important domains of youth culture'. The term 'intoxigenic social environment' is used by these authors 'to refer to the discursive social practices that engage with and utilize pro-intoxication talk to create and maintain expectations, norms and behaviours around alcohol consumption'. They further argue that this is a context created largely by the marketing of alcoholic beverages:

> These data show multiple instances in which young participants make meanings from alcohol marketing that create and maintain social environments where drinking to intoxication is the norm and the expectation. Participants enjoy, value, identify with and make social use of the alcohol marketing messages that are used to create positive valence for specific products. We argue that, in their own cultural spaces, young people combine these elements into lived ideologies of alcohol intoxication.

Young people are often caste as consumers *par excellence* and the marketing of alcohol to young people is both controversial and understandable from a marketing perspective. Newburn and Shiner (2001, 20), for example, suggest that since the 1990s there have been trends and development in marketing alcohol to young people that have 'witnessed a diversification of the drinks market as concerted efforts were made by the drinks industry to exploit the youth market'. These trends included the 'development of "designer drinks", followed by the emergence of alcopops – also known as alcoholic soft drinks'. These new forms of beverage and the accompanying marketing, have been 'characterized by a high alcohol strength and have stimulated particular concern because of the belief that they appeal particularly to young people. It has been suggested that designer drinks were part of the drinks industries' response to the emerging 'Ecstasy culture' which involved a rejection of alcohol in favour of illicit drugs'.

Newburn and Shiner (2001, 21–22) cite Hughes et al.'s (1997; see Appendix B) claim that the 'attitudes of 12–17 year olds towards designer drinks varied quite distinctly with age and this reflected attitudes towards, and motivations for, drinking'. The argument here is that the 'brand imagery of designer drinks, unlike that which was used for more mainstream drinks, tended to match 14 and 15 year olds' perceptions and expectations of drinking. The popularity of these drinks peaked between the ages of 13 and 16, while more conventional drinks became consistently more popular with age'. This research claims that 'designer drinks tended to be consumed in less controlled circumstances and were associated with heavier alcohol intake and greater drunkenness'. Further support for this argument is provided by research undertaken by Forsyth et al. (1997; see Appendix B) who suggested that 'under-age drunkenness was most strongly associated with white ciders, fruit wines and vodka, although it is worth noting that the first two categories included designer drinks such as Electric White, Ice Dragon, White Lightning, and Mad Dog 20/20' (cited in Newburn and Shiner 2001, 22).

To this point the discussion has been related to young people as the population that appears to cause or be the object of most concern in relation to intoxication and drunkenness and their meanings and consequences. Indigenous communities are also a common target for interventions designed to curb alcohol abuse and familiar stereotypes abound in media commentary on these communities. In the following section we provide a sketch of the type of ground covered in these accounts. A point to stress at this stage is that we do not set out to provide an extensive review of concerns with intoxication and drunkenness in Indigenous communities. Such a task is beyond the scope of our discussions. Our intention is to present an outline of concerns so as to illustrate our claim that the meanings and understandings of intoxication and drunkenness shift and change in relation to contexts, settings, different populations and differing purposes.

Intoxication and drunkenness in Indigenous communities: Media commentary and the popular imagination

The New Zealand and Australian news media dedicate substantial time to discussing the issues of drinking and drunkenness in Indigenous communities in the two countries. The main elements regarding much of this commentary include identifying the causes of the current problems with

Indigenous drunkenness, with cataloguing those problems, and suggesting possible solutions to them. We are not able in this space to discuss other indigenous communities, though populations such as Native American communities do feature in media commentary (Fields 2007).

Much of the commentary in the New Zealand and Australian news media considers it self-evident that the causes of contemporary social disorder in Indigenous communities can be traced to the introduction of alcohol by European settlers, the 'mapping' of whose arrival Louis Nowra (2007) calls 'one of the most depressing exercises in Australian history'. As John Stapleton (2004) writes, if we want to understand the causes of the disorder that mars the Sydney suburb of Redfern, we must recognise such suburbs as being marked by 'tableaus of dereliction which have as much to do with alcoholism and addiction as the vexed subject of race'. For Malcolm Brown (2007), the deaths of young Aborigines on Palm Island are symptomatic of the destruction wrought on Indigenous communities by white Australia. He writes:

> Maybe the Palm Islanders were happy once. They probably were in 1770 when, as the Manbarra people, they saw James Cook's Endeavour sailing by... Things were destined for major change in 1914 when the Queensland government gazetted Palm Island as an Aboriginal reserve... Over the next 20 years, some 1,630 Aborigines regarded as troublemakers in the Queensland communities and elsewhere in Australia were sent to Palm Island. The island quickly became known as "Punishment Island" and the disaffected individuals, who came to represent more than 40 tribal groups, lived in squalor.

The plight of Palm Islanders is taken to represent the problems with alcohol abuse in Indigenous communities across Australia generally (see Hodge 2003; Mann 2008; Pryor 2001; Skehan 2003). A story in *The Australian* describes Palm Island as 'a lawless place with horrific degrees of theft, domestic violence, sexual assaults against children and abject drunkenness [which is] a typical result of boredom, aimlessness, lack of education, absence of role models and complete loss of self-worth' (Koch 2004). In Brown's (2007) account of the problems on Palm Island, he traces the cause of the despair currently plaguing Palm Island to the introduction of alcohol to the island in 1973: an event which only brought 'drunkenness, violence and arrests'. Over time, 'the island fell more deeply into the welfare mentality, with its associated feelings of hopelessness and desperation'. The 'old paternalism' of the Queensland government, which subsequently introduced an 'alcohol management plan', only exacerbated the problem, for 'what else can islanders do but drink?' It is even suggested that the situation on Palm Island is indicative of a country whose black imprisonment rate has reached '(pre-Mandela) South African dimensions' (Farrant and Ambrose 2000). Indeed, in one account *The Sunday Age* points to the experiences of a Father Raass, who believes that conditions in Indigenous communities are equivalent to 'the poorest parts of Africa' (Skelton 2006).

A story in *The Age* suggests that 'even in Victoria most Aborigines and Torres Strait Islanders felt the colour of the skin was influencing the way police treated them' (Farrant and Ambrose 2000). Farrant and Ambrose (2000) suggest that there are specific cultural factors that have contributed to the scale of alcohol abuse amongst Aborigines:

> Many Aborigines like to meet and socialise with friends and extended family members in the street or other public areas, a practice that draws more attention in country towns than, say, Melbourne. That has led to troubled relations in recent years in several country Victorian towns, such as Mildura and Robinvale... In Mildura, the magistrate's position is rotated regularly – a wise idea... in a town where the visiting magistrate can quickly feel pressures to "deal with the Aboriginal problem".

Robinvale is a town in regional Victoria that, according to a story in *The Age*, has 'fallen off the page' in terms of government assistance (Nader 2008; see also Skelton 2006). It is said to suffer from one of the highest suicide rates amongst Aboriginal youth in the state. The problem, write Farrant and Ambrose (2000), is again cultural: 'The question of cultural difference is one that may never be reconciled in a country whose justice system is based on Judaeo–Christian tenets and British historical practice. Aboriginal customary law, for example, is not formally recognised by the official justice system at all'.

Writing in *The Australian*, Louis Nowra (2007) offers an example of the incompatibility between the two cultural and legal systems. According to Nowra, Aboriginal men often try to explain the 'epidemic of male violence and sexual abuse' that is 'obliterating' Indigenous communities by deferring to what they claim to be their own cultural traditions in order to – literally – 'get away with rape and murder'. He recalls one case in particular:

> Even when Aboriginal men go to court, many receive lenient sentences when using the defence of intoxication combined with customary law.

[An Indigenous man] was convicted of manslaughter, not murder, yet no alcohol was involved in the crime and he was breaching the conditions of his parole at the time. There is no doubt that some judges still consider that Aboriginal men's treatment of their women should be viewed differently from how the rest of society treat women. The defence does work.

It has also been suggested that alcohol has been at the heart of the racial divisions in New Zealand. Commentary there suggests that in contrast to the settlers, 'Maori were one of a very few cultures who had not developed alcoholic drink'. And while it took the Maori time to develop a taste, liquor 'was soon pouring in with the pioneers and has since soaked into our way of life as if into a sponge' (*New Zealand Herald* 2003b). The extent to which alcohol became a part of daily life in New Zealand was made clear by the historian Stevan Eldred-Grigg, who estimates that in the 1840s, Pakeha (settler) men 'each drank around 45 litres of licit spirits a year' (*New Zealand Herald* 2003b). It is argued that New Zealanders are still living with the legacy of this period of developing a drinking culture.

What is striking about Australian and New Zealand news commentary on alcohol abuse in Indigenous communities is the willingness to recognise the roles that European settlement has played in the disorder that plagues Indigenous communities. This stance reflects a sense of the double-sided nature of alcohol – that it can be both 'a "faithful companion"', as well as being as 'responsible for "nine-tenths of the evils of society"' (*New Zealand Herald* 2003b). The Australian news media identifies similar *evils* in Indigenous communities in Australia. A story in *The Sydney Morning Herald* claims that, 'across Australia, booze cuts a swathe through the indigenous population, killing 1,145 people between 2000 and 2004' (Farrelly 2007). An account in the *New Zealand Herald* (2007b) claims that alcohol abuse, along with 'poor health... drug abuse, pornography, unemployment, poor education and housing, and general disempowerment', have contributed to the collapse of morality in Aboriginal communities, and has led to the 'sexual abuse of men and women and, finally, of children', incest and violent rape, and the organised prostitution of teenage girls as young as 12.

While the *New Zealand Herald* is quick to point out the many problems that stem from 'endemic alcohol and drug addiction' in Aboriginal communities, the newspaper is also eager to discuss possible solutions to the problem. Its discussion of the then Liberal/National party coalition government's (the Howard Government) intervention into Aboriginal communities is equivocal. The paper both celebrates the fact that something is being done but is critical about what it is, and offers little in the way of real alternatives. The newspaper variously describes the Howard Government's intervention into Aboriginal communities as a 'mission to rescue the children', an 'invasion', a 'crusade', 'draconian', and as heralding 'the end to Aborigines' rights to control access to their land' (*New Zealand Herald* 2007b; see also Shanahan 2007; Toohey 2008a). Moreover, the newspaper dismisses the government intervention as lacking innovation since it is modelled on the success community elders had in bringing about a decline in drunkenness, assaults, domestic violence 'and other ills of alcohol' a decade ago (see Toohey 2008b). In all, the Howard Government's actions are seen as belonging to a long history of government responses to problems in Aboriginal communities that are 'ineffective, culturally inappropriate or inconsistent, and met with mistrust' (*New Zealand Herald* 2007b).

Research on intoxication and drunkenness in Indigenous populations in Australia

The ways in which intoxication and drunkenness are defined and understood in indigenous populations around the world is a topic that is outside the limits that we have set for this discussion. Rather, our interest is with Indigenous Australians and the ways in which intoxication and drunkenness are used, defined and interpreted by researchers of Indigenous issues. We review research and debates about legality and public drunkenness as they relate to Indigenous Australians; the controversy surrounding sobering-up centres, particularly in relation to defining and understanding intoxication and drunkenness; and finally we examine the notion of drunken comportment and intoxicated aggression in Indigenous communities.

The legality of public drunkenness is different in different places. For example, 'being intoxicated in a public place has not been an offence in the ACT since 1983' (McMillan 2008, 1). In this jurisdiction police may detain a person intoxicated in public only if intoxication is accompanied by disorderly conduct, behaviour likely to cause injury or damage to property, or an inability for the intoxicated person to protect themself from physical harm. Throughout Australia the impetus to decriminalise public drunkenness was, in part, due to the recommendations of the Royal Commission into Aboriginal Deaths in Custody in 1991 (McMillan 2008, 12). Victoria is the only state in Australia where public drunkenness is still an offence, despite reports and recommendations over the years (see Appendix B) suggesting this law be reconsidered. While public drunkenness laws impact on everyone in a community, it is argued that they have greater impacts on Indigenous populations. The Victorian Aboriginal Legal Service argues strongly for the decriminalisation of public drunkenness due to the negative experiences of Indigenous Australians. They argue that these laws result in 'over policing' leading to a 'lack of holistic facilities for those with substance abuse problems; and the fact that the offence is a "gateway" to further charges and entrenchment in the criminal justice system' (Guivarra 2008, 19). For these researchers, public drunkenness is not foremost a legal issue but a public health, medical and welfare problem and they argue that the fact that public drunkenness laws in most states in Australia have been abolished is testament to this view. Guivarra (2008, 20) argues that public space is used differently by Indigenous Australians and 'homelessness and low income levels both contribute to Indigenous Australians being highly visible to police. Physical presence in public spaces as a precursor to arrest is supported by the figures which show that public drunkenness arrests do not correlate with drinking trends'.

Taylor and Bareja (2005, 14) claim that public drunkenness continues to be a major reason for being detained in police custody:

- in 2002, 12 per cent of all incidents of police custody were due to public drunkenness;
- in the jurisdictions where public drunkenness has been decriminalised (all jurisdictions except Victoria and Queensland), incidents involving public drunkenness generally involved people being placed in detention for purposes of protective custody;
- among Indigenous custody incidents, 19 per cent were for public drunkenness whereas this figure was eight per cent for non-Indigenous incidents;
- Indigenous people comprised the vast majority of all public drunkenness custody incidents in the Northern Territory (92%) and Western Australia (83%);
- incidents of custody relating to public drunkenness were much more likely to involve Indigenous than non-Indigenous persons.

However, while the numbers of custody incidents relating to public drunkenness are high, the proportions of all incidents which involve public drunkenness for both Indigenous and non-Indigenous people have been decreasing since 1995:

- in 1995, 34 per cent of all Indigenous custody incidents involved public drunkenness compared with 19 per cent in 2002;
- for non-Indigenous incidents, 15 per cent involved public drunkenness in 1995 compared with only eight per cent in 2002.

This research suggests that police cells are being used as a temporary solution to the problem of public drunkenness rather than other alternatives, such as sobering-up shelters (Taylor and Bareja 2005, 14).

For Weatherburn (2008, 92) the problem of disproportionate Aboriginal arrests for public drunkenness, and more generally alcohol-related crime, is a problem of supply (measured by consumption, expenditure on alcohol, liquor outlet density or liquor trading hours): 'The Royal Commission's [The Royal Commission into Aboriginal Deaths in Custody 1991; see Appendix B] own research revealed that 46% of all Indigenous detentions by police were for public drunkenness [see McDonald 1992; Appendix B]. In the years that followed, the evidence linking alcohol abuse to Indigenous arrest and imprisonment continued to mount'. This is an argument for the decriminalisation of public drunkenness. However, as Guivarra (2008, 20) explains:

> There are two streams of argument against decriminalisation. One is the long running position that abolition of public drunkenness law can only happen once there are enough sobering-up centres available. The other is that, in the interests of community safety, police and local councils need every weapon available to them, including bans on public drinking, and "move on" laws.

In 2003, the role of Aboriginal people in the problem of public drunkenness in Townsville was under debate. Hoolihan (2003, 9) explains the controversy:

> When public drunkenness and the bad behaviour associated with it are mentioned in Townsville most people think about Aboriginal people in our parks. The reality is that the nightclub strip in Townsville generates more incidents of violence and bad public behaviour than exists in our parks. Despite this Townsville politicians scapegoat Aboriginal people as the cause of the public drunkenness problem when they politicise the issue leading up to elections. They then fail to take action once elected to office. This has led to a public debate being drawn out… [over] many years without any hope of dealing with the issue successfully. Furthermore, the negativity that is generated by such a public debate fuels racism, negative stereotyping, and negative social interaction between the Indigenous and non-Indigenous communities.

Hoolihan (2009) argues that the high cost of living, racism in the housing sector, poor health status (resulting from low socio-economic status) and unemployment all contribute to a constellation of issues which are the root causes of public drunkenness. These issues, Hoolihan (2009) argues, are swept aside in local debate about how to fix the problem of public drunkenness.

Margolis et al. (2008, 104) describe a study about supply reduction in remote Indigenous communities: 'An Australian review by d'Abbs and Togni (2000) [see Appendix B] concluded that supply reduction was effective in reducing alcohol consumption and related harm including drunkenness, interpersonal violence, and property damage'. Here drunkenness is defined as a harm related to alcohol consumption and this term was not used again in the evaluation of alcohol management plans in four remote areas of the Northern Territory. Instead, alcohol-related harms and the impact of different methods of alcohol restriction were considered.

In other research Putt et al. (2005, 1) use data from two different surveys to consider the impact of intoxication on crime rates among Indigenous and non-Indigenous offenders. Their report claims that 'overall it is alcohol that seems to be most directly associated with adult Indigenous male offending, as alcohol intoxication was directly attributed as a cause of the most recent crime by many Indigenous male offenders'.

As we have suggested, the question of the decriminalisation of public drunkenness has been closely linked to the establishment, use and support of sobering-up centres since the 1980s. Brady et al. (2006, 201) argue that they provide 'an alternative to individuals being arrested and held in police cells and watch houses'. Brady et al. use case study data to examine the benefits of sobering-up centres and argue that their study provides 'supporting evidence of the important role of sobering-up centres in averting the known harms of a custodial response to public drunkenness, as well as avoiding the potential harm of alcohol-related injury among vulnerable Aboriginal people' (Brady et al. 2006, 201). However, despite lobbying since the 1950s, the 2002 National Police Custody Survey reported that 'police cells, in spite of efforts to the contrary, continue to be used as temporary sobering-up shelters in the absence of other alternatives' (Taylor and Bareja 2005, 5).

Sobering-up centres are of interest to us here as an instance of the variety of responses of Australian communities to public drunkenness and also the ways in which intoxication is defined. Brady et al. (2006, 202) explain how intoxication was defined and recorded at a sobering-up centre in South Australia: 'Staff estimated blood alcohol concentrations using a Lion Alcometer S-D2. Readings were recorded as percentage of blood-alcohol concentration (eg. 0.050% is equivalent to 50 mg of alcohol per 100 ml of blood)'. The staff also recorded a qualitative assessment of patients' condition upon arrival. Table 3 provides behavioural indicators and the estimated blood alcohol range associated with those behaviours.

Table 3. Scale and indicators used to determine condition upon arrival at 'sobering up' centre

Scale	Indicator	Estimated blood alcohol concentration range (%)
Condition 1	Presenting reasonably normal, steady on feet (balanced), reasonable coordination of eyes and limbs, clear speech, able to follow instructions, able to blow on the Alcometer, undress, shower and dress unaided. May be anxious or aggressive on occasions.	0.000–0.100
Condition 2	Somewhat unsteady on feet (unbalanced), slurred speech, some difficulty in following instructions, may need some help in showering, not mentally alert, may be anxious or aggressive on occasions, can blow on the Alcometer but may need encouragement.	0.100–0.200
Condition 3	Presenting unbalanced, difficulty talking and following instructions. Slow response time. May be sick, with strong alcohol breath. Disoriented, anxious, may be aggressive and violent, poor coordination of eyes and limbs, will need assistance in showering and going to bed, may have some breathing difficulties.	0.200–0.300
Condition 4	Very unbalanced, unable to follow instructions, cannot undress, shower and dress for bed unassisted. Strong alcohol breath, difficulty breathing, drowsy, incontinent, poor coordination of eyes and limbs, crying.	0.300–0.400
Condition 5	Comatose. Seriously unwell. Need to transfer to hospital for care.	>0.400

Source: (Brady et al. 2006)

Brady et al. (2006, 204–205) suggest that the clients who were using the sobering-up centre were highly intoxicated, defined by both the assessment of their behaviour as well as the estimated blood alcohol concentrations. They found high levels of intoxication among females, and explained this as perhaps being linked to 'the way in which women's bodies process alcohol (the fact that they generally have less fluid and more fat in their bodies), rather than indicating that they are consuming more alcohol'. Linking intoxication to risk, Brady et al. argue strongly in support of sobering-up centres:

Non-Aboriginal clients were fewer in number and generally presented with lower intoxication levels. These findings support national survey data estimating that 82% of all Indigenous current drinkers consume at risky or high risk levels compared to 28% of non-Indigenous drinkers [see Commonwealth Department of Human Services and Health 1996; Appendix B]. In view of the levels of intoxication documented here, it is likely that these individuals would be at high risk of injury, abuse or death if they were not offered the humane care and safety of this facility.

While acknowledging that some may see sobering-up centres as simply 'rewarding drunken behaviour' Brady et al. (2006, 205) argue that the use of such services by police acts to reinforce 'the message that public intoxication is socially unacceptable'.

In their ethnographic study, Shore and Spicer (2004, 2510) take seriously the influence of socio-cultural factors on drunken comportment. In their examination of an Australian Aboriginal community they argue for 'a model for examining intoxicated aggression that includes societal/cultural framing, personal factors, pharmacological effects of alcohol and drinking context/environment'. Such a model should also seek to 'explore the ways in which culture actually can pattern drunken behavior in the context of additional factors and the extent to which the patterning of such drunken behavior in one Aboriginal community actually conforms to the predictions of the "time out" function of drunkenness'. These authors claim that the literature on Aboriginal alcohol use tends to use social constructivist readings or functionalist accounts of the role of alcohol in Indigenous communities. From these perspectives drinking plays a major role in the construction of Aboriginal culture, and that it serves to promote particular functions, such as powerlessness or social cohesion, in those communities. Their project consisted of three months of intensive fieldwork in an anonymous Aboriginal community in rural north-eastern Australia (including numerous formal and informal interviews) and a written survey to examine the relationship between alcohol and violence. Shore and Spicer (2004, 2519) argue that intoxication and drunkenness are events and states of being which are understood in an Indigenous community as a part of the overall interactions of the community:

> In this Community, rather than functioning as an excuse for behavior, drunken comportment functions as a medium through which tensions and conflicts are played out. Violent acts committed while drinking in

the Community may be partially explained through this system, but are never excused. Alcohol-mediated violent acts are remembered in the Community, and often lead to increased tensions between individuals and kinship groups, and hence more fights and conflicts, even at times when people are sober. In this manner, alcohol-mediated violence seems to be integrated within the larger structure of Community interactions, rather than being a removed and special situation.

Gender and the problem of intoxication and drunkenness

In this section we move to a discussion of the ways in which intoxication and drunkenness are often imagined and debated in gendered terms. In this discussion we see that intoxication and drunkenness are most often framed in masculine terms. When women, young and old, enter discussions of intoxication and drunkenness it is as if the terms take on new meanings, as the old ways of making sense – of both intoxication and drunkenness, and of femininity – become problematic.

Much media commentary, for example, has a difficult time figuring out how to discuss women and drunkenness. On the one hand, many accounts continue to cast women as the victims of men's aggressive drunkenness, and, yet, also spend time discussing women's drinking itself (see Phipps 2004). So, while women are represented as being susceptible to men's aggression, women are also depicted as being more susceptible to *drunkenness* than men. The *New Zealand Herald* (2007c), for example, cites statistics that suggest that women might be 'taking over' from men in 'in the alcohol stakes' (see also Burchill 2001), while a story in *The Guardian* reports that female drunks are 'more aggressive' than men (Saner 2008). In another account a student welfare officer at Georgetown University in Washington D. C. is quoted observing that 'women are not just drinking more, they are drinking ferociously' (Vulliamy 2002). Carol Midgley (2001b) also suggests that studies are showing that 'young women are drinking themselves to death'.

In her reckoning of women's drinking Jane Brody (2002) seeks a physiological rather than social explanation to what she calls the 'ferocity' of such drinking. Brody argues that women's smaller bodies are less able to break down alcohol before it reaches the blood stream compared to men. As a result, consuming the same quantity of alcohol will result in greater levels of intoxication for women than for men (see also Critchley 2008). In these sorts of narratives, women 'develop alcohol dependency at about half the rate of consumption than men, with almost the same proportion for liver damage and brain injury' (Minogue 2001). Meanwhile, Bachelard (2008) claims that the culture that has produced a 'generation of 'strong, independent, [and] liberated' young women, has also led them 'to believe, wrongly, that they can safely adopt the drinking patterns of the boys around them'. This is the 'dark side of sexual equality', writes Ed Vulliamy (2002) in *The Guardian*, and it could well turn out that 'alcohol problems are the price women pay for emancipation' (Minogue 2001; see also Wolf 2007).

This dilemma is personified in the figure of Gina Mallard – a notorious middle-aged woman from Lincoln (UK) who had a high public profile for anti-social behaviour and public drunkenness. Mallard featured in a story in *The Guardian* on women with serious drinking problems. Mallard's drunkenness is variously described as 'colourful', 'loud-mouthed', 'frightening' and 'intimidating'. What Mary O'Hara (2004) calls the 'Mallard question' concerns precisely the relationship between drunkenness and whether women are to be seen as victims or aggressors in drunken violence and crime: 'The "Mallard question", it is fair to say, has divided the community. Some local people regard her merely as an irritant or public nuisance. Others believe she is an aggressive, violent terror whose antics make their lives a misery'. The example of Gina Mallard, however, is no longer exceptional. In a story in *The Sydney Morning Herald* Jordan Baker (2008) claims that, while the 'number of women arrested for domestic violence is soaring', it is not clear whether they are the aggressors or whether the victims of this crime (Baker suggests that many women arrested for domestic violence 'are trying to defend themselves'). The relationships between women and drunkenness have long been a topic of interest for media reporting and commentary. For example, the *The New York Times* recounts how, long before celebrities such as Paris Hilton and Lindsay Lohan became notorious for their drinking, the popular press of the late-eighteenth century published pamphlets such as 'Characters of the present most celebrated courtesans exposed, with a variety of secret anecdotes never before published', which included stories about the 'sordid affairs' of well known people (Grose 2007). More than two centuries later, the drinking habits of young women – the 'Bridget Jones generation', as Claire Phipps (2004) writes – are again a favourite topic for the press, and young women's drinking is being discussed with the same paternal concerns as young people's drinking:

> Young women have got the government worried. Our drinking is, apparently, out of control. And so the No 10 strategy unit report on alcohol misuse, due this month, is expected to recommend a public

information campaign aimed at the "Bridget Jones generation". Concerned department of health officials will back this up with a new *Hello!*-style magazine, *Your Life!*, packed with celebrity-endorsed, cautionary tales about the dangers of binge drinking.

According to Phipps (2004), the problem with the rush to demand government intervention into women's drinking habits is much the same problem as trying to find government solutions to the problem of youth drinking: the press and government simply do not understand why they drink. Phipps (2004) writes that the press and government in Britain are judgmental, and they 'demand explanations for women's drinking that we don't ask of men's, as if falling over after a few pints were an exclusive male right':

> The strand of opinion that recoils from the sight of ladies stumbling along the pavement late at night, laughing loudly and perhaps even singing, would obviously prefer their eventual abstinence to come sooner rather than later. It is hard to imagine young male bingers responding to such pressure. But come one Friday night soon, you might find that those young women who are usually perched in the corner with a couple of Martinis have finally tired of the scrutiny and gone home in disgrace.

The differences between intoxication and drunkenness in men and women have received much attention in the research literature as well. Both qualitative and quantitative studies inform the search to better understand both how intoxication and drunkenness are defined by men and women differently, and also how intoxication is thought to affect them differently. Research has shown that 'drinking continues to be a male-dominated activity, men outnumber women in almost every category of drinking behaviour investigated in research: consumption, frequency of drinking and intoxication, alcohol abuse and dependency. Men are also less likely than women to be aware of the recommended daily limits' (Mullen et al. 2007, 151).

Wang et al. (2003, 910–915) conducted a study with 'twenty right-handed healthy subjects – 10 female subjects (mean age, 36.1 +/- 8 years; range, 21–50 years) and 10 male subjects (mean age, 40.6 +/- 8 years; range, 25–53 years)' of similar socioeconomic background and education levels. They examined 'metabolic decrements' in the brain to compare gendered responses to alcohol use. They 'hypothesized that female subjects would have larger metabolic decrements than male subjects when given alcohol because it is believed that women are more sensitive to the behavioral effects of alcohol than men'.

They further hypothesised that the 'decrements in regional brain metabolism would mediate, in part, alcohol's behavioral effects'. They found that 'global and regional brain glucose metabolism at baseline did not differ between genders'. However, while 'alcohol consistently decreased whole-brain and regional brain metabolism in both genders, ethanol-induced decrements in brain glucose metabolism were significantly smaller in female than in male subjects'. That is, Wang et al. explain, 'despite the [unexpected result of] significantly blunted metabolic response to alcohol in female subjects when compared with male subjects, they showed greater self-reports for intoxication, high, dizziness, and sleepiness'. For these researchers 'alcohol-induced disruptions in motor performance also tended to be greater for female than for male subjects' (Wang et al. 2003, 915).

Psychological differences have also been identified between intoxicated men and women. Olge and Miller (2004, 60) argue that:

> intoxicated men tend to be more aggressive toward men than toward women and that women do not show this differential response pattern… Through multiple steps of social information processing, intoxicated men evidenced more processing alterations related to aggression when the provocateur was male and the apparent intent hostile. This relation was absent in the case of intoxicated women.

Olge and Miller (2004, 60–61) offer psychologically-based explanations for this difference, arguing that 'women tend to experience more empathy for provocateurs and more anxiety and guilt upon showing aggression, which decreases the potential for aggression so that where men show aggressive response, women present anxiety and guilt'. They suggest that the *real-world* ramifications of this divide are obvious when considering that intoxicated women 'ranked hostile male scenarios significantly lower in hostility than all other groups did'. The authors suggest that since:

> women may have been more empathic toward provocateurs and may experience more guilt and anxiety toward their own aggressive behavior, it may be that alcohol impairs processing ability by forcing processing into a more schema driven stereotypical mode. This would account for intoxicated men's increased hostile representation and women's decreased hostility compared with non intoxicated men and women, respectively.

A number of qualitative studies have examined how men and women understand the role of intoxication and drunkenness in their own lives.

Lyons and Willott (2008, 695), for example, argue for a different approach to gender arguing that:

> Rather than viewing and measuring gender in terms of static roles and personality traits, a more fruitful approach is provided by social constructionist theory. This posits that women and men think and act how they do because of concepts about femininity and masculinity that they adopt from their culture (Courtenay 2000 [see Appendix B]). Thus, gender resides not in the person but in social transactions and daily activities defined as gendered (Crawford 1995 [see Appendix B]). As Measham (2002 [see Appendix B]) has stated, "masculinities and femininities are not something imposed upon men and women, but something men and women accomplish themselves on an ongoing basis, constructed in specific social situations in which people find themselves" (p. 351).

In a study of masculinity and drinking in Glasgow (UK), Mullen et al. (2007) examined 'links between excessive alcohol consumption' and masculinity. Mullen et al. (2007, 157) consider how this masculine role plays itself out in the context of 'drinking and drunkenness' amongst 16–24 year olds in Greater Glasgow with ten focus groups and 12 in-depth 'life-trajectory' interviews. As other studies have shown (see for example Harnett 2000), drinking is important in different ways at different times of life. Being drunk becomes less acceptable as men get older. However, Mullen et al. argue that, 'a certain level of intoxication is valued when you spend time with friends or are trying to meet a sexual partner' even as men got older. Nonetheless, drunkenness was still considered to be risky.

In this study Mullen et al. (2007, 153) argue that many men 'are not only compelled toward intoxication due to it being "deeply rooted in expectations of male behaviour" but also that not drinking is not an option for men as it would be seen as "weak and feminine"'. Not only is drinking excessively important to constructing a masculine identity, but there is a gendered imperative for men to do so 'without becoming intoxicated'. However, the authors suggest that a drunken comportment is becoming a more complicated area for young people to navigate as the social milieu keeps shifting. Mullen et al. (2007, 162–163) claim that 'drunkenness is a key theme' in their findings, but that the link between traditional masculinity, which was enacted largely around only other men, is shifting and the rules of drunken comportment are becoming more complex. This research identified a shift from a preference for drinking in homogenous groups to mixed-gendered groups. In this context a good night out explicitly involves 'some intoxication', it 'markedly contrasts with the experience of their fathers and grandfathers': 'The young men in our study could feel uncomfortable about a young women getting drunk, initiating sexual contact, or being loud and "emotional", but they tend to prefer drinking in mixed-sex groups in comparison to the experience of their fathers'. Mullen et al. (2007, 162) suggest that 'we are witnessing a move away from the conventional hegemonic masculine role to a more pluralistic interpretation'.

For much of our discussion to this point the concept of 'intoxication' has referred to a state attained through the consumption or ingestion of alcoholic beverages. However, Bogran (2008, 97–98) sees intoxication 'in broader terms as an instance of an experience of ecstasy, where ecstasy indicates transcendence of regular or everyday limits or frames'. Bogren suggests that 'gender is linked to ecstasy through the idea that transcendence and escape from the everyday' provided by intoxication 'is said to be a concern only for men'. Bogren links the 'escape' from the mundane to sex, but coming back to alcohol use, she suggests that 'women do not "need" sexual transcendence as men do, that is, women do not need or want no-strings-attached sex with many sexual partners, women rather want love and security'. Bogren explains her argument further:

> I suggest that we hypothesize that women's drinking and intoxication is subject to more strict social control because one image of drinking women places women closer to nature than men. Evolutionary theory links women's sexuality to pregnancy and child care, and because contemporary alcohol prevention campaigns and news reports target women – but not men – for their role in reproduction, these cultural ideas together contribute to the positioning of women as "closer to nature".

Partanen (2006, 193–194) argues that in Japan, drinking alcohol has long been considered men's business. In her description of the male drinking session, Partanen explains how a 'wall of etiquette' is erected in social situations which is then 'unwrapped' in the drinking of alcohol, allowing communication to flow more freely. It has been noted that during a night of drinking, men are encouraged to speak and laugh loudly, sing and clap, but when the party is over, sobriety is regained 'almost instantly' and everyone 'acts almost like a different person, like a group of actors leaving the stage after the curtain comes down'. Despite this immediate switch to sobriety at the end of a festive night, Partanen explains: 'The inebriated are to be humored and cared for, and most often this is women's task. Tolerating inebriated men and being concerned about their safety is a part of Japanese women's routine'.

Labelling Japanese men's drinking as 'heroic' (defined as both heightened sociability and intoxication), Partanen understands alcohol's role in a variety of cultural practices and highlights the idea that alcohol's effects are more than simply physiological and depend upon more than the alcohol itself.

In a US study Montemurro and McClure (2005, 279–286) analysed so-called *bachelorette* parties to consider gendered assumptions about drinking behaviour. They conducted in-depth, qualitative interviews with 51 women over 21 years old. From the standpoint of symbolic interactionism they understand alcohol as a symbol through which meaning is created for the women at the bachelorette party. In fact, they argue: 'The bachelorette party is the only pre-wedding event in which it is expected and planned that women will become intoxicated – and really the only secular ritual focused on women's alcohol consumption'. Montemurro and McClure argue that public intoxication by women is both under-researched as well as stigmatised, however, these ideas and understandings may be changing, as 'public intoxication may no longer be perceived as deviant by young women and/or by society at large'. Indeed it is argued that intoxication at this 'event is the norm' and it is used by women for a number of reasons in this context: for stress reduction during the planning of the wedding, as well as to alleviate the stress of becoming a wife and taking on a new role: 'Any anxiety or stress she may have about getting married is not appropriate for public display or discussion. Thus, the bachelorette party provides a much needed release for women'. So, intoxication provides a space where the stresses of a wedding and a changing role for women are allowed to be relieved by alcohol use, even to intoxication, which has otherwise been shown to be a stigmatised practice for women. Montemurro and McClure (2005) propose that bachelorette parties provide a space for women to deviate from and resist traditional gender norms in that they are, in particular, drinking in public, and drinking to excess; two things that are seen as traditionally male activities. This, they argue, enables women to 'use alcohol as a symbol of power and equality'. This study of bachelorette parties indicates that intoxication plays a vital role. 83 per cent of respondents (n=118) described parties at which the bride-to-be was intoxicated. For the purposes of their analysis, Montemurro and McClure defined 'trashed' as an intense kind of intoxication, 'in which the bride-to-be passed out, blacked out, or got sick from drinking too much':

> It seems that the women in this sample used alcohol as an excuse for their actions. In other words, if they were able to dismiss or legitimate

their behavior by claiming intoxication, to say that behavior was neutralized in some way, their 'real' self or identity would not be marred by their actions at the bachelorette party.

In another study Lyons and Willott (2008, 705) conducted qualitative research in New Zealand with eight focus groups with 32 participants (16 women, 16 men, mean age 24.6 years). Women reported drinking less than men but, as in other studies, drunkenness was part of what it was to be social and having shared stories/histories with your social network. Lyons and Willott were interested in the increase in women's drinking and how gender relations and identities are constructed in the context of alcohol consumption: 'Specifically, this study aimed to explore contemporary constructions of femininity, and how young women are (re) defining their gender identities in relation to men and the traditional masculine ethos of consuming alcohol in public'. Women's drunkenness was found to be monitored in particular ways; it was acceptable, but only 'up to a certain point'. Lyons and Willott argue: 'Once very drunk, however, women are looked down upon, considered embarrassing and also "slutty"'. They explain 'that participants know they hold this double standard themselves, and that women see themselves as holding it even more than men'. In the quote below Lyons and Willott argue that, in New Zealand, men's drinking is strongly tied to the pub and sport. Tracy interjects to claim that women can only get drunk to a certain level of drunkenness. For Lyons and Willott this suggests that respectability 'remains an issue for women':

> Simon: *We're still, I think as Matthew was saying before, it's, I think we're still, we're adjusting to, to different, um, gender roles basically. Like, that it's OK for women to be getting drunk but I think*

> Tracy: *To a level of drunkenness*

> Simon: *Yeah, but, but I don't, I think probably there'd be people who would look down more on the young girls stumbling around the Viaduct, than the young guys stumbling out of the pub, do you know what I mean, after watching the rugby. Like, there's still some disparity there.*

The relationships between men and women and intoxication were explored in a study by Abrahamson (2004, 13–23). The research comprised two to three hour (same gender) focus groups with men and women and involved a total of 56 participants. Abrahamson argues that 'the role of alcohol in the flirtation game has a similar meaning for both women and men. The implications of picking up/being picked up in the context of intoxication, on the other hand, are different for men and for women and are described in different terms'. For men: 'Unbridled intoxication is described as a liability-free zone where other rules apply and where alcohol offers absolution'. Women however describe a different experience: 'The women feel themselves to be under observation and also are constantly observing themselves. They continually guard themselves against going too far and set themselves invisible boundaries. For women, alcohol offers no excuses' (Abrahamson 2004, 22). One of Abrahamson's participants, a young woman of about 20 years of age explains that if she was seen flirting when she was sober she believed that she would be viewed as 'desperate' but, 'under the cover of intoxication... flirting can be presented as partly serious and partly in jest'. Many of these twenty-something women spoke about the need for alcohol, and the need to be at least 'somewhat intoxicated' as something that they required when they were 'younger', because it facilitated socialising when they felt too shy to do so without it.

While we have shown that intoxication and drunkenness are gendered concepts, evidenced by both qualitative and quantitative research, the studies we review here do not enable us to better understand, as Lyons and Willott (2008) argue we should, how society works to underpin these gendered constructions of intoxication and drunkenness And indeed there are signs in some studies that females are starting to act more like males in terms of public displays of intoxication and drunkenness.

Conclusion

In this chapter we have reviewed media commentary and the research literature that focus on different populations and the problem of intoxication and drunkenness. As is evidenced throughout our discussion these terms are rarely defined and are therefore open to differing interpretations depending on the context of their use.

Although popular perceptions of alcohol use and intoxication and drunkenness tend to rely on generalisations it is clear that there are important differences between and within groups. For example, from our discussion of media commentary and the research literature on young people as a population who present particular concerns in relation to intoxication and drunkenness, we could suggest that not all young people, male or female, in different geographical locations and cultural settings, regularly drink to intoxication and even if they do, their patterns of consumption – the context of their drinking and even the types of alcohol consumed – is different in different geographical locations. The same is true for Indigenous groups. What is missing in this research is the absent (silent) majority who drink responsibly or do not drink at all.

We have also presented a limited account of media commentary and research on the raft of issues that are associated with understandings of intoxication and drunkenness with Indigenous populations (in this case in Australia). These issues present a minefield for review and discussion. The political, the cultural, the social and the economic dimensions of the history of colonialism, dispossession, and marginalisation of Indigenous populations in Australia are things that make an appearance in this commentary and research. The complexities we have indentified in relation to the meanings and consequences of intoxication and drunkenness take on an altogether different dimension in this context. Our only contribution here is a very modest attempt to highlight this complexity.

We have also presented a discussion of the research literature on gender differences related to intoxication and drunkenness. The sociological literature, we argue, holds the promise for more nuanced portrayals of lived experiences and cultural differences in drinking behaviours. These are not dependent on describing physiological or psychological harms, nor do they attempt to measure these harms by using various scientific formulae. Sociological approaches make it clear that different rules and moral codes still apply to the ways in which men and women drink, often to levels of intoxication and drunkenness. For the most part intoxication and drunkenness appear to be expected of males and are seen as deviant in females. These differences in expectations of course, as has been shown elsewhere in this review, are not new, but they do find purchase in new ways in the contemporary context. This is not to say that male intoxication and drunkenness is not seen as a problem though, and particular groups are the targets of legal interventions, particularly related to issues around public safety. There is evidence, however, that young women are adopting more traditionally male drinking styles and the reasons for this are not yet well known.

Chapter 5

The management of intoxication and drunkenness: Crime and issues of regulation

Introduction

As we have seen so far many of the concerns that give meaning and shape to intoxication and drunkenness are related to the actual and possible consequences for the behaviours of individuals and groups/populations. These consequences are often related to individual and public health concerns (physical and mental), and/or various adverse outcomes in work, education and relationships. In this final chapter we present a discussion of the ways in which the problems of intoxication are understood, interpreted and acted upon when they become issues or concerns to be managed, regulated or subjected to legal considerations and judgment.

The discussion in what follows takes a number of directions. In the first instance we turn to an account of some of the ways in which media commentary tends to focus on the anti-social, even criminal, consequences of intoxication and drunkenness, and, for the media, the always incomplete, problematic and ineffectual ways that governments respond to and attempt to manage these issues. This background discussion leads to a review of the legal and criminological research and commentary on issues such as: the ways in which intoxication and drunkenness may mitigate personal responsibilities and accountabilities; the particular nature of choice, consent and responsibility in cases of sexual assault when intoxication is a factor; the dilemmas associated with various regulations related to the promotion and policing of the Responsible Serving of Alcohol (RSA) in various contexts; and the relationships between intoxication, violence and gender.

Anti-social behaviour, crime and the need for government action: The news media and its concerns with intoxication and drunkenness

At the heart of the news media's understandings of intoxication and drunkenness is the question of the law. *The Washington Post* and the *Otago Daily Times*, for example, publish weekly crime and court reports that catalogue convictions and cases for 'disorderly intoxication' and 'senseless drunkenness' – that is, alcohol abuse that affects people other than the drinker. Much media commentary tends to spend a great deal of time examining the legal implications of intoxication, and whether impairment of 'perception risk' due to 'self-induced intoxication' – which is to say, drinking to intoxication can be used as a defence in court (see for example McFadden 2006; Sontag and Alvarez 2008; *Otago Daily Times* 2003; *The Times* 2003a; 2005; Cornwell 2006; Power, 2007a, *The Washington Post* 2002). There are a range of issues explored in articles dealing with the legal implications of self-induced intoxication including:

- a *New York Times* story that examined the implications of intoxication on murder trials, and whether it could be judged that the murderer 'was sufficiently sober to have formed the intent to kill the victims' (Zhao 2003);

- a law introduced in New Hampshire that enabled police to take young people into custody for alcohol that was already in their body (Fahrenthold 2006);

- a *New York Times* report about a driver who was charged with driving 'while impaired by alcohol', even though his blood alcohol level of 0.09 was under the legal limit for intoxication (*The New York Times* 2001);

- the liability for gun murder as a result of intoxication (Santana 2001);

- the liability of drunk drivers (Lueck and O'Donnell 2004; *Otago Daily Times* 2004a; 2005a; 2006b);

- whether drink driving that kills can be tried as murder (Vitello 2006), or as manslaughter (Jackman 2000);

- the legality of breath testing – for while it is accepted that a driver's breath test is admissible in a US court as proof of intoxication, there are questions about whether a breath test taken hours after drinking is reliable (Elliott 2000a; 2000b; Helliker 2006).

In addition to these sorts of concerns recent media commentary in settings such as the UK and New Zealand has canvassed the possibilities that Anti Social Behaviour Orders (ASBOs) can provide an effective governmental response to a range of problems associated with intoxication and drunkenness. These sorts of stories reference a growing body of health experts who argue that government intervention will never be able to solve the problems of alcohol abuse, since government intervention can only treat the problem on a society-wide level. At the same time commentators increasingly support calls for approaches that treat the individual drinker. For these commentators this might take place either through the introduction of ABSOs, or by supporting non-governmental groups such as Alcoholics Anonymous.

For example, some commentary in New Zealand has suggested that the introduction of ASBOs in that country mirrored the example set by Britain, where ASBOs were 'introduced to act as a deterrent and to help rid local communities of troublemakers' (O'Hara 2004). In Britain they can be served on anyone who is 10-years-old or over for a variety of offences (Horowitz 2005). The same attempt to regulate the behaviour of young drinkers prevails in New Zealand, where the term ASBO has come to be 'a catch-all term for hooning, drunkenness, out-of-control youth, petty crime, unruly neighbours, intimidation and other acts of boorishness' (*New Zealand Herald* 2007a).

Commentators such as Mary O'Hara (2004) suggest that ASBOs were introduced to act as a deterrent to the kinds of 'nuisance' crimes that governments fear can escalate into more serious crimes. They were designed to 'rid local communities of troublemakers'. But a problem drinking culture is, she writes, 'bigger than the person'. Any form of government intervention must therefore design 'more appropriate help for people with drink-related problems' than ASBOs, which seek to 'address' problem drinking merely by removing problem drinkers from sight (O'Hara 2004). Some in the media attack ASBOs, moreover, for the way they often impose 'ridiculous' restrictions on people. O'Hara (2004) cites examples including a person who was, apparently, given an ASBO for being sarcastic, and a boy who was banned from using the word 'grass' in England until 2010. ABSOs 'set people up to fail', she writes, 'especially vulnerable individuals – who... need rehabilitation, not time inside'.

Media commentary also suggests that the British and New Zealand governments discovered how difficult it is to regulate drinkers' behaviour when they introduced ASBOs. In considering the introduction of ASBOs to New Zealand, some news stories sought to point out the many legal difficulties the government would encounter in using them. Chief amongst these was the complaint that ASBOs contravene human rights. In some accounts commentators were critical of the way ABSOs are heard in civil courts, which means that 'complaints do not have to be proven beyond reasonable doubt, merely judged on the balance of probability' (*New Zealand Herald*, 2008c; see also 2007a). Not only do ASBOs rely on 'naming-and-shaming tactics [that] take away the child's right to privacy' (see also Button 2005), but ASBOs are often used by police to manage people with mental health problems, when treatment would be more appropriate. There is also criticism of the way anti-social behaviour has been defined so broadly that it results in orders bordering on the ridiculous. The *New Zealand Herald* (2008c) cites some examples of this:

> [A] 23-year-old woman who repeatedly threw herself into the Avon was banned from jumping into rivers or canals. A man with mental health problems was banned from sniffing petrol anywhere in Teesside... A 17-year-old was forbidden to use his front door. Then there was the evangelical preacher banned from London's Oxford Circus, the football-mad teenager told to stop kicking a ball in the street, and the neighbour prevented from playing Dido albums over and over again.

The ambivalence and ambiguity characteristic of much media commentary about anti-social behaviours and drunkenness – and what governments should or can do about these concerns – is evident in the ways that Simon Jenkins (2006), writing in *The Guardian*, demands the British government intervene into the drinking culture of young people. Jenkins then laments that Britain is 'the world capital of insufferable paternalism', led by a government that 'no longer trusts communities to exercise self-discipline through bylaws and licensing' (see also Armstrong 2000). These criticisms are also evident in Australian media commentary. Malcolm Brown (2007) argues in *The Sydney Morning Herald* that the same kind of 'old paternalism' is responsible for the failure of a succession of Queensland government interventions into alcohol abuse in Aboriginal communities. A story in *The Australian* (Price 2006), in contrast, broadly supports the call of the former federal Health Minister, Tony Abbott, for a 'form of paternalism' to tackle the problems of alcohol abuse in Indigenous communities. Elizabeth Farrelly (2007) supports the 'counter-intuitive' strategy of 'giving people more freedom and responsibility', arguing that it 'can make them behave less like children, [and] more like civilised adults' (see also Brown 2007; *New Zealand Herald* 2007b). Ultimately, according to Julie Burchill (2001), government intervention in 'people's self-destructiveness actually makes the situation far worse'.

Central to media accounts of the consequences of drunkenness is the assumption that drunkenness causes harm. Concerns in these narratives include the role that drunkenness plays in promoting both 'nuisance' crimes such as 'graffiti, drunkenness, intimidation and abuse' (Button 2005; see also Phillips 2000; Hsu 2002), and 'serious' crimes, such as violence, addiction, rape and racism (*New Zealand Herald* 2008c). Drinking, so this narrative goes, leads first to minor or 'nuisance' crimes, which, if not addressed, ultimately develop into more serious crimes. The *New Zealand Herald* (2008c) looks at how crime can escalate from a seemingly innocuous beginning to becoming a significant social problem. The question the newspaper asks is: 'Does graffiti cause murder?' The idea that crime is spawned from disorder comes from the 'Broken Windows' theory outlined in a 1982 *Atlantic Monthly* article. The *New Zealand Herald* presents the following account of this theory: 'Consider a building with a few broken windows. If the windows are not repaired, the tendency is for vandals to break a few more. Eventually, they may even break into the building, and if it's unoccupied, perhaps become squatters or light fires inside'. The theory sees crime as an epidemic. A broken window can be a signal that no one cares, that anything goes and before long anarchy rules. According to the 'broken windows' theory of social disorder, if a society tolerates 'nuisance crimes' such as graffiti, or leaving buildings with broken windows, then its sensibilities will be stretched to the point where, in time, the nuisance of graffiti escalates into more serious crimes.

The *New Zealand Herald* (2003a) reported on one successful example of attacking nuisance crimes in the hope of preventing an escalation into serious crime in its report on how Baltimore overcame its history of violent crime (see also Rosen 2000):

> Four years ago, Baltimore had the grim distinction of having the highest rates of violent crime and drug addiction of any big American city. Baltimore's fortunes were transformed when its mayor, Martin O'Malley, ordered a blitz on the low-level offending that scarred communities. The city's agencies were given targets for tackling vandalism and drunkenness and were repeatedly judged on them. He cites that as a driving factor behind Baltimore's 26 per cent fall in violent crime since 1999.

This narrative is neither particularly new, nor unique to New Zealand. In a 2002 story in *The New York Times*, Santora (2002) suggests that the same concerns occupied the city's Assembly in 1685: 'The Assembly was "worried about the spillover from New Yorkers" drinking, and felt compelled to raise the fine on public intoxication, describing "that Louthsome and Odious sin" as "the root and foundation of many other Enormous Sinnes as bloodshed, stabbing, murther, swearing, fornication, Adultry, and such like'". The *Otago Daily Times* (2005b) also suggests that intoxication escalates into crime, and further intoxication. The problem with intoxication, the court reporter writes, is that it can lead to a 'lack of consequential thinking which leads to offending, then guilt and further intoxication'. The newspaper cites the behaviour of students at Otago University in Dunedin as an example arguing that 'if the culture of couch-burning, drunkenness and general mayhem is allowed to continue, the numbers seeking enrolment here will drop and an increasing proportion of those who do come will be predisposed to disorderly conduct, since that will have become the main attraction' (*Otago Daily Times* 2006a). In such accounts drunkenness and intoxication are implicated as causes of social disorder (see also Bowditch 2006; Miles 2002a; 2002b). This is reflected in *The Washington Post*'s preoccupation with cataloguing convictions for 'disorderly intoxication' in its weekly crime reports. Any attempt to address social disorder is therefore necessarily an attempt to address drunkenness and intoxication in society. But as the *New Zealand Herald* (2008c) argues, one of the problems with an approach to policing that seeks to deter the kind of escalation of disorder described by the 'broken windows' theory is that it gives the police 'carte blanche to stomp out minor offences', with a focus on punishment rather than rehabilitation:

> The aim is not to reform the disorderly, but to punish, exclude and get them off the street. The idea was fervently taken up in the mid-1980s by the New York Transit Authority determined to remove graffiti from the subway. Line by line, car by car, graffiti was painted over or removed with solvents on a daily basis. A message was sent to graffiti vandals that their handiwork would never see the light of day. Similar strategies were applied to fare-beating. And in 1994, when Rudolf Giuliani was elected mayor, the strategy broke out above ground – a city-wide crackdown on street disorder, ranging from drunkenness to "squeegee men" washing car windows at intersections.

In contrast to the commentary on various forms of government intervention cited above, the Australian news media regularly carries stories about the problems facing individual drinkers. In one such story in *The Australian* it is claimed that the onus must be on helping the individual drinker: 'The best thing to do is to stop taking substances by getting appropriate help. Short of living in a dry community, utopian or dystopian, the only way to stop addictive behaviours is for individuals to learn how to refuse alcohol… when faced with the opportunity of taking it' (Gaughwin 2008). In spite of some commentators claiming that the onus must be on helping the individual drinker, it is rare for media stories to support organisations that seek to do that. As Fitzgerald (2007) writes, 'psychologists and other health professionals consistently undervalue the proven effectiveness' of organisations such as Alcoholics Anonymous in helping individual drinkers. He suggests that this is because 'these groups are non-professional lay organizations that involve alcoholics and other addicts from all walks of life helping each other and, in so doing, helping themselves' (see also Writer 2005; Power 2007b; Aratani 2007). In his account of how Alcoholics Anonymous helped him to beat his problem drinking, Andy Mayer (2001) writes that he only turned to the organisation after government facilities and the NHS failed to help him.

Governments tend to face intense scrutiny and criticism in media reporting of the consequences – intended or otherwise – associated with their attempts to regulate and manage issues related to intoxication and drunkenness. While *The Washington Post* pushes for Government intervention to help problem drinkers, the newspaper is quick to criticise when government agencies 'miss' the deaths of three homeless people (Kovaleski and Chan 2001). In another story *The Washington Post* criticises the police for their mishandling of a case involving two people who froze to death after being taken into custody for public drunkenness (Brown 2003). In Australia the Northern Territory government was also heavily criticised in a story in *The Australian* when its Department for Community Development failed to intervene to prevent the death of an Aboriginal baby (Wilson 2006). Simon Jenkins (2002), writing in *The Times*, suggests that the problem with relying on government intervention is that government alcohol policy 'is driven not by reason or "the right thing to do". It is driven by fear of the media, fear of a minority of public opinion, fear of message, image and spin'. The problem, in short, is that 'there might be broad agreement about the problem – binge drinking, hospitalization and violence – but there is no agreement on how to fix it' (see, also, Bachelard 2008).

The role of government intervention

Some of the more informed debate encountered in the press relates to the role – and extent – of government intervention in addressing the consequences of problem drinking. In a story in *The Age*, Associate Professor John Fitzgerald (2008) identifies the question at the heart of the public debate over the need for government intervention into drinking behaviours. He writes: 'The biggest question… is to what extent we want our laws to control our desire to get drunk. Do we want government to control drinking behaviour, to educate us on responsible drinking, to protect us from alcohol-related violence?'

Julian Baggini (2004) writing in *The Guardian* provides a particular response to this type of question. In discussing the merits of government paternalism in relation to regulating alcohol policy, he argues that John Stuart Mill 'was right that no actions that harm only ourselves should be illegal', although there is, Baggini admits, a difference 'between regulation and banning outright'. He continues: 'That is why there is no mixed message in calling for a lift on absolute prohibitions on illegal drugs, while at the same time legislating to encourage responsible drinking and coming down hard on those whose intoxication risks harm to others'.

Simon Jenkins (2006), also in *The Guardian*, argues that in the context of finding solutions to binge drinking, the role of government must be to introduce laws and policies that limit the capacity for young people to access alcohol. If we want to understand why '24% of 15-year-olds' claim they have been 'drunk 10 times or more in the past year', and how it is that 'the UK ranks as the third highest out of 35 European countries in this particular league table' (Travis 2007), we must first look at public policy'. After all, he asks: 'What is Government for?' (Jenkins 2007; see also Jenkins 2000; Riddell 2003).

But such *behaviour modification* is problematic according to Fitzgerald (2008), who argues that to rely too heavily on government intervention is 'naïve', especially in light of the 'spate of violence in Melbourne's CBD' and other failures of the Victorian Government to control alcohol-related harm (see also Tippet 2008). And even when a government takes deliberate steps to regulate problem drinking, as the Howard Government did in 2007 in its intervention in Northern Territory Indigenous communities, whether such interventions can be successful is far from clear. For instance, in two reports on the Howard Government intervention, published only three months apart, *The Australian* gives contradictory accounts of whether the intervention is working. In July 2007, the newspaper described '"rivers of grog"…still flowing as strong as ever' through Aboriginal communities (Kearney 2007a). In October of the same year, the paper writes that the intervention 'has put food on the table and taken grog off the streets in Aboriginal communities' (Kearney 2007b; see also Langton 2008; Skelton 2007).

In the UK and Australia media commentary has at different times focused on two proposed forms of government intervention in particular, but then criticised them both for being counter-intuitive. The first – the introduction of 24-hour drinking licenses in Britain – was aimed at curbing the trend identified by Jack Straw (the then-UK Home Secretary), whereby drinkers are forced to drink as much as possible before pubs close at 11 pm. Paradoxically, it was claimed that forcing pubs to close earlier in this way could actually lead to increased drunkenness and increased violence (Neilan 2000). The rationale for introducing 24-hour drinking licenses taps into the kinds of stories the news media often tells about the drinking cultures of other countries. In particular, they draw on the perception that 'continental-style' drinking is 'civilised', as Ian Jack (2005) writes in *The Guardian*. But he is also sceptical as to whether emulating a 'European' drinking culture will work in Britain, since what is essentially British about the British drinking culture is that for the British, getting drunk is only the means to 'something more' (*The Guardian* 2004b). In contrast, the image of the 'civilised', 'contented drunk' European simply does not appeal to the British drinker. Jack (2005) argues that:

> I am with the many other sceptics who disbelieve that England's new relaxed licensing hours will encourage more "continental-style" and "civilised" drinking, which is the government line. It won't. There is in this country, the United Drunkdom of Great Britain and Northern Ireland, a singular pride and pleasure in the mass abandonment of sobriety. You might argue that the old ways, the privacy of the dark bar and its 10 o'clock bell, are what kept it in check.

A story in *The Guardian* also highlights the apparent contradiction involved in allowing pubs to be open 24 hours. This policy of 'liberalisation' is an odd tactic, argues Riddell (2003), because it will only *exacerbate* problem drinking rather than reduce it:

> The Government says flexibility will stop a mass exodus of drunks at closing time. It hints that continental timetabling will substitute legless alcopoppers for Jean-Paul Sartre in Les Deux Magots or Italians with a meager Chianti habit and a grandma in tow. You don't have to be a temperance freak to acknowledge that the real result could be city centres run as alcohol theme parks producing the big profits, and the odd dead child.

In another account *The Guardian* (2004b) is unequivocal in its position on this proposal: it will not work, the newspaper argues, because it is attempting to 'make us both more free and more responsible' in a system that has effectively taught the nation's drinkers that they cannot be trusted 'with a drink after the hour of 11pm'. These contradictions are, for a range of media commentators, the product of an 'insufferable paternalism' (Jenkins 2006) with 'unpleasant Big Brother overtones' (Devine 2008), which has shaped a 'draconian' and 'archaic' approach to alcohol policy: a situation in which 'the nation's youth, to say nothing of its more mature citizens, have grown up under an effective curfew and a semi-prohibition. In these rushed and draconian circumstances, it's no wonder that we have developed an unhealthy relationship with booze' (*The Guardian* 2004b; see also Jenkins 2001). Alan Travis (2007) argues that the proposal to introduce 24-hour drinking licenses is inconsistent with other forms of government intervention. He suggests that while the 24-hour licensing proposal will make alcohol more readily accessible, it contradicts other policies designed to tackle Britain's binge drinking culture such as 'cracking down on the promotional sale of cheap alcohol and happy-hour discounts': and where alcohol is readily accessible from 'supermarkets, late night shops and petrol stations' (see also Macaskill and Gordon 2007; Knight 2008). The risk of 24 hour drinking licenses is, in these arguments, that they will end up promoting 24-hour binge drinking, and subsequently the escalation of the crime that it is meant to deter. Such concerns are to be found in much media reporting including the following account of the contradictions that *The Guardian* (2004b) identifies in the ways that Nottingham's (UK) local council understands the problems of, and solutions to, public drunkenness:

> In the interim, it might help if our towns and cities began to catch up with modern life. Fourteen years ago, Nottingham Safer Cities Project published a report to combat alcohol-related crime. It set out to reclaim the city centre for non-drinkers, or at least non-drunks, and recommended that transport, museums, galleries, cinemas, sporting facilities and bookshops should be encouraged to open later. A few weeks ago I saw about 100 bars and three restaurants, and nothing else that was functioning after dark in the heart of Nottingham. The local council told me that it had no plans to extend the tram's working hours or even to build a public lavatory... In other words, the intention, and one that extends way beyond Nottingham, is to treat late-night city-centre visitors like unsocial drunks and just hope that they don't behave that way. And if they do, well, that must be a problem for the police. Really, it's enough to turn you to drink.

Some media accounts in Australia also suggest that allowing pubs to stay open for such long hours will encourage 'pub crawling'. A story in *The Sydney*

Morning Herald argues that longer opening hours encourages 'thousands of... young Sydneysiders [to] drift from pubs to clubs in the early hours of the morning'. The newspaper therefore supports government calls to introduce curfews, in order to 'crack down on alcohol-fuelled crime, violence and anti-social behaviour' (Jacobsen 2003).

At another level there is substantial support in some parts of the Australian news media for government intervention in the form of raising taxes on the drinks that are most popular with problem drinkers. Health practitioners and researchers argue that raising taxes are the 'single intervention best supported by evidence' (Bachelard 2008). This is the so-called 'Scandinavian' approach to regulating alcohol consumption, which 'imposes extremely high taxes, state control of advertising and state ownership of alcohol retailing outlets' (Bachelard 2008). The logic of this approach is quite straightforward: 'If alcohol causes harm, make it harder to get' (Farrelly 2007; see also Shaver 2007).

While much media commentary responds to social incidents of intoxication and drunkenness, calling for some form of government response, in doing so, it reinforces particular ways of understanding intoxication and drunkenness as they relate to government, policy and the law. This commentary can also be productive of public concerns about intoxication and drunkenness. It can set the agenda in relation to these issues, and drive this agenda in particular directions. These directions can be contradictory and produce more uncertainty and complexity in terms of understanding intoxication and drunkenness, their consequences, and the nature of possible responses and forms of regulation.

Legal definitions of intoxication and drunkenness: Choice and mitigation of personal responsibilities?

As we have indicated, intoxication and drunkenness, and the difficulty of defining them, have a number of implications for the law. Unlike public health and medical discourse, where the study of intoxication and drunkenness is framed in scientific discourse and these terms are often defined with relation to counting drinks or measuring blood alcohol content, in legal discourse the volume, or amount of alcohol consumed is not the central focus of debate. This divergence points to the myriad ways in which expertise is constructed and mobilised by different disciplines in relation to these two terms. In the following discussion we are concerned particularly with various aspects of understanding intoxication and drunkenness in the context of legal discourses from Australia and New Zealand, the UK and the US.

Levi and Valverde (2001, 835) explain some of the difficulty of defining such a slippery concept as intoxication:

> The legal entity of intoxication has an inherent tendency to undermine, and indeed to deconstruct, the opposition between opinion and fact evidence. Eyewitnesses can and do give evidence that they saw Mr. X consume three beers or, more commonly, that Mr. X was swaying while walking, had bloodshot eyes, or whatever. But the addition of a few such observations so as to produce the aggregate, somewhat diffuse, category of intoxication is a tricky epistemic operation.

Levi and Valverde (2001, 836) further argue that intoxication is not a fact of the kind developed from scientific investigation, and that 'courts are pretty well united in allowing that nonexperts can indeed give an opinion about intoxication, and that scientific knowledge about alcohol and behavior is not required (Miller 1999 [see Appendix B])'. This interpretation is counter to much of what we have considered so far in this book. The suggestion that intoxication cannot be scientifically defined is very different to work undertaken and reported on here from the fields of health and medicine and social science which seeks to develop strict definitions of intoxication. We examine then, how the legal field approaches intoxication and drunkenness.

In the first instance we consider the use of intoxication in mitigating the level of responsibility for various criminal offences, including sexual assault cases. There are a number of factors to be considered in understanding how intoxication is understood and mobilised in a court of law. We examine the idea that intoxication can be either voluntary or involuntary and the possibility of making a free choice with relation to intoxication. In sexual assault cases, legal definitions of intoxication must consider the notion of consent in sexual encounters, and the role of intoxication in those instances.

Although the 'intoxication doctrine' states that intoxication is never a defence, Simester (2009, 6) argues that 'it is surely preferable to accept the facts of the matter, and proceed on the basis of truth rather than pretence'. This argument suggests that to ignore the fact of intoxication is to misrepresent the facts of a case. As we discussed in Chapter 1, the question of responsibility while intoxicated is one that has been considered for centuries – especially in the philosophical discourses of Immanuel Kant and John Locke. For Kant, 'the actions, for example, of a madman or a drunkard can be attributed, though not imputed to them. In imputation the action must spring from freedom. The drunkard cannot, indeed, be held accountable for his actions, but he certainly can, when sober, for the drunkenness itself' (cited in Nicholls 2006, 136). Nicholls (2006, 136–137) finds Kant's work relevant to notions of freedom and reason:

> When freedom, reason and legal responsibility are inextricable one is, when drunk, neither properly free nor properly a subject. When drunk, one is neither subject *to* the law nor entirely outside of the law... when the ground of responsibility is the capacity for reason, then intoxication, incontrovertibly, presents mitigation. The locus of legal responsibility, therefore, becomes the sober individual who *chooses* to become drunk. It is here, however, that the problem of addiction comes into view, for to apply this principle the law needs to ask to what extent individuals are entirely free to choose whether or not to drink in the first place.

Of interest in this discussion is the link between criminal behaviour and the responsibility of intoxicated persons in the eyes of the courts. While there is a belief that alcohol use causes criminal behaviour, no evidence has been established about the causal link between intoxication and criminality. Despite this difficulty, intoxication is often raised as a mitigating factor. For example, one may claim that the crime committed and the level of intoxication is atypical of the defendant's character. However, any history of offending while intoxicated, it is argued, 'implicitly makes the individual more culpable, because he or she would be aware that such conduct can follow drinking' (Dingwall and Koffman 2008, 339). To what extent past wrongs should influence sentencing for current wrongdoings is an issue that has long divided philosophers and legal theorists. In the mid-nineteenth century John Stuart Mill claimed:

> Drunkenness, for example, in ordinary cases, is not a fit subject for legislative interference, but I should deem it perfectly legitimate that a person who had once been convicted of any act of violence to others under the influence of drink should be placed under a special legal restriction, personal to himself; that if he were afterwards found drunk, he should be liable to a penalty, and that if, when in that state, he committed another offence, the punishment to which he would be liable for that other offence should be increased in severity. The making himself drunk, in a person whom drunkenness excites to do harm to others, is a crime against others. (1859: 167 [see Appendix B]; cited in Dingwall and Koffman 2008, 339)

More recently a report titled *Intoxication and Criminal Responsibility* examined this question of the degree to which intoxication can be used as an excuse for criminal behaviour. The author points out that the law is not consistent across states in Australia and claims that some laws relating to intoxication are 'uncertain, illogical, inconsistent, unprincipled and unduly complex' (Bradfield 2006, 7). In 1996 the Australian High Court 'abolished the common law defence of intoxication' and 'the Australian common law position… that intoxication, whether voluntary or otherwise, is a circumstance relevant to the establishment of the mens rea of any criminal offence'. Essentially, this new legislation claims 'intoxication is irrelevant except in the case of offences that involve a specific intent' (Howie 2004, 57).

It has been argued that intoxication makes it more difficult for the individual to assess the danger of a situation, therefore causing her/him to overreact or act out of mistaken beliefs of impending harm: 'The criminal law has had to respond to a number of cases where an intoxicated individual attacked someone (and often killed him) in the allegedly mistaken belief that the victim was about to attack him' (Dingwall 2007, 127). Reporting on recent activity in the Court of Appeals in the UK, Dingwall (2007, 127) examines the case of *R* v. *Hatton*. In this case it was found that, 'if the defendant mistakenly believed that force was necessary to defend himself and that this mistake was caused by voluntarily induced intoxication, the defendant could not rely on self-defence'. The more specific question of the voluntary nature of the intoxication is considered below. However, here we see an example of how, when one makes the choice to drink to intoxication, the individual is to be held accountable for violent outcomes.

The amount of leniency an intoxicated defendant should receive is a matter of some debate. Dingwall and Koffman (2008, 340) explain that 'some retributivists might argue that a first-time, intoxicated offender deserves a lesser sentence' implying that one is less responsible for his/her first intoxicated encounter with the law. However: 'After a certain number of offences the offender would lose all mitigation'. In this sense we encounter a third possible interpretation of intoxicated crime: it is an individual's responsibility for being intoxicated in the first place. Dingwall and Koffman (2008, 346) argue that the mitigation plea is not nuanced enough to cover all possible offences that occur while individuals are intoxicated:

> Not every individual who offends while intoxicated deserves that intoxication to be treated as mitigation. An individual who gets intoxicated and offends for the first time can justifiably be distinguished from an individual who gets intoxicated and offends, having done so previously. The former deserves to be punished, but deserves mitigation

on the basis that the consequences of his conduct were less foreseeable. An individual who has offended while intoxicated before is aware of the possible (though not necessarily the probable) consequences of intoxication. Accordingly, a deliberate decision to continue getting intoxicated precludes the use of this factor as a mitigating argument if he subsequently offends.

The question remains: is *any* mitigation to be expected by a repeat offender? Dingwall and Koffman (2008, 346) continue to argue that the repeat offender 'forfeits the right to mitigation. By deliberately following a course of action that he knows from personal experience may result in the commission of a criminal offence, he is as culpable as an individual who commits that offence while sober'. Following a rationalist approach to human behaviour, based on ideas of free will and a responsible individual, Dingwall and Koffman (2008) argue that mitigation for intoxicated behaviour should be graduated.

This theme is taken up by Tolmie (2001, 694) who argues that the 'model of criminal responsibility that purportedly underpins the criminal justice system is premised on the notion that people have free will and rationality'. However, she suggests that intoxication can impair one's capacity for choice, potentially on a number of levels. For instance, accountability is reduced:

> in those situations where a person is deprived, at least to a significant degree, of free choice in relation to their actions, either because of mental impairment (diminished responsibility or insanity), emotional pressure (provocation), emergency (duress, necessity or self-defence), separation from their body (automatism), or irresistible impulse (diminished responsibility).

Echoing a Kantian position, Tolmie questions how much one's choice to drink alcohol is a freely made choice. While these factors are taken into account concerning responsibility and accountability for criminal behaviour, moral culpability nonetheless remains, as alcohol consumption is most often considered a choice. Tolmie (2001) examines differences in relation to the responsibility and culpability of alcoholics when one adopts different models for understanding alcoholism (for example, as a habit versus a disease), and resultant intoxication when criminal activities are committed under the influence of alcohol. Although her overall arguments in relation to alcoholism are not of direct interest here we do consider the theoretical complexity in developing a stable, unified and comprehensive definition of intoxication or drunkenness that takes into account the notions of both responsibility and the voluntary (or involuntary) nature of alcohol consumption. In this context Dingwall and Koffman (2008, 338) can argue that: 'The problem is not so much one of retributive theory but a lack of clinical agreement'.

The question of insanity is one that has been raised for intoxicated defendants and has been the topic of some debate for many years. What is known as the M'Naughten standard for a successful insanity defense defines insanity as 'a defect of reason, from disease of the mind' (Feix and Wolber 2007, 172). Therefore, does a defendant who is extremely intoxicated meet the criteria for insanity in a court of law? In Feix and Wolber's (2007, 172) *Intoxication and Settled Insanity* they argue that in the US, it does not. It is useful in the context of our discussion to present some details of this claim. They point out:

> The American Law Institute's criterion for a successful insanity defense requires that the defendant be so affected by mental illness that he could not conform his behavior to the requirements of the law. Therefore, whether a defendant was using drugs or alcohol while committing a crime should matter little, if at all, to the question of insanity when the criteria for an insanity defense have not been met.

As Feix and Wolber (2007, 173) explain, there are a wide range of interpretations of this criterion across state courts in the US: 'Interpretation could range from the prohibition of any defense when there is evidence of voluntary intoxication to allowing the insanity defense when voluntary intoxication has resulted in only temporary exacerbation of an existing psychosis'. In particular, the criterion is best met if it can be shown that the intoxication has made worse an existing symptom which exists independent of the intoxication itself. For example, in the US, in the case *State* v. *Wicks*, the court found that 'the only time that drugs or alcohol may be successfully used for an insanity defense is when the influence of alcohol or drugs triggers an underlying psychotic disorder of a settled nature'. However, Federal Courts in the US rule out the use of the insanity defense when intoxication is deemed to be voluntary:

> The United States Congress enacted the Insanity Defense Reform Act in 1984, which narrowed the definition of insanity that had developed in case law (and shifted the burden of proof to the defense at the "clear and convincing" level). The Senate Judiciary Committee, in discussion

of the Act, stated that, "the voluntary use of alcohol or drugs, even if they render the defendant unable to appreciate the nature and quality of his acts, does not constitute insanity".

In these sorts of circumstances Griffith (2008, 3) outlines a number of important considerations, including:

> evidence of intoxication may be used by the defence to establish that the person did not act voluntarily, thus negativing the *actus reus* of the offence. Evidence of intoxication can also be used for the purpose of negativing *mens rea*. The *actus reus* refers to the act (either a positive act or an omission to act) as defined by the offence, that is required to attract criminal liability. A second element of a criminal responsibility is the *mens rea* (the guilty mind) of the accused. The *mens rea* of most serious crimes is generally expressed as an intention to bring about the requisite *actus reus* of the offence. Without the requisite intention, it is argued, the accused cannot be guilty of a criminal offence. The question is whether a state of intoxication can be said to prevent the formation of the required intent.

There are, then, cases in which voluntary intoxication may be considered a partial defence. For Feix and Wolber (2007, 173) this is relevant:

> when the alleged offense requires a specific intent, or *mens rea*, which the defendant may argue that he could not have possessed due to the effects of intoxication. In most states, defendants are not held responsible for crimes committed under the influence of involuntary intoxication, because they are considered "unconscious" and unable to formulate the *mens rea*, or criminal intent, to commit the offense.

Feix and Wolber (2007, 173) provide an example to illustrate this point:

> In the case of *State* v. *Bush*, the defendant appealed two first-degree murder charges arising from the killing of his former girlfriend and her boyfriend. He lost the appeal, but the court did record that: Voluntary drunkenness is generally never an excuse for a crime, but where a defendant is charged with murder, and it appears that the defendant was too drunk to be capable of deliberating and premeditating, in that instant intoxication may reduce murder in the first degree to murder in the second degree, as long as the specific intent did not antedate the intoxication.

English courts define 'involuntary' on a case by case basis and there are three main types of scenarios considered involuntary with only one relating to alcohol consumption – in this scenario, the individual has become intoxicated by fraud or coercion (Tolmie 2001, 696). Involuntary intoxication is also of concern for deciding consent issues in the law. In the UK involuntary intoxication is considered in section 61 of the Sexual Offences Act of 2003. This section states that 'it is an offence for a person to administer a substance to another person, B, knowing that B does not consent and with the intention of stupefying or overpowering B, to enable any person to engage in sexual activity that involves B' (cited in Elvin 2008, 153).

In this sense, argues Griffith (2008, 3–6), for a defendant to be considered liable, the nature of the act in question must been understood to be voluntary, or, 'the product of the will or the conscious mind'. Intoxication, as we have seen makes these ideas problematic: 'Perhaps intoxication impairs consciousness to such an extent that one could not be considered as acting from one's own conscious will when intoxicated'. In fact, 'evidence of self-induced intoxication is not raised very often because it is extremely difficult to establish that a defendant was so intoxicated that he or she was unable to form any intent'. It could be argued then that intoxication is difficult to define in a precise enough way for courts of law. Despite the need for clear definitions, even the law seems to conflate the terms intoxication and drunkenness. As Griffith indicates, 'it is reported that the Government intends to "remove intoxication as a defence or a mitigating factor in crime – particularly assaults". Instead, drunkenness would become an "aggravating factor" in sentencing'.

There are similar challenges for courts and legal processes in Australia. For example, in deciding the relevance of intoxication to assault cases the New South Wales (NSW) courts made a decision in the context of broader social concerns about the misuse of alcohol. In the *Criminal Legislation Further Amendment Act of 1995* it was decided that an excuse of intoxication was unacceptable. The court found that 'to excuse otherwise criminal conduct… because the accused is intoxicated to such an extent, is totally unacceptable at a time when alcohol and drug abuse are such significant social problems'. In conclusion, it was decided that if intoxication is undertaken voluntarily, individuals 'should be responsible for his or her actions' (Griffith 2008, 4). While the court takes the broader social world into account here, there is no consideration of the impact of the social or cultural environment on individual defendants, or more broadly, the culture of intoxication in which the defendant acts.

Dingwall and Koffman (2008, 335–337) argue that liability for criminal charges is attributed differently in different jurisdictions, however, these differences matter little since 'very few individuals are sufficiently intoxicated to meet the extremely high threshold required to evade criminal liability in those jurisdictions where this is theoretically possible'. Where intoxication does really matter, according to Dingwall and Koffman, is for sentencing: 'Whatever the provisions of the substantive criminal law, a high proportion of individuals will claim that they were intoxicated, at the time of offending, when it comes to the sentencing process'. They explain that in sentencing there is a requirement to assess the offender's culpability and that: 'It is, therefore, a question of real practical importance whether intoxication should affect a sentence… and if so, whether intoxication should be considered as a mitigating or as an aggravating factor' (Dingwall and Koffman 2008, 336–337).

Sexual assault, intoxication and consent

In this section we outline and discuss a number of issues important to any discussion of the fraught relationship between intoxication, sexual practices and consent. Some of these elements are especially evident in media commentary. Indeed, the connection between drinking and sex is ingrained in the news media's imagination, as is evident in a report in *The Australian* about the 'lucrative booze and bonking cruise market' (Lee and McDonald 2003; Stewart 2006). That there exists a connection between drinking and sex was confirmed, according to a story in the *New Zealand Herald* (2008b), by a 2005 study which concluded that unsafe sexual behaviour and regret of sexual behaviour were two of the outcomes of British binge drinking for 14- to 17-year-olds (see also Macaskill 2008). For Suzanne Goldenberg (2006) these concerns are heightened in that particular combination of drinking as a form of male bonding (especially in sporting teams), drunkenness, unsafe sexual behaviours and escalations of this into rape (see also Toynbee 2005; *New Zealand Herald* 2006a).

For the law, issues about levels of risk are not central to the facts of the case. Instead, the voluntary nature of intoxication and how permissible the use of intoxication is as a defence in a court of law, are issues that come up in a discussion of the legal understandings and implications of intoxication and drunkenness. In cases of sexual offence, where intoxication is involved, consent is a particular issue. In the UK, a case which went through the Court of Appeals, *R v. Bree*, illustrates many of the issues related to men and women voluntarily drinking heavily then having intercourse, resulting in a case of disputed consent. In these legal processes the notion of responsibility and risk are mobilised very differently to the ways in which they are used in other disciplines. We can identify a marked divergence in the court summary from the approach to notions of intoxication and drunkenness in public health and medical literature, as well as popular media, which emphasise the moral and health dimensions and consequences of young adults and alcohol use. As Rumney and Fenton (2008, 283) explain:

> The court was at pains to emphasise that both parties were free to choose how much to drink and free to have intercourse if they wished: indeed "there is nothing abnormal, surprising, or even unusual about men and women having consensual intercourse when one, or other, or both have voluntarily consumed a great deal of alcohol". It also pointed out that "it is not a question whether either or both was behaving irresponsibly".

When it comes to legal processes involving alcohol consumption and claims of sexual offences, consent is a particular problem. Referring to *R* v. *Bree*, Elvin (2008, 153) explains that this case has established some working understandings of what intoxication is in relation to sexual assault and rape cases, particularly that 'it does not necessarily deprive a person of the capacity to consent': 'drunken consent is still consent'. However, there is no clear definition of when exactly intoxication has occurred. That is, 'it does not make it clear when a person lacks the capacity to consent because of intoxication'. Importantly, and quite in contrast to much of the literature reviewed in other chapters of this book, the judge ruling in this case decided that it was inappropriate to define intoxication in a generalisable way, by, for example, counting the number of drinks consumed:

> it would be unrealistic to endeavour to create some kind of grid system which would enable the answer to these questions to be related to some prescribed level of alcohol consumption. Experience shows that different individuals have a greater or lesser capacity to cope with alcohol than others, and indeed the ability of a single individual to do so may vary from day to day. The practical reality is that there are some areas of human behaviour which are inapt for detailed legislative structures. In this context, provisions intended to protect women from sexual assaults might very well be conflated into a system which would provide patronising interference with the right of autonomous adults to make personal decisions for themselves. (Rumney and Fenton 2008, 286)

Elvin (2008, 154) rejects this finding offering that the law has set a quantifiable limit to intoxication through drink driving laws, in order to 'provide a clear and unambiguous definition of consent'.

The law in the UK states that a person retains the ability to consent if voluntarily intoxicated and still conscious. However, as Rumney and Fenton (2008, 288) point out from the ruling itself, 'the capacity to consent may evaporate well before a complainant becomes unconscious'. While responsibility and risk are not explicitly written into the law, section 75 of the Sexual Offences Act of 2003 in the UK provides conflicting levels of support for complainants:

> if the victim is intoxicated due to the defendant's actions then she merits the protection of section 75; if, however, she intoxicates herself she is denied this advantage and left to the "mercy" of the jury and the well-documented extra-legal factors which may come into play.

In other words, they argue the law implies that, 'the "ideal" victim does not get herself drunk, she is able to control her own intoxication and if she does not do so, she does not deserve the protection of the law' (Rumney and Fenton 2008, 288).

A case in the US at a private university further illustrates the complexities and ambiguities that are so evident in the consideration of the notion of consent while intoxicated. Wertheimer (2001, 377–378) explores the meanings of the Brown University Code of Student Conduct which finds a young man guilty of having sex with a girl who was intoxicated, despite her seemingly active involvement at the time. Here, again, it seems the notion of consent while intoxicated is not straight forward:

> Sara (a pseudonym), a Brown University freshman, consumes approximately 10 shots of vodka in her dorm room one Saturday night. She walks a few blocks to a Brown crew party, then to a fraternity house to see someone she had been dating. Adam finds Sara in a friend's room lying next to some vomit. Adam asks Sara if she wants a drink of water. Sara says yes. Adam gets her some water. They talk. Adam asks Sara if she wants to go to his room. She says yes. Sara follows Adam to his room without assistance, kisses him and begins to undress him. Sara asks Adam if he has a condom. He says yes. They have sex. They talk, smoke cigarettes, and go to sleep. In the morning, Adam asks Sara for her phone number, which she provides. "It took a while for it to actually set in", Sara says. "When I got home, I wasn't that upset.

The more I thought about it, the more upset I got". Three weeks later, and after Sara sees a "women's peer counselor" in her dormitory, Sara brings charges against Adam Lack. According to the Brown University Code of Student Conduct, one commits an offense when one has sexual relations with another who has a "mental or physical incapacity or impairment of which the offending student was aware or should have been aware".

The expectancy effects of alcohol consumption such as increased sexual arousal and aggression 'allow people who have consumed alcohol to blame their actions on the intoxicant, but also encourage third party observers to excuse their behaviour or to deal with them more leniently where they know that they have been drinking' (Finch and Munro 2007, 594). In fact, the difference is not only between defendant and complainant but, as Finch and Munro (2007, 593) argue, between the differences in expectancies and placement of blame between men and women. Citing Stormo et al. (1997), Finch and Munro describe these differences: "'the female's intoxication is viewed as sufficient grounds for her partial condemnation, while for the male perpetrator, intoxication is regarded as a mitigating circumstance warranting at least some clemency in judging his behaviour" (Stormo et al., 1997: 303 [See Appendix B])'. They further suggest that:

> The extent to which this is true is only magnified, moreover, by the existence of the one apparent exception to this rule, which arises where a sober defendant "takes advantage" of a drunken complainant. Here, despite her intoxication, it seems that the complainant will not be deemed to be more responsible (Wall and Schuller, 2000 [see Appendix B]) and it is more likely that observers will conclude that a rape has occurred (Norris and Cubbins, 1992 [see Appendix B]), since the defendant's sobriety removes scope for leniency.

For Finch and Munro (2007, 593) intoxication is not explicitly defined but used conceptually in opposition to 'sober' and at one point in their analysis intoxication is opposed to someone having consumed 'a few beers'. Here, though, we are interested in highlighting the ways that intoxication is mobilised differently between men and women in different scenarios. Not only is intoxication a factor for assigning responsibility to defendants of sexual assault cases, but it is also considered in assessing the involvement of complainants. Further, observers of such situations have been found to be influenced by the intoxication status of the individuals involved: 'In a recent, and highly publicized, report (Amnesty International, 2005), for example, 30 per cent of respondents indicated that they would hold a complainant who was intoxicated at least partially responsible for having been raped, with four per cent holding her completely responsible'. Finch and Munro draw on social psychology to argue that intoxication impacts on interpretations of observers in this way and that this kind of interpretation is gendered. There is 'a double standard that renders intoxicated defendants less responsible for intercourse than their sober counterparts while holding intoxicated complainants more responsible'. The ability to consent when intoxicated and how these abilities are interpreted by others are also, as we have seen, not straightforward issues. In the UK, section 74 of the Sexual Offences Act of 2003 states that: 'For the purposes of this Part, a person consents if he agrees by choice, and has the freedom and capacity to make that choice'. Participants in the study by Finch and Munro (2007, 601) concluded that it is often the complainant's responsibility to maintain her 'freedom and capacity to make that choice'.

The dilemmas of the responsible serving of alcohol

The issues outlined here point to the difficulty in legal discourses of defining intoxication simply and universally. This uncertainty about the definitions, meanings and interpretations of the understandings of intoxication is also seen in the realm of hospitality. We consider some of the potential problems with responsible serving of alcohol laws in the US, Australia and New Zealand. In many countries people who serve alcohol in retail contexts are obliged by law to assess the buyer's level of intoxication and refuse service to individuals who appear to be intoxicated. Linking intoxication to high-risk or harmful outcomes, the service industry is seen to be important for the management of intoxication.

In a review article, Graham (2005) illustrates a historical connection in Europe to what has come to be known as the 'responsible serving of alcohol' (RSA), and, like Levi and Valverde (2001), argues that it was not inevitable that those serving alcohol would become responsible in ways that they have for public order and personal levels of drunkenness: 'The defining of this responsibility for publicans in early modern Germany is a clear precursor to the expanded legal and regulatory expectations placed upon servers of alcohol in recent times' (cited in Graham 2005, 47–48). He argues that the placement of responsibility on the servers of alcohol is not inevitable and that it may be a particularly Western outcome. It is in this context that Levi and

Valverde (2001, 824) describe the history of what they call a 'devolution of responsibility' to the very people subject to regulation. They argue that this devolution relies on the application of 'nonexpert knowledge'. They suggest that 'at the heart of the logic of licensing, it is assumed that untrained persons have the knowledge necessary to govern their own activities, as well as those of their clients or customers, or will at least acquire the necessary knowledge in order to retain their license'. They continue by considering what it takes to govern in this way:

> The license holders are held responsible for their own actions and those of their employees, not just in terms of civil liability but also in terms of what one might call a semilegal "duty to know". The knowledge useful for averting future dangers is of course often of an expert, professional kind. But, contrary to the tendency of sociolegal scholars to make knowledge coterminous with science and/or expertise, the knowledge that is expected of people such as bartenders (and for that matter of drinkers who own cars) is not scientific. It is a prescientific, qualitative, commonsense type of knowledge.

This type of knowledge, what Levi and Valverde (2001, 826) call 'common knowledge' is said to:

> impute knowledge to lay people that they may not in fact have (or of which they may, in fact, have a specific and contrary knowledge). Common knowledge, then, is more of an ideal type than it is empirically verifiable, and it is also impossible to refute or contest on the basis of empirical investigation of what people actually know...

Importantly, Levi and Valverde (2001, 835) argue that this 'subcontracting of paternalistic police powers to a group of entrepreneurs and workers who are not a self-regulated profession' is important because 'it suggests that the obligations envisaged by police regulations – the obligation to monitor, observe, and manage spaces and activities regarded as inherently problematic – are not monopolized by state officials or by members of expert, licensed professions'. In fact, under these sorts of regulatory regimes 'ordinary citizens can and do participate in the regulation of urban nuisances and disorders'.

In Australia this responsibility is referred to as the Responsible Serving of Alcohol and courses are offered at various locations (through private companies and TAFEs) to potential service employees throughout the country. In New South Wales, 'liquor laws place the onus on the licensees and their staff to serve alcohol responsibly'. Specific sections of the *Liquor*

Act 1982 and the *Registered Clubs Act 1976* 'stipulate that a licensee shall not permit intoxication, or any indecent, violent or quarrelsome conduct on his or her licensed premises' (Briscoe and Donnelly 2002, 3). More recently, through the Liquor Act 2007, it has become an 'offence for a licensee to permit intoxication on licensed premises, or for a licensee or an employee to sell or supply alcohol to an intoxicated person' (Griffith 2008, 1).

Some of the dilemmas and complexities associated with the possibilities of non-expert owners, managers and employees of licensed premises policing the intoxication of patrons through the responsible serving of alcohol are examined in research by Briscoe and Donnelly (2002, 4–5). They use data from a telephone survey of 1090 people, of whom 758 had drunk more than the 2001 NHMRC drinking guidelines (safe drinking at that time was considered no more than six standard drinks per day for men and four standard drinks for women) on at least one occasion during the previous three months, and were therefore included in the survey. They argue that the lack of a 'statutory definition of "intoxication" in either the Liquor Act 1982 or the Registered Clubs Act 1976' meant that 'licensees and their staff generally must rely on some set of objective behavioural signs to assess a patron's level of intoxication'. For this study, 'eligible respondents were asked to indicate whether they showed any of the following five signs of intoxication: (1) *loss of coordination*; (2) *slurred speech*; (3) *staggering or falling over*; (4) *spilling drinks*; and (5) *loud or quarrelsome behaviour*'. While recognising the limitation of such a definition, they also claim that 'these five signs are also consistent with information on signs of intoxication supplied to licensees in a Department of Gaming and Racing information sheet discussing important elements of serving alcohol responsibly on licensed vessels'. Survey respondents were asked how staff responded to their intoxication with the following eight options:

> (1) they refused to serve me any more alcoholic drinks; (2) they asked me to leave the premises; (3) they called the police; (4) they advised me on or organized transport home; (5) they suggested I buy low- or non-alcoholic drinks; (6) they suggested that I buy some food; (7) they suggested that I stop drinking and (8) they continued to serve me alcoholic drinks.

Briscoe and Donnelly (2002, 5) administered their survey in the following way:

> Items one through seven for this question were rotated across respondents, however item eight (relating to the continual service of

alcohol) was always asked last. Items one through three were included because both the Liquor Act 1982 and the Registered Clubs Act 1976 define these as "reasonable steps" to prevent intoxication. Items four through six were included as they were consistent with guidelines issued in a Licensing Court Practice Direction relating to harm minimisation.

Briscoe and Donnelly (2002, 13) argue that the results showed that much of the drinking that occurs at licensed premises takes place when young adults are intoxicated: 'Over half reported showing at least one of the five signs of intoxication investigated, while almost one in five reported showing three or more signs'. Furthermore, they found 'only limited evidence of staff intervention to prevent the serving of alcohol to these people'. They suggest that:

> Of those who said they exhibited at least one sign of intoxication, less than 3% were refused service and less than 4% were asked to leave the premises. For those who reported showing three or more signs of intoxication, less than 4% were refused service and only about 6% were asked to leave the premises. The most common response of licensed premises staff was to continue serving alcohol. Indeed, a higher percentage of those who reported showing three or more signs of intoxication said that they were continued to be served alcohol than those who reported showing one or two signs of intoxication.

Scott et al. (2007, 6) repeated this survey in 2006, with a slightly larger sample size, to assess changes to the provision of RSA in NSW after a number of initiatives were undertaken to improve the responsible serving of alcohol. In this follow up study a sample of 2427 young adults (aged 19–39) were asked the same questions as in the initial survey about their last drinking occasion at a licensed premises. Few changes were found, and still about 50 per cent reported at least one of five signs of intoxication. Similarly there were no significant changes found to the provision of RSA initiatives. However, this study did indicate a number of outcomes which seemed to suggest improvements on the findings of the initial research:

> Firstly, the proportion of young adults drinking at a licensed premises who reported three or more signs of intoxication significantly decreased from around 19 per cent in 2002 to around 14.5 per cent in 2006. Secondly, the provision of RSA to this more intoxicated group of patrons increased across the two survey occasions. While less than 12 per cent of this group reported having received at least one of seven

RSA interventions from bar staff in 2002, this increased to almost 28 per cent in 2006. In other words, while the likelihood of an intoxicated young adult receiving an RSA intervention was only around one in ten in 2002, this had improved to be better than one in four in 2006.

Hammersley and Ditton (2005, 499) identify and examine some of the unintended consequences of laws that require hospitality workers who serve alcohol to assess the drunkenness level of their customers and deny them if they believe they have had enough. They argue that 'this may paradoxically encourage "non-drunken comportment" and may thus unintentionally promote high intake over many hours as long as overt signs of drunkenness are absent'. These researchers are concerned that focusing on public drunkenness is only one way in which policy must attend to the public health issues inherent in alcohol use. Here, drunkenness seems to be used as a term to describe the *effects* of intoxication, where drunken-comportment can be managed to hide the level of intoxication.

Other research considers whether hospitality employees are *able* to make such an assessment on the spot, given the lack of consensus of what actually constitutes drunkenness in licensed venues. Using the three physical displays of drunkenness which are used by the UK police to identify drunkenness (gait, eyes and speech) Perham et al. (2007, 379) compared subjective measures of drunkenness and blood alcohol concentration (BAC) obtained with an alcometer. Gait was categorised as normal, staggering or severely impaired, eye appearance was either clear or glazed and speech was considered clear, slurred or incoherent, rating overall drunkenness along a 10-point Likert scale where 1 was sober and 10 was 'heavily intoxicated'. This study used a BAC of 0.15, 'staggering gait on its own and a combination of any two, or all three physical attributes of drunkenness' to 'indicate that a drinker has consumed an excessive amount of alcohol and should be refused further alcohol'. They suggest that while staggering gait was 'the most reliable indicator of drunkenness' the other physical displays of drunkenness are useful indicators that may reliably be used by bar staff to assess whether a patron should continue to be served alcohol.

Recognising intoxication in others, and then being able to do something about it in the conditions and spaces that are characteristic of many licensed premises are not simple matters. One study tested the ability or willingness of American bartenders in a university town to serve pseudo-customers at varying levels of intoxication (non-intoxication, ambiguous intoxication, and obvious intoxication). This study defined intoxication levels in the following ways: Level 1, no signs of intoxication, yet knocking over a beer; Level 2, the pseudo customers portrayed two 'ambiguous signs of intoxication (e.g. loudness and leaning on bar)' before knocking over a beer, asking for another and then fumbling with money; and Level 3, portrayed five obvious signs of intoxication (e.g. swaying/leaning on bar, talking slowly, forgetting bartender's name right after asking, poor eye contact, slurred speech), then knocking over a beer, followed by 'three more signs of intoxication (e.g. fumbled while reaching for knocked over beer, difficulty finding money in pocket, dropped money while paying bartender) prior to asking for another beer' (Goodsite et al. 2008, 547). A further illustration of the difficulties associated with predicting or recognising intoxication in others comes from Rosenberg and Nevis (2000, 34) who claim that 'previous research... has found that years of experience as a police officer, bartender, or alcoholism counselor are not correlated' with accurately judging another person's level of intoxication. Likewise, in an attempt to find out if university students can be taught to recognise alcohol intoxication by their peers, Rosenberg and Nevis found that 'most university students are unable to recognise moderate intoxication that results from binge like drinking (i.e., 3 to 5 standard drinks in 1 hr)'.

Kypri et al. (2007, 2594) conducted research related to New Zealand's version of RSA which is called the Sale of Liquor Act (1989). The Act 'prohibits pubs, bars and clubs from admitting intoxicated persons to the premises, from serving patrons to the point of intoxication, and from allowing intoxicated persons to remain on the premises'. Their study examined the limitations of this law, starting with the lack of a definition of intoxication or drunkenness. They argue that this ambiguity in definition 'may make it difficult for licensees to comply with the law, for police to collect suitable evidence, and for a prosecution to be effected when a case is brought to court'

In the US, Responsible Beverage Service (RBS) programs 'train alcohol servers to identify and refuse service to minors and intoxicated persons, and train establishment managers to implement policies and procedures to support servers' intervention techniques'. The popularity of such laws is indicated by Mosher et al. (2002, 91): 'A recent nationally representative survey of adults age 18 and over indicates that 89% of the population is in favor of policies mandating server training, and 88% are in favor of manager training to increase responsible service of alcohol'. Mosher et al. (2002) conducted a broad survey of 23 states in the US and varying programs in each state and suggest that there is much variability in the requirements throughout the country. Decisions about who must be trained, servers, managers or owners; whether only new businesses will have to train or all existing businesses;

whether training is mandatory or voluntary and, whether incentives are given to encourage training are all issues that vary from state to state.

While the US has a number of laws relating to RSA, it has been shown that many of the same problems around identifying intoxicated patrons and refusal of service are common. The main reason for these problems is the common issue of the lack of an operational definition of intoxication that is useful to staff in busy venues, particularly with experienced drinkers 'who have learned to manage (and therefore who have the ability to hide) physical symptoms of intoxication, such as slurred speech and difficulty walking, well enough to "pass" as not intoxicated' (Reiling and Nusbaumer 2006, 654). Reiling and Nusbaumer (2006, 655–662) argue that some servers knowingly serve beyond intoxication due to 'outside pressure or influence that overrides their concern for legal or socioemotional consequences of their behavior, such as guilt'. For example, staff may be pressured by 'management to sell as much alcohol as possible or to keep the customer happy, or they could be willing to continue to serve rather than discontinue receiving tips'. The authors also suggest that economic interest in selling more alcohol by serving intoxicated customers influences the attitudes and practices of servers. For some of Reiling and Nusbaumer's participants their own drinking practices impacted on their 'willingness to over-serve'. Other factors have been found to influence servers as well. This study found that servers who are concerned about the consequences of liability laws may change their serving habits, but those who do not share such concerns are unlikely to be influenced simply by the laws.

The specifics of RSA laws are different in different places. As a consequence, civil liability laws that are related to RSA practices are always being redefined and challenged in the courts. In the following section we examine how definitions and understandings of intoxication are negotiated through the civil liability laws in Australia and the United States. Again, the discussion here is not meant to be extensive, but illustrative of a number of issues that are relevant to the concerns that we are exploring.

Civil liability for the consequences of intoxication in New South Wales and Queensland

The civil liability laws in both NSW and Queensland have been criticised for the way in which they uphold an 'individual focus' (Watson 2004, 131). Here we consider the implications of such an approach. The definition of 'intoxication' in the Civil Liability Act 2002, NSW s50 is: 'a person being under the influence of alcohol or a drug (whether or not taken for a medicinal purpose and whether or not lawfully taken)'. Watson explains that in this context, the term '"influence" is not defined in terms of degree or any specific measure, such as blood alcohol content' (Watson 2004, 127). Despite laws such as drink driving laws which define a certain level of BAC as intoxicated, Watson (2004, 128) explains that: 'Experts largely agree that with a blood alcohol level of 0.02 or 0.03, alcohol will have some minimal influence on the drinker, although the legal limit in NSW for driving offences is set at 0.05'. The *Civil Liability Act 2003* of Queensland also deals with intoxication and is similar to the NSW Act.

The ambiguous and vague ways in which much legal discourse treats definitions of intoxication and drunkenness has meant that some legal theorists have explored the possibilities offered by the sorts of bio-medical, scientific definitions that we canvassed earlier. Hamad (2005, 16), for example, uses these sorts of definitions and calculations to describe the effects of intoxication on pedestrian behaviours. What is defined as low levels of alcohol consumption (BACs between 0.02 to 0.05 g dL^{-1}) is known to reduce peripheral vision, and impair speed and distance perception. This is opposed to high levels of alcohol consumption (such as BACs > 0.15 g dL^{-1}), at which glare resistance is significantly reduced compared to a sober person. High levels of alcohol consumption are understood to further impact on motor coordination and balance, perception and response time. To better understand a case in which an intoxicated pedestrian was hit by an oncoming car, Hamad (2005, 17) provides some background on pedestrian collisions:

> The incidence of moderate to high dose alcohol involvement (BAC > 0.10 g dL-1) among pedestrians appears to be greatest during the night, at weekends, and in collisions where the pedestrian was struck while crossing the road at some distance from a traffic control device (such as a pedestrian crossing)… amongst the motorists involved in the deaths of 95 intoxicated pedestrians on Australian roads in 1992, only 10 were intoxicated.

Given the drunken status of the pedestrian in these scenarios Hamad (2005, 18–19) indicates that the intoxicated 'pedestrian may choose to initiate legal proceedings against the driver of the motor vehicle. In order to succeed, the intoxicated pedestrian must establish that the driver breached the general duty of care which drivers owe to all pedestrians'. This duty of care is surprisingly broadly defined. For example, 'the fact that the driver was travelling in accordance with road traffic regulations or conditions at the time of the collision may not prima facie relieve the driver of liability in negligence'. Drivers are expected to 'take account of the possibility of inadvertent and negligent conduct on the part of others'. With respect to intoxicated pedestrians, Hamad considers that they may be:

> more readily noticeable to oncoming traffic through her or his lack of balance and co-ordination and/or irregular movements in stumbling along footpaths and in traversing the roadways. However, in other instances, diminished visual perception and cognition resulting from high-level alcohol consumption may make the intoxicated pedestrian's road behaviour more difficult to predict.

Despite the difficulty described here, Hamad (2005, 19–22) notes that 'in the majority of cases, the courts have tended to find a breach of duty where there was something in the conduct of the intoxicated pedestrian to alert the driver to the *possibility* that the pedestrian was engaging or may engage in aberrant behaviour'. In such instances the courts may assert the responsibility of the driver, not the intoxicated individual pedestrian. As Hamad goes on to suggest, the role of intoxication in cases such as these is specific to the character of the law. For each case, the courts consider 'whether the consumption of alcohol, in particular the consumption of alcohol that gives rise to the blood alcohol reading detected in the intoxicated pedestrian subsequent to the collision, is... indicative of contributory negligence on the part of the intoxicated pedestrian'. Bio-medical definitions of intoxication are referenced in these contexts and intoxication *as a physical state* is defined via behavioural signs (for example, staggering), or 'expert psychopharmacological evidence as to how the pedestrian's intoxication (obtained from a blood alcohol reading) would have affected either the physical coordination or the mental processes of the pedestrian immediately prior to the collision'. So, it is not a clear cut case of whether intoxication does or does not inform decisions of the court in the apportioning of responsibility, or liability to respective parties. Instead, it is a factor which is 'weighed in the scales when apportioning responsibility'.

The high profile case of *Cole* v. *South Tweed Heads Rugby League Football Club Ltd* ('*Cole*') illustrates some of these dilemmas. In this case, Australia's High Court 'considered the liability in negligence of a registered club for injury to a patron injured shortly after leaving the club in a state of extreme intoxication'. The Court held by a majority of four to two 'that the appeal should be dismissed, there being no breach of any relevant duty of care' (Dixon and Spinak 2004, 816). In this case, the customer who drank became 'grossly intoxicated' at the club, then walked home, rejecting the servers' offers to call her a taxi, after they declined to serve her more alcohol and asked her to leave (Hamad 2005, 30). She left by foot and was hit by a car while walking along a road. In what follows we spend some time reviewing the court's decision because of a number of ideas central to the case and our discussion, including: responsibility and expectations around responsibility for intoxication; questions of public policy; issues of privacy and individual consumption; and the role of the community in monitoring and regulating individuals and their consumption of alcohol. The decision in this case was that the intoxicated pedestrian 'should be held legally and morally responsible for her or his own predicament' (Hamad 2005, 39). Linking intoxication with individual responsibility, free will and personal autonomy, Hamad (2005, 39) argues that in a social context of 'ever-increasing insurance premiums and personal injury suits, such a portrait may resonate with public opinion' but the responsibility of commercial venues is diminished.

The High Court's ruling highlights, above all, the role of personal responsibility and the problems with regulating at that level: 'The Chief Justice [Gleeson] started from the proposition that the law protects the individual freedom of mature adults to make choices regarding the consumption of alcohol' and continued to argue that the imposition of a duty of care on persons serving alcohol to prevent consumers becoming dangerously or excessively intoxicated would interfere with that freedom' (Dixon and Spinak 2004, 818). Furthermore, it was argued that: 'To impose liability on the server of alcohol for voluntary choices by the consumer, in the face of obvious dangers to them from such consumption, would be to fail to respect values of personal responsibility' (Dixon and Spinak 2004, 818). Referencing understandings of the voluntary nature of intoxication, Justice Callinan stressed 'that the decision to drink carried with it the known risk that the capacity to make decisions about further consumption would be progressively impaired' (Dixon and Spinak 2004, 819). As such, the duty of care was not found to rest with the club and individual responsibility remained paramount. Adults could not 'be expected to be ignorant of the intoxicating effects of the alcohol they voluntarily consumed' (Dixon and Spinak 2004, 819–820).

However, in this case there were dissenting views which called for increased consideration of the duty of the venue, which, it is argued, relieves the plaintiff of some responsibility, given that 'the common law does not hold the plaintiff absolutely responsible for their choices' (Dixon and Spinak 2004, 820). In Justice McHugh's view, since the club became aware of her high level of intoxication in the early afternoon before the accident:

> its duty was then to take steps to prevent her drinking – not only by refusing to serve her alcohol, but also by warnings, by ensuring that she was not served alcohol purchased by others, and if need be, by removing her from the premises at that time. Having breached its duty in the early afternoon [because Cole's drinking continued into the evening] it was irrelevant that the appellant later refused the offered transport (the very thing that might have been expected from allowing her to consume further alcohol) or that the Club relied on assurances by third persons. (Dixon and Spinak 2004, 820)

Watson (2004, 115) explains how Justice McHugh proposed:

> that the duty of an occupier "to protect members and customers from injury as a result of consuming beverages must extend to protecting them from all injuries resulting from the ingestion of beverages… [including] injury that is causally connected to ingesting beverages". If the supply of alcohol to a customer gives rise to "a reasonable possibility" of that customer suffering a type of injury not likely to be suffered by a sober customer, the club will be liable where the exercise of reasonable care would have avoided the injury. As he had pointed out in a previous case, "[o]rdinarily, the common law does not impose a duty of care on a person to protect another from the risk of harm unless that person has created the risk". Here, the server had created the risk.

We cite this judge's reasoning at length because it specifically addresses our concern to better understand legal definitions and understandings of intoxication, particularly with respect to responsibility. The dissenting view is that there is a duty of care by the club and that duty extends quite broadly. However, in the majority view:

> Their Honours held that, once a person chooses to engage in an activity with known risks, the fact that they become increasingly unable to form judgments and take actions to avoid those risks does not diminish their moral responsibility for the consequences of their actions. Choices to assume a risk have a once-and-for-all character, rather than a more gradated or contextual meaning (such as, for example, a series of

decisions to attend the breakfast, to drink the alcohol supplied, and to buy more alcohol after the alcohol supplied was consumed). (Dixon and Spinak 2004, 823)

Watson (2004, 109) argues that the majority decision in this case reflects 'a distressingly narrow, individualistic approach to injury and duty in the context of intoxication; and that in so doing they have ignored the social implications of their stance'. Furthermore, Watson claims that:

> attributing some responsibility for alcohol-related injury to those who both benefit from and are in a position to control alcohol abuse, would promote safety, deter irresponsible self-interested conduct, and set meaningful standards of acceptable behaviour. The result could be a much needed cultural and social shift towards more responsible alcohol practices.

Watson (2004, 115) goes on to argue that for cases where intoxication is an issue or concern an economic argument against holding venues liable for their customers' well-being is not defensible: 'the risks of injury are high, extreme intoxication is easily detected, and occupiers are in a very favourable position to take simple precautions against injury, as well as to pass on any extra costs to a broad client base'. Interestingly, in this legal analysis, intoxication is not defined, and is considered 'easily detected' despite the difficulty of definition and detection illustrated in the public health literature and the struggle of other legal theorists to define this term. Nonetheless, intoxication for Watson (2004, 116) is an individual state that extends beyond the consumption of alcohol served in a venue. In this argument there should be 'an affirmative duty imposed on servers to prevent patrons from drinking to excess' and that this 'is a protective duty derived from the server's control of both the premises and the supply of alcohol'. It is concluded, therefore, that this duty extends to both 'injury on the premises and for the duration of the intoxication, which would include the journey home'. Watson (2004, 116) argues that by finding that intoxication is a problem for the individual rather than the community, 'the High Court missed a clear opportunity to send a message about corporate responsibility in hazardous contexts'. Watson (2004, 131) reminds us that these decisions create a relationship to intoxication that could be imagined otherwise:

> Talk of personal responsibility and autonomy in the context of alcohol service operates as a justification for denial of community responsibility for activities of dubious social worth, which benefit strong commercial

interests and provide government revenue. Canada and the United States have demonstrated that contrary choices are readily available.

Watson (2004, 118–120) suggests that laws in the US which make venues or retailers of alcohol liable for injuries incurred by intoxicated patrons, on or off their property, are more favourable to the communitarian approach. As in Australia, in the US, laws related to alcohol intoxication are managed state-by-state. Generally, Southern states have laws which make venues least liable for intoxicated patrons, and, at the other end of the spectrum, California's laws make venues much more liable. Illinois law, for example, states that 'Every person who is injured within the state in person or property by any intoxicated person has a right of action in his or her own name, severally or jointly, against any person… who, by selling or giving alcoholic liquor… causes the intoxication'. This law is comprehensive in that no 'proof that the defendant knew or should have known that the patron was intoxicated' is required and 'every person who sold the patron alcohol can potentially face liability'. Watson argues that 'Such broad liability is intended "to place responsibility for damages caused by intoxicants on those who profit from the sale of alcohol" [and] to protect the health, safety, and welfare of the people from the dangers of traffic in liquor'. However, even in these contexts and jurisdictions defining intoxication is not straightforward. 'Obvious intoxication' can involve 'significantly uncoordinated physical action or significant physical dysfunction' in Missouri, or, in Texas, 'a patron must be so obviously intoxicated that he presents a clear danger to himself or others'. However, 'A narrower example comes from Minnesota, where dram shop laws impose liability only when an illegal sale of alcohol directly results in harm to an innocent third party, specifically personal injury, property damage, loss in means of support and "other pecuniary loss"'.

Liability laws vary from place to place, but the underlying debates are related. There is a shared need to apportion responsibility between individuals who consume alcohol and those who provide it. At the core of these concerns are two issues central to our discussion: how intoxication is defined and how it is understood. And there is no agreement or consensus on either of these questions.

Intoxication, violence and gender

As we have shown, the relationship between intoxication and the legal system is complex. We turn now to a discussion of the ways in which the relationship between intoxication and violence is framed in various settings.

Media commentary on the consequences of drunkenness often focuses on violence. The connection between nuisance and serious crimes involving violence appears in a range of ways in the media in countries such as the US, UK, Australia and New Zealand. Often this occurs in discussions of sport and the behaviour of sports fans (see Barnes 2005; Felten 2008). The well-documented and publicised hooliganism of English soccer fans over the last 20 or so years is often referenced as being illustrative of the disorder and violence brought about by drunkenness (see Dudman 2008; Laville 2004; Lyall 2008; Marrin 2003; Riddell 2003; Sweeney 2008; Syed 2008; *The Times* 2003b). Sandra Laville (2004) describes a typical scene:

> Stripped to the waist and drinking pints of lager from plastic glasses, England fans gathered in their hundreds on the Algarve yesterday for the crucial Switzerland match. At Lineker's Bar and every neon-lit pub along a three-quarter of a mile promenade known as the Strip in Montechoro, the scene was the same. Snatches of Rule Britannia mingled with a chorus of Three Lions and chants of "Eng-er-land" in the countdown to the game. Two miles away, in a courtroom in Albufeira, the hangover from other nights like this had paraded in front of the judge to face accusations of hooliganism. As the referee's whistle blew to a mass rendition of the national anthem on the Strip, the 33 fans arrested on Wednesday morning for alleged rioting were being bundled into police vans outside the court... The supporters, who were seized in a night of violence late on Tuesday and early on Wednesday, were asked by the magistrate whether they would volunteer to deportation. They all agreed and were asked for written affidavits in their defence to be logged at the court in 30 days' time. Charges against them were adjourned.

Indeed, the figure of the football hooligan as the personification of the disorder caused by drunkenness – *The New York Times* calls football hooligans and 'so-called lager louts' the 'public face of overconsumption' (Lyall 2004) – has even penetrated into the otherwise docile world of petanque. In his discussion of some of the challenges facing the petanque establishment, such as alcohol-fuelled racism (see also Mydans 2003), Berlins (2007) invokes the figure of the football hooligan:

> Gentle petanque had been tainted with the maladies usually associated with football supporters – drunkenness, brawling, hooliganism and violence – to the extent that, since the beginning of May, all competitions

in the department of Nievre, in Burgundy, have been prohibited. There have been demonstrations by deprived players in the streets of Nevers, the departmental capital. The petanque establishment is asking for more protection from the local police, who answer by demanding that the sport put its own inebriated house in order. A touch of racism has entered the picture, with some blaming Gypsy travellers for starting the troubles in that area.

The Weekend Australian also ran a feature on the incidence of alcohol-related assaults and drink-driving convictions in rugby league, concluding that the code 'is losing its battle against the bottle' (Honeysett 2008). The same trends are also noted amongst Australian Rules teams (Jacobsen 2003). In 2001, for instance, *The Age* published a comprehensive list of the alcohol-related charges committed by AFL players (Munro 2001; see also Smith 2001; Tippet 2000). Others have argued that 'the evidence shows that alcohol intoxication by itself is not a sufficient condition for alcohol-related violence, but can increase the risk in situations where there is a degree of conflict or frustration around human interactions' (Stockwell 2001, see also Farke and Anderson 2007).

Whether alcohol causes violence has been a matter of some debate (Tryggvesson 2004; Tryggvesson and Bullock 2006). One recent Victorian report, the Victoria's Alcohol Action Plan 2008–2013 (2008, 33; see Appendix B) suggests the link between intoxication and criminal behaviour: 'The relationship between alcohol, crime and violence is complex. While intoxication does not always lead to offending, it has been estimated that 47 per cent of all perpetrators of assault and 43 per cent of all victims of assault were intoxicated prior to the event'. Nicholls (2006, 147) concludes that: '"The drink question" remains confused. Objections to acts of violence which may follow alcohol consumption, and concerns over health issues which can arise from certain patterns of alcohol consumption, continue to be conflated with associated, but distinct, concerns over intoxication'.

So, while the relationships between intoxication and violence are complex and ambiguous, there has been a significant amount of research that explores different dimensions of these relationships. In one study Olge and Miller (2004, 55–59) examined the effects of gender and acute alcohol intoxication on social information processing of hostile provocation scenarios. In their study they hypothesised that 'when responding to each hostile provocation scenario, intoxicated individuals, compared with nonintoxicated individuals, would attribute greater hostility to the provocateur'. The authors also investigated the role of gender differences and hypothesised that intoxicated men would show greater hostile-aggressive processing alterations than intoxicated women in all domains as well as 'greater differential hostile-aggressive processing on the basis of provocateur gender than intoxicated women'. The researchers claimed that male aggression was evident: 'Intoxicated men evidenced more attribution of hostility than all other groups for both hostile male and hostile female scenarios and intoxicated men were sensitized to the hostility within the hostile provocations and interpreted the intentions of the provocateur as more hostile than any other group did'.

Male aggression is not only associated with violence toward others. In another study McCloskey and Berman (2003, 309) have suggested that intoxicated men also show signs of increased self-aggression, though, the causal link between intoxication and self-aggression is not clear. Their research involved 40 men (aged 21–45 years) with no history of drug or alcohol dependence or severe psychological problems. Using self-administered electric shocks, self-aggression was defined through the level of shock chosen. Participants who had ingested alcohol before the test 'self-administered higher mean shock compared with participants who did not ingest alcohol, with alcohol accounting for about 33% of the variance in shock selections. Intoxicated participants also chose a "severe" shock at substantially greater rates than their non-intoxicated counterparts'.

In another study Tomsen (2005, 285–293) considered the nature of young men's intoxication related violence. Tomsen was interested in a range of issues, relationships and practices that may have had some influence on the use of alcohol and intoxication and violence. These included such things as:

> male identity, drinking histories and styles and the subjective experience of drinking and intoxication, especially in peer groups, perceptions of threat in public space and drinking contexts, the contrast between scenarios of violence and nonviolence, and the drinker's own interpretations of the causes and pattern of aggressive and physically violent encounters.

Tomsen (2005, 285–293) conducted focus group interviews comprising 6–10 participants (aged 18–25 years) in NSW in 2002. Seven were in full-time employment and seven in part-time work. Ten were full or part-time students and six were unemployed. Participants were recruited from groups of men who drank regularly in local venues and a smaller number of security officers and venue staff who were employed in these locations. The participants ranged from university educated men to working class men whose 'style of "disrespectable" working class protest masculinity was apparent in coarse and sometimes distinct language (e.g., more swearing and language such as "flogging" as a term for assault), overt sexism, racism and disrespect for authority'. Tomsen argues that violence was understood by these groups as linked to intoxication, because, as participants claimed, some people are "'idiots when they get drunk" or "bad drunks"'. Similarly, the men in this study considered the intoxicated aggression of others something to ridicule and laugh at, rather than participate in.

For one social group examined by Tryggvesson (2004) intoxication is not only a useful excuse for violent behaviour, it is also an acceptable one. Tryggvesson (2004) conducted focus group interviews with a total of 47 young Swedes (26 females; 21 males). Although this study did not examine the gendered implications of violence and drunkenness, it does discuss the influences of drunkenness and gender on young people's understandings of violence. As Tryggvesson (2004, 250) explains:

> A sober aggressor would be judged as mentally ill, but a drunk aggressor is a normal person who does stupid things. The drunkenness, however, protects him, so the stupid act does not transform him into a stupid person. Drunkenness also has a neutralization effect that implies that the act is viewed differently when the aggressor is drunk. With a drunk aggressor [violence] is just something that happens; with a sober aggressor, however, the act would be more severe – then it is an assault, and you report it to the police.

While no firm conclusions could be drawn on the use of intoxication as an excuse for behaviour that would otherwise be considered wrong, there were, nonetheless, limits to its use. That is, the more serious the act, the less leeway one receives for the excuse of drunkenness. This study found that sexual aggression, for example, could never be excused through drunkenness. On the other hand, 'alcohol is the only explanation needed to make a fight appear rational and understandable' (Tryggvesson 2004, 252). There were some contradictions in the way in which these young Swedish people were willing to accept drunkenness as an excuse and there were limitations to this approach. While believing that, generally, alcohol is not an excuse for bad behaviour, they were still willing to use it as an excuse when describing their experiences. Interestingly, Tryggvesson (2004, 254) reconciles this contradiction by suggesting that: 'It is enough to understand that they can hold both of these beliefs, and that they tell us different things – that there are limits for what you can admit and other limits for what you can do'.

These themes were further explored in later research that surveyed over 1000 young Swedish men and women aged 16 to 25. Tryggvesson and Bullock (2006, 61–67) examined how intoxication works as an excuse in two ways: how much blame would be attributed to the aggressor and whether or not the incident would be reported to police. Respondents were presented with a vignette about provoked male assault in which two males, unknown to each other, meet at the local pub and following a brief argument one of them behaves violently. The researchers asked if alcohol was understood as an excuse for such aggressive behaviour. A number of variables were manipulated in the study to ascertain more precisely the role that intoxication plays. For example, the researchers changed the level of intoxication of the perpetrator: 'he was described as either sober, feeling the effects (tipsy) or very drunk'. The severity of the violence was also altered: 'In the low-severity version, the perpetrator pushed the victim so that he fell, and in the high-severity version he punched him until his nose started to bleed'. Finally, the relationship between the perpetrator and the victim was manipulated so that the participants were either best friend of the aggressor or the victim.

Tryggvesson and Bullock (2006, 73–74) argue that the link between intoxication and violence is a socially sanctioned outcome: 'A drunk person becomes involved in violence because society approves of his drunkenness as an excuse for his behaviour'. While some variables, such as the relationship to the aggressor, did not influence attribution of blame (as shown in a study by Finch and Munro 2007), the victim's alcohol consumption may 'reduce blame for the aggressor'. In this study, 'the range between highest and lowest attributed blame was smaller when the perpetrator was drunk compared to when he was sober'. These results were interpreted as indicating that the intoxication status of the perpetrator impacts the interpretation of events: specifically, 'when the perpetrator was drunk the violence was something qualitatively different'. The authors suggest that:

> When sober people fight, people recognize the difference between levels of severity, and it matters whether they are friends with the perpetrator or the victim. But when both are drunk, they are just drunk, and the fight is not a fight, it is just two drunks who behave as drunken people do.

In a study of Scottish men, masculinity and alcohol use, Mullen et al. (2007, 159) argued that intoxication plays a role in male violence. They suggest that it 'tended to facilitate fight escalation, although the relationship was complex'. The complexity was found in the ways in which intoxication 'can lead to impulsive behaviour, to assessing situations in simplified terms and to not thinking through the consequences of actions'. In a similar way to that claimed by Tryggvesson (2004): 'intoxication was offered as an excuse. The man might claim that his behaviour would have been different if he had been sober'. For example:

> [T]his guy was slagging off my friend because she's Irish, because of her Irish accent. It was just a wee cat-fight. There wasn't anything physical. It was verbal. It was drink. I wouldn't have done that if I was sober. I would have ignored it. I was really annoyed that he was slagging her off.

Each of these studies finds that intoxication can be framed in different settings as a legitimate excuse for violence, and that behaviour which would not otherwise be tolerated is acceptable because it is believed that this kind of behaviour is an expected outcome of intoxication. Indeed, as Tyrggvesson (2004) and Tyrggvesson and Bullock (2006) argue, intoxicated violence might be interpreted as qualitatively different from sober violence.

Conclusion

In this chapter we have examined legal interpretations, definitions and understandings of intoxication and drunkenness as these emerge in a contested and debated manner, as well as, in a variety of settings, situations and contexts. In the complex, contested and contentious nature of these definitions; in the applications and uses of these definitions in different settings; in the ways in which these definitions are used to determine the truth of the matter in cases of sexual assault, violence and anti-social behaviour, we witness again the seemingly intractable dilemmas that have framed much of our discussion in this book.

Expert definitions and lay definitions, and the use of these definitions to account for personal and/or organisational/corporate responsibility for the range of consequences of intoxication and drunkenness are all involved in what at times appears as a noisy chorus of claim and counter claim. In such a contest we are left with little common ground on which to make judgments. We discuss what this complexity and ambiguity means, and where it might leave us, in our concluding chapter.

Conclusion: Smashed?

So what have we learned about the many meanings of intoxication and drunkenness from this review of media commentary and research findings from across a number of disciplines? What, if anything has been smashed? Or is the title of this book little more than a play on words that might be slightly amusing, or even a little forced? To answer the last question first: we would not want to claim that we have smashed anything in terms of understanding the complexities and ambiguities that circulate around, and actively construct, what we might mean when we talk about intoxication and drunkenness. The title then *is* largely a play on words (amusing and/or forced). Instead then, we might claim that our review of media commentary and research findings has at least provided a map (possibly a list) of the complexity and ambiguity associated with the many meanings of intoxication and drunkenness. In another sense it may not be that we have provided a map *of* this complexity, but, rather, a map that *reveals* complexity and ambiguity. Or, possibly, makes this complexity more apparent than it might be if our primary recourse to understanding intoxication and drunkenness was to be found in the media commentary. Or in the policy and political discussions that emerge on a frequent basis in response to twenty-first century public health, social (dis)order, crime or regulatory issues that are often connected to diverse understandings of intoxication and drunkenness.

This is not to say that we, in our discussion, and the ways that we have chosen to frame and present this discussion, would deny any relationship between intoxication and drunkenness and these issues. That would be both a misreading of what we have tried to do here, and a folly on our part in the face of the commentary, research data and evidence that we have reviewed and presented. But in returning to the first question, what have we learned about the many meanings of intoxication and drunkenness?

To begin with we introduced a claim that in the history of discussions about intoxication and drunkenness we can identify a number of themes that appear to recur – often in different, but related forms – at a number of points during the seventeenth, eighteenth and nineteenth centuries, and which continue to echo through the late twentieth and early twenty-first centuries. These themes include the following: the ways in which understandings of intoxication and drunkenness become attached to, and articulated with, particular concerns about sinfulness, delinquency and/or vice; the shifting and unstable ideas about the responsible, autonomous self who may be more or less accountable for states of intoxication and drunkenness and a range of consequences that might flow from these states; the ways in which personal and social consequences of intoxication and drunkenness – often related to concerns about health, public order, the regulation and licensing of the production, distribution, sale and consumption of alcohol, and ideals associated with prohibition and temperance movements – have tended to be filtered through concerns about the supposed moral delinquency of certain groups, social classes, and ethnic populations. *Plus ça change, plus c'est la même chose.*

Our account of the ways in which psychological, biological and medical expertise struggles over definitions of intoxication and drunkenness revealed attempts to develop more sophisticated ways to identify, define, measure and quantify states of intoxication and drunkenness. These attempts, we suggested, are characterised by an emphasis on what might be called objective, quantifiable, generalisable, 'scientific' measures, and the applications of these in various medical and psychological contexts in which the physical and mental health and safety dimensions of intoxication and drunkenness are of primary interest. What is apparent in any examination of these processes is that in spite of an emphasis on calculation, measurement and scientific objectivity, these psychological, biological and medical discussions of intoxication and drunkenness do not, indeed, remove ambiguity, uncertainty and imprecision from these debates and discussions. In these discourses there may be only minor disagreements about some of the physical and mental health and well-being and safety issues associated with states of intoxication and drunkenness. If there is a strong degree of agreement at the level of the range of physiological, bio-medical and psychological harms that are a consequence of intoxication and drunkenness, it tends to disappear when discussion turns to attempts to calculate and measure levels of intoxication and drunkenness, or who is most able to make these calculations, and what measures are most suited to this task.

We have argued that the social and symbolic dimensions of alcohol consumption are important for understanding drunkenness and intoxication. Our review suggests that there is ample evidence that definitions of intoxication and drunkenness vary according to cultural context, geographic location and drinking settings. In both the popular imagination and social science literature there are considerable anxieties and ambivalence about cultures that value intoxication and drunkenness. Media commentary often relies on, and reproduces somewhat simplistic cultural stereotypes about *bingeing* British and Australians, *easygoing* southern Europeans and *sensible* Nordic cultures to criticise public behaviour and imagine alternative cultural arrangements in relation to the use of alcohol and the consequences of intoxication and drunkenness. These simplifications are sometimes even reproduced in the social science literature. However, recent research also questions these cultural differences, and processes of globalisation may result in the distinction between 'wet' and 'dry' cultures becoming less useful.

As we also demonstrated there are strong indications that intoxication and drunkenness are often social practices rather than simply individual practices; and getting drunk with others is valued in some social groups and settings. Drinking settings strongly linked with drunkenness and intoxication include the night-time economy in post-industrial cities, university colleges/ fraternities and private parties. For example, the new culture of intoxication identified in the UK literature describes the phenomenon of large numbers of young people drinking rapidly to intoxication as a means to pleasure, escape and loss of control. Pleasure and escape from everyday life are also key elements of so-called *alcotourism*.

This discussion led us to examine the ways in which particular groups and populations – young people, Indigenous communities in Australia and women – tend to dominate concerns, in media commentary and in the research literature, about the nature of intoxication and drunkenness and their consequences. We explored the ways in which media commentary represents the problem of intoxication and drunkenness in relation to young people, Indigenous communities in Australia and men and women. These accounts are located alongside, and in contrast to the ways in which the psychological, scientific and sociological research literature understands intoxication and drunkenness in relation to these populations. Our discussion suggested that the population that attracts the greater focus in all of these accounts is young people. Media commentary tends to be sensationalised and to reinforce stereotypes. In this sense we encountered stories about Indigenous people, young people and women, and the problems that stem from 'their' drinking. The research literature also, often sees certain populations as posing particular problems in terms of intoxication and drunkenness. Our review of this research suggested, however, that there are a number of attempts to explore, discuss and understand these issues in ways that can account for the symbolic, social and cultural meanings that drinking, intoxication and drunkenness may have for individuals in these groups. This research points to the shifting, and often contested, meanings that individuals attach to drinking, intoxication and drunkenness.

In the preceding chapter we presented an examination of the ways in which the problems of intoxication are understood, interpreted and acted upon when they become issues or concerns to be managed, regulated or subjected to legal considerations and judgment. In that discussion we tried to account for some of the ways in which media commentary tends to focus on the anti-social, even criminal, consequences of intoxication and drunkenness. And how, for much of this media commentary, the ways in which governments respond to and attempt to manage these issues is always incomplete, problematic and ineffectual. From there we presented a review of the legal and criminological research and commentary on issues such as: the ways in which intoxication and drunkenness may mitigate personal responsibilities and accountabilities; the particular nature of choice, consent and responsibility in cases of sexual assault when intoxication is a factor; the dilemmas associated with various regulations related to the promotion and policing of the Responsible Serving of Alcohol (RSA) in various contexts; and the relationships between intoxication, violence and gender. The story here was much the same: the meanings and understandings that attach to and produce different accounts of intoxication and drunkenness are subject to much debate and are characterised by complexity and ambiguity.

If this, then, summarises some of the key points that have emerged from this review, which, indeed, might be seen as things that have been learned: *What next?* This is a question that a number of people in the organisations that provided initial funding for this review have asked us. The answer to that depends, in part, on what it is imagined that this sort of review is meant to, or is able to, achieve in the first place. For example, it would be a vain hope to suggest that the sort of mapping/listing that we have undertaken here can provide some sort of way out of the complexities and ambiguities that attach to, and produce, the multiple understandings of intoxication and drunkenness that are revealed in this book. Such an outcome is not possible, and is certainly beyond any purpose that could be reasonably imagined for our review. But that doesn't mean that a review such as this cannot make some contribution to the debates and discussions about the health and well-being and safety and social order issues, risks and hazards (individual and community) that bear some relationship to intoxication and drunkenness and their consequences. Or, indeed, to discussions about the pleasures and the sense of sociability, belongingness, and shared (hi)stories that many individuals and groups talk about when they are asked about drinking alcohol – sometimes to levels that result in them or others getting *smashed*.

A number of prominent sociologists and social theorists have, over the last 20 or 30 years, grappled with the ways in which a range of issues in the increasingly globalised, interconnected and complex environments at the start of the twenty-first century – from global poverty and inequality, to the prospects of sustainable development in the under-developed world, to the *facts* of climate change and what to do about it – appear as intractable, unsolvable, not resolvable. So many competing interests, world views, rationalities, ideologies (call them what you will, they are just something else to debate) appear to make any chance of agreement or consensus about such issues beyond the capacities of a *reasonable* humanity. For Anthony Giddens (1994; see also 1990, and Ulrich Beck 1992; 1994), the ways in which the diverse issues facing humankind (in a global context, but also in more local settings), and the ways we understand these issues as being more complex, can be imagined in terms of what he calls *manufactured uncertainty*. This manufactured uncertainty is different to the uncertainty and unpredictability that has always been a characteristic of human existence. It is not so much that contemporary existence is less predictable, more uncertain that it might have been at other times in human history. Rather, it is the source of this uncertainty that is different. For Giddens and Beck the uncertainty that we face in terms of so many of the issues that we confront is created by our own knowledge. The more knowledge that we produce does not produce more certainty; paradoxically, it produces more uncertainty and doubt. Scientific disciplines and discourses, political rhetorics and posturing, media commentaries and public discussions clamour to be heard in any number of these and other debates. And a major challenge to emerge from this cacophony is: *How is it that we might make judgment about anything that attracts and produces such noise, such complexity, such ambiguity?*

And so it is with the always heated, always contentious, always political, always social and cultural arguments about intoxication and drunkenness and their meanings and consequences.

What next, then? Well, these debates and discussions will go on. What this review offers, in the end, is a list or map of many of the characteristics, the contours, the limits and possibilities of these debates. Those who have an interest in these debates, or who want to participate in them, may look to this list to provide ways of thinking about and contributing to the conversations that will continue to be had in a variety of settings and contexts, and with a variety of purposes. If that is the case then we would conclude by making clear that given our approach, and the things that we have discussed and revealed, understandings of intoxication and drunkenness need to be situated in particular historical, social, cultural and political contexts. Intoxication and drunkenness need to be understood and defined with due regard to these contexts and with an appreciation for the influences such things as social class, age, gender, ethnicity and race, and geography have on constructing these multiple meanings.

Appendix A: Methodology

Approach and scope of the literature review

This book emerges from a literature review that has two distinct elements. In the first element we reviewed published academic literature from a variety of fields and for a specified time frame (more details below). In the second element we reviewed particular elements of the print news media in Australia, New Zealand, the UK, Europe and the US. We chose these areas because they are culturally similar yet, importantly, they also have distinct social contexts (more details below). In this section we provide detail of this review process, the manner in which it was conducted, a justification for this approach, and a discussion of its limits.

Search strategy

This review includes published material only. While we acknowledge that many unpublished reports and reviews would be relevant to our research question we have chosen to narrow the search results in this way. We have also not reviewed books. The limitation in terms of time and the prolific nature of studies in the broad field of alcohol use meant that we limited the search to published academic articles.

Databases were identified in the following disciplines (the figures show the number of databases identified). However there was overlap between disciplines, with some databases being repeated in different disciplines:

- Anthropology (11)
- Cultural studies (15)
- History (9)
- Linguistics (11)
- Medicine, public health, ethics (16)
- Philosophy (10)
- Politics, law (13)

- Psychology (13)
- Sociology, criminology (26)

Discipline	Database
Anthropology	Academic Research Library
	Anthropology Plus
	British Humanities Index Expanded Academic Index
	IBSS: International Bibliography of the Social Sciences
	Libraries Australia – includes Australian Government
	Public Anthropology
	Sociological Abstracts
	Periodicals Archive Online
	Project MUSE – scholarly journals online
	ProQuest Dissertations and Theses
	Web of Science – Social Sciences Citation Index
Cultural Studies	Academic Research Library
	Australian Public Affairs – full text
	Blackwell Reference Online – includes 300 reference works
	Brill Online
	British Humanities Index
	Communication & Mass Media Complete
	Current Contents Connect
	Expanded Academic Index
	Family & Society Plus
	IBSS: International Bibliography of the Social Sciences
	International Encyclopedia of Marriage and Family
	Libraries Australia – includes Australian Government
	MAIS: Multicultural Australia and Immigration Studies
	PAIS International
	Sociological Abstracts
History	Academic Research Library
	Arts & Humanities Citation Index
	British Humanities Index
	Current Contents Connect
	Historical Abstracts
	Libraries Australia – includes Australian Government Periodicals archive online
	Project MUSE – scholarly journals online
	ProQuest Dissertations and Theses

Linguistics	Australian Public Affairs – full text
	BHI: British Humanities Index
	Blackwell Reference online
	Communication & Mass Media Complete
	ERIC
	Expanded Academic ASAP
	IBSS: International Bibliography of the Social Sciences
	Informaworld: Journals
	Linguistics and Language Behavior Abstracts
	MLA International Bibliography
	Periodicals Archive Online
Medicine/Public Health	AMED: Allied and Complementary Medicine
	Australasian Medical Index (AMI)
	BioMed Central
	Cochrane Library:
	Cochrane central register of controlled trials
	Cochrane database of systematic reviews
	Database of Abstracts of Reviews of Effects (DARE)
	EBM Reviews
	Encyclopedia of Drugs, Alcohol & Addictive Behaviour
	H&S: Health & Society Database (Australian)
	Faculty of 1000 Medicine
	Libraries Australia – includes Australian Government
	Meditext (Australian)
	NDLTD – online US Theses
	Ovid MEDLINE
	ProQuest Health & Medical Complete
	Scopus Web of Science
Philosophy	Academic Research Library
	Arts & Humanities Citation Index
	Australian Public Affairs – full text
	BHI: British Humanities Index
	Philosopher's Index
	Current Contents Connect
	JSTOR: The scholarly journal archive
	Libraries Australia–includes Australian Government Oxford Scholarship Online: Philosophy
	Periodicals Archive Online
	Project MUSE – scholarly journals online

Politics/Law	Academic Research Library
	Australian Public Affairs – full text
	AGIS Plus Text (Australia)
	British Humanities Index
	CaseBase (Australia)
	Expanded Academic Index
	IBSS: International Bibliography of the Social Sciences
	LAWLEX
	LegalTrac
	Libraries Australia – includes Australian Government Worldwide Political Science Abstracts
	Political Science: a SAGE full-text collection
	Sociological Abstracts
Psychology	Academic Research Library
	Expanded Academic ASAP
	Cochrane Library:
	Cochrane central register of controlled trials
	Cochrane database of systematic reviews
	Current Contents Connect
	Database of Abstracts of Reviews of Effects (DARE)
	DRUG: Drug Database
	Libraries Australia – includes Australian Government
	Ovid MEDLINE
	PsycINFO
	PsycBOOKS
	Psychology: a SAGE full-text collection
	Web of Science
Sociology/Criminology	**Australian Databases**
	AEI: Australian Education Index
	AFPD: Australian Federal Police Digest
	AGIS Plus Text
	Australian Bureau of Statistics
	Australian Public Affairs – full text
	CINCH: Australian Criminology Database
	DRUG: Drug Database
	Family & Society Plus
	Informit e-library: Humanities & Social Sciences Collection
	Libraries Australia – includes Australian Government Publications and Theses

Sociology/Criminology (cont'd)	MAIS: Multicultural Australia and Immigration Studies
	Overseas Databases
	Academic Research Library
	Blackwell Reference Online – includes 300 reference works including the International Encyclopedia of Marriage and Family
	British Humanities Index
	Communication & Mass Media Complete
	Contemporary Women's Issues
	Criminal Justice abstracts
	Criminology: a SAGE full-text collection
	The Gallup Organisation
	IBSS: International Bibliography of the Social Sciences
	Mass Observation Online
	PAIS International
	ProQuest Dissertations and Theses
	Social Services Abstracts
	Sociological Abstracts
	Studies on Women and Gender Abstracts online
	Web of Science – Social Sciences Citation Index
Multidisciplinary	**Australian Databases**
	Australian Public Affairs – full text
	Australian Bureau of Statistics
	Libraries Australia – includes Australian Government Publications and Theses
	Informit e-library: Humanities & Social Sciences collection
	Publications.gov.au – Government Publications
	Overseas Databases
	Academic Research Library
	Blackwell Reference online – includes 300 reference works
	Cambridge Journals online
	Current Contents Connect
	Expanded Academic Index
	IBSS: International Bibliography of the Social Sciences
	Informaworld: Journals
	JSTOR: The scholarly journal archive
	PAIS International
	PAIS Archive (1915–1976)
	Periodicals Archive Online
	Project MUSE – scholarly journals online

Multidisciplinary (cont'd)	ProQuest Dissertations and Theses
	Scopus
	Web of Science – citation indexes for all subjects
	News sources
	eLibrary Australasia (includes newspapers and radio transcripts
	Factiva (overseas newspapers)
	Newsbank Newspapers: Australia and the world
	TVNews – All major news and current affairs television programs (indexed)
	Data Archives
	CESSDA, Council of European Social Science Data Archives
	Economic and Social Data Service (ESDS), UK social science research
	Inter-university Consortium for Political and Social Research (ICPSR)
	ASSDA – Australian Social Science Data Archive

Overall, 53 databases were searched. Sixteen were not available from the university at which the search was undertaken. 77 per cent of the librarians' list was searched in the review. The databases not consulted included:

1. DARE (which was covered by EBM reviews)
2. Encyclopaedia of Drugs, Alcohol and Addictive Behaviour
3. Faculty of 1000 Medicine
4. NDLDT–online US theses
5. British Humanities Index
6. CaseBase
7. IBSS: International Bibliography of the Social Sciences
8. Arts & Humanities Citation Index
9. Periodicals Archive Online
10. Contemporary Women's Issues
11. Mass Observation Online
12. PAIS International
13. Studies on Women and Gender Abstracts Online
14. International Encyclopaedia of Marriage and Family
15. Anthropology Plus
16. Public Anthropology

The most relevant and useful databases (number of articles used) were:

1. Academic Research Library (20)
2. Current Contents (18)
3. Expanded Academic (15)
4. AGIS (the Attorney–Generals Information Service) (9)
5. Scopus (6)
6. ProQuest (5)

Biomed Central, Cochrane Database, Ovid Medline and others were also valuable sources.

Although we consulted many journals in our search, some of the most common were:

1. Contemporary Drug Problems
2. Journal of Studies on Alcohol and Drugs (formerly, Journal of Studies on Alcohol)
3. American Journal of Epidemiology
4. Addiction

The databases in each set were searched by using, firstly, the term 'intoxicat*' and, secondly, 'drunkenness'. The search terms were paired with search options such as 'all fields', 'citation and abstract', 'keywords', or similar options, to achieve a high return rate; the full text search option was not used to ensure that the literature screened for relevancy had intoxication or drunkenness as a main theme. 'Intoxic*' and its variants were considered but if 'intoxic*' or drunkenness were not present in the article it was usually rejected. For example, a study on the social context of drinking norms and heavy drinking (Wild 2002) defined heavy drinking specifically as five or more drinks at least once a week or more, yet the study did not specifically address intoxication or drunkenness, and therefore it was left out of this review.

In cases where the search produced hundreds or thousands of returns the search was refined. The first step involved adding "defin*" ('definition', with the possibility of 'define', 'defining' etc.) to the search terms. The second step in refining a search was to search intoxication and drunkenness in combination with 'understand*' (to enable 'understanding').

The searches were limited by the time frame 1 January 2000 to 15 January 2009 and, where possible, to papers which had been peer-reviewed. The lists of articles and reports answering the search terms in each database were examined, initially, by title. If the title suggested an item to be relevant to the literature review, the abstract, if available, (or an executive summary in the case of a report), was read; a document was selected if the abstract included any of the following:

- a description of the instruments used to measure alcohol intoxication or drunkenness;
- an explanation of a research design to obtain people's understandings of intoxication or drunkenness;
- thematic content such as ethnicity, race, gender, age, culture or class in relation to intoxication or drunkenness.

In cases where the sought information was not contained in the abstract, but there was good reason to believe that the article or report was nonetheless relevant, the full text was examined and paragraphs or pages of interest were noted. This process of selection produced a new, shorter list.

Full text versions of selected literature were downloaded for future reference and details of each entered into *Endnote*. The program was used to record additional information of interest:

- The 'Label' field was used to indicate (a) the discipline a paper/report belonged to and (b) whether a document represented an expert view of drinking or the view of a population group.
- The 'Keyword' field was used to indicate (a) whether a paper/report had and Australian or an international focus, (b) whether it contained a definition or 'understanding' and (c) any thematic content.

The age of drinkers of alcohol was a point of major interest and, in response, the keywords 'school student' or 'university student' were noted as a refinement of the 'age' theme.

We include a Further Reading section (Appendix B) which includes articles that are referenced in the sources we review, but are not specifically reviewed by us and which we deem particularly useful. We also include references that were found in our search but not included in the analysis in the review

As explained, we began by simply searching for our keywords: 'intoxication' and 'drunkenness' however, we found that meanings change through time. For instance, in the last few years the term 'binge' has grown in importance in this area. As we explain in the review, the definition of a binge is itself contested and may imply intoxication and/or drunkenness, but the relationship between these terms is only implied, not explicitly defined.

Therefore, an article about binge drinking but not explicitly referring to intoxication and drunkenness was considered peripheral and therefore not included in the review.

Print news media

Our review of the print news media draws primarily on a review of a number of key, mass circulation newspapers in the US, the UK, Australia and New Zealand. Our reasons for these limits are largely pragmatic, and determined by the fact that the print media presents a readily accessible archive in relation to these concerns. In addition, in these media spaces we are able to identify a number of concerns that we examined in greater detail in the review of the academic literature. This review of the print news media also sheds some light on the differing cultural and symbolic dimensions of the meanings and understandings associated with intoxication and drunkenness.

This review has been drawn from a pool of 928 articles drawn from the following newspapers:

Australia	New Zealand	United States	United Kingdom
The Age	New Zealand Herald	The New York Times	The Guardian
The Australian	Otago Daily Times	The Wall Street Journal	The Times
The Herald Sun		The Washington Post	
The Sydney Morning Herald			

Search strategy

This media literature review is focused on newspapers from Australia, New Zealand, the US, and the UK. These newspapers were selected on the basis of three criteria: (a) their large readership; (b) their international renown; and (c) to achieve a balance between broadsheet and tabloid commentary.

The Factiva database was used to search specific newspapers. When given a choice to search the print version, online version, or print *and* online versions of a newspaper, only the print version was searched since that was the only option that was common to all the newspapers. For each newspaper, the database was searched on a year-by-year basis, starting from 1 January 2000 and running to 15 January 2009. 'Intoxication' and 'drunkenness' were searched separately as keywords for each newspaper and searches were limited to articles of at least 1000 words (or more than 999 words) with the "wc>999" keyword. This criterion was included to limit the results to more substantial commentary.

The articles returned from these searches only indicated that they included the word 'intoxication' or 'drunkenness' somewhere in the article. As a result the articles were reviewed to identify those which were specifically related to drinking, as opposed to those which merely mentioned intoxication or drunkenness in passing, or in a different context. The 928 articles that were deemed relevant for this review were then sorted according to the orientation that the article took in relation to intoxication and drunkenness.

The sources and references that we have cited in this review were deemed to be directly related to issues of intoxication or drunkenness, and which provided insight into the definitions and understandings of these terms and states in this public arena. The Factiva database provides versions of the articles unpaginated, so for the purposes of this literature review we have cited the references without specific page numbers. Information provided in the citations at the end of this review will be sufficient to lead the reader to the source.

Appendix B: Further reading

Chapter 1

Barr, A. 1995. *Drink*. London: Bantam.

Brandt, A M. 1987. *No Magic Bullet: A Social History of Venereal Disease in the United States since 1880*. New York: Oxford University Press.

Burns, E. 2004. *The Spirits of America: A Social History of Alcohol*. Philadelphia: Temple University Press.

Eckersley, R. 1992. *Youth and the Challenge to Change*. Carlton South: Australia's Commission for the Future.

Engels, F. 1844/1987. *The Condition of the Working Class in England*. London: Penguin.

Gately, I. 2008. *Drink: A Cultural History of Alcohol*. New York: Gotham.

Greenaway, J. 2003. *Drink and British Politics since 1830: A Study in Policy-making*. New York: Palgrave Macmillan.

Holt, M P., editor. 2006. *Alcohol: A Social and Cultural History*. New York: Berg.

Hunter, I. 1994. *Rethinking the School*. St. Martins Press: New York.

Kant, I. 1978. *Anthropology from a Pragmatic Point of View*. Trans. Dowell, V L. Rudnick, H H, editor. London: Feffer and Simons.

Levine, H G. 1978. 'The discovery of addiction: Changing conceptions of habitual drunkenness in America'. *Journal of Studies in Alcohol* 39: 143–174.

Monkkonen, E H. 1981. 'A disorderly people? Urban order in the nineteenth and twentieth centuries'. *The Journal of American History* 68: 539–59.

O'Malley, P; Valverde, M. 2004. 'Pleasure, freedom and drugs: The use of "pleasure" in liberal governance of drugs and alcohol consumption'. *Sociology* 38: 25–42.

de Toqueville, A. 1835/2002. *Democracy in America*. Trans. Mansfield, H C; Winthrop, D. Chicago: The University of Chicago Press.

Chapter 2

Australian Institute of Family Studies (AIFS). 2000. *Patterns and Predictors of Teenagers' use of Licit and Illicit Substances in the Australian Temperament Project Cohort*. Australia: University of Melbourne.

Miller, W R; Heather, N; Hall, W. 1991. 'Calculating standard drink units: international comparisons'. *British Journal of Addiction* 86: 43–47.

Chapter 3

Bell, D. 2006. 'Commensality, urbanity, hospitality'. In *Critical Hospitality Studies*, edited by Lashley, C; Lynch, P; Morrison, A. London: Butterworth-Heinemann.

Christie, N. 1965. 'Scandinavian experience in legislation and control'. *National Conference on Legal Issues in Alcoholism and Alcohol Usage*. Boston: Boston University Law-Medicine Institute: 101–122.

Douglas, M., editor. 1987. *Constructive Drinking*. Cambridge: Cambridge University Press.

Hemstrom, Orjan. 2001. 'Informal alcohol control in six European countries', presented at a conference on Alcohol Consumption and Harm and Policy in the European Union, Public Health Institute, Stockholm, 17–18 March.

Home Office. 2005. *Drinking Responsibly: The Government's Proposals*. Accessed 2 July 2009. Available from: http://www.homeoffice.gov.uk/documents/2005-cons-drinking/.

Kneale, J. 2001. 'The place of drink: Temperance and the public 1956–1914'. *Social and Cultural Geography* 2 (1): 43–59.

Olsson, B. 1990. 'Alkoholpolitik och alkoholens fenomenologi' ('Alcohol policy and alcohol's phenomenology: opinions as articulated in the press'). *Alkoholpolitik – Tidskrift för nordisk alkoholforskning* 7: 184–194.

Ramstedt, Mats. 2001. 'Alcohol consumption and the experience of adverse consequences – a comparison of six European countries', presented at a conference on Alcohol Consumption and Harm and Policy in the European Union, Public Health Institute, Stockholm, 17–18 March.

Rose, N. 2007. *The Politics of Life itself: Biomedicine, Power and Subjectivity in the Twenty First Century*. Princeton: Princeton University Press.

Tonkiss, F. 2004. 'Urban cultures: Spatial tactics'. In *Urban Culture: Critical Concepts in Literary and Cultural Studies*. Jenks, C., editor. London: Routledge.

Wilson, T. 2005. 'Drinking cultures: Sites and practices in the production and expression of identity'. In *Drinking Cultures*, Wilson, T., editor. Oxford: Berg: 1–24.

Chapter 4

Commonwealth Department of Human Services and Health. 1996. *National Drug Strategy Household Survey Urban Aboriginal and Torres Strait Islander Peoples Supplement 1994*. Canberra: Australian Government Publishing Service.

Courtenay, W H. 2000. 'Engendering health: A social constructionist examination of men's health beliefs and behaviours'. *Psychology of Men and Masculinity* 1: 4–15.

Crawford, M. 1995. *Talking difference: On gender and language*. Thousand Oaks, California: Sage.

D'abbs, P; Togni, S. 2000. 'Liquor licensing and community action in regional and remote Australia: A review of recent initiatives'. *Australian and New Zealand Journal of Public Health* 24: 45–53.

Drugs and Crime Prevention Committee: Parliament of Victoria. 2001. *Inquiry into Public Drunkenness*. Accessed 2 July 2009. Available from: http://www.parliament.vic.gov.au/dcpc/Reports%20in%20PDF/Drunkenness_final_report.pdf.

Forsyth, A; Barnard, M; McKeganey, N P. 1997. 'Alcopop Supernova: Are alcoholic lemonades (alcopops) responsible for under-age drunkenness?' *International Journal of Health Education* 35 (2):53–8.

Hughes, K. MacKintosh, A M; Hastings, G; Wheeler, C. 1997. 'Young people, alcohol and designer drinks: Quantitative and qualitative study', *British Medical Journal* 314: 414–18.

McDonald, D. 1992. 'National police custody survey'. In *Deaths in Custody Australia, 1980 –1989: The Research Papers of the Criminology Unit of the Royal Commission into Aboriginal Deaths in Custody*, Biles, D; McDonald, D. eds. Canberra: Australian Institute of Criminology: 303–50.

Meashan, F. 2002. '"Doing Gender" –"Doing Drugs": Conceptualizing the gendering of drugs cultures'. *Contemporary Drug Problems* 29 (2): 335–73.

Moore, K. 2004. '"Sort drugs make mates": The use and meanings of mobiles in dance music club culture'. In *Reinventing Music: Social and Collaborative Aspects of New Music Technology*, Brown, B; O'Hara, K. eds. Bristol: Hewlett-Packard.

Moore, K; Miles, S. 2004. 'Young People, Dance and the Sub-Cultural Consumption of Drugs'. *Addiction Research & Theory*. 12: 507–523.

Royal Commission into Aboriginal Deaths in Custody, National Report. 1991. Vol. 1. Canberra: AGPS.

Chapter 5

Mill, J S. 1859/1974. *On Liberty*. London: Penguin.

Miller, C J. 1999. *Annotation: Competency of Nonexpert Witness to Testify, in Criminal Case, Based upon Personal Observation, as to Whether Person Was under the Influence of Drugs*. American Law Reports. Vol. 4, 21: 905–17.

Norris, J; Cubbins, L. 1992. 'Dating, drinking and rape: Effects of victims' and assailants' alcohol consumption on judgments of their behaviour and traits'. *Psychology of Women Quarterly* 16: 179–91.

Stormo, K; Lang. A; Stritzke, Q. 1997. 'Attributions about acquaintance rape: The role of alcohol and individual differences. *Journal of Applied Social Psychology* 27 (4): 279–305.

Summary Offences Act. 1966. 'Victoria's Alcohol Action Plan 2008–2013'. (Vic) 5813, 14 and 16. Accessed 5 June 2009. Available at: http://www.health.vic.gov.au/drugservices/downloads/action_plan.pdf.

Wall, A; Schuller, R. 2000. 'Sexual assault and defendant/victim intoxication: Jurors' perceptions of guilt'. *Journal of Applied Social Psychology* 30 (2): 353–74.

References

Aalto, M; Seppä, K. 2007. 'Primary health care physicians' definitions on when to advise a patient about weekly and binge drinking'. *Addictive Behaviors* 32: 1321–1330.

Abbey, A; Buck, P O; Zawacki, T; Saenz, C. 2003. 'Alcohol's effects on perceptions of a potential date rape'. *Journal of Studies on Alcohol* 64: 669–677.

Abbott, T. 2009. 'The end of the disaster narrative and the new consensus on Aboriginal affairs'. *The 2009 Annual Earl Page College Politics Lecture*. Presented on 1 September 2009: The University of New England. Accessed 25 April 2010. Available at: http://blog.une.edu.au/news/2009/09/02/abbott-tells-of-new-consensus-on-indigenous-affairs-at-earle-page-college-politics-lecture/.

Abdul-Ahad, G. 2005. '"How can you establish a free media in such fear and anarchy?": Last week Fakher Haidar al-Tamimi became the 36th Iraqi journalist to be killed since the start of the war. His friend Ghaith Abdul-Ahad explains how, in the postwar carnage, his fellow countrymen have become the softest targets'. *The Guardian*. London.

Abel, G; Plumridge, E. 2004. 'Network "norms" or "styles" of "drunken comportment"?' *Health Education Research* 19: 492.

Abrahamson, M. 2003. 'Perceptions of heavy drinking and alcohol problems among young adults'. *Contemporary Drug Problems* 30: 815–837.

Abrahamson, M. 2004. 'Alcohol in courtship contexts: focus-group interviews with young Swedish women and men'. *Contemporary Drug Problems* 31: 3.

Australian Bereau of Statistics (ABS) 2008. 'Risk taking by young people'.

Ahern, J; Galea, S; Hubbard, A; Midanik, L; Syme, S. 2008. '"Culture of drinking" and individual problems with alcohol use'. *American Journal of Epidemiology* 167: 1041–1049.

Amnesty International. 2005. 'Sexual Assault Research Summary Report'. Prepared by ICM.

Andersen, A; Holstein, B; Due, P. 2007. 'School-related risk factors for drunkenness among adolescents: Risk factors differ between socio-economic groups'. *The European Journal of Public Health* 17: 27–32.

Anderson, P. 2006. 'City sees another big night out of it'. *Herald Sun*. Melbourne.

Aratani, L. 2007. 'Taking treatment message to the streets'. *The Washington Post*. Washington D. C.

Armstrong, S. 2000. 'Looking for a little club class?'. *The Sunday Times*. London.

Asthana, A. 2008. 'Drink-fuelled antics? Not our fault, say students'. *The Observer*, Sunday 30 March 2008. Accessed 25 April 2010. Available at: http://www.guardian.co.uk/education/2008/mar/30/highereducation.uk.

Australian Institute of Health and Welfare. 2004. 'A Guide to Australian Alcohol Data'. Canberra.

Babor, T; Caetano, R. 2005. 'Evidence-based alcohol policy in the Americas: Strengths, weaknesses, and future challenges'. *Revista Panamericana De Salud Publica-Pan American Journal of Public Health* 18: 327–337.

Bachelard, M. 2008. 'Hitting the drink'. *The Sunday Age*. Melbourne.

Baggini, J. 2004. 'It's in our interests to be nannied'. *The Guardian*. London.

Bainbridge, B. 2004. 'You light up my life'. *The Times*. London.

Baker, J. 2008. 'Women pushed to the brink'. *The Sydney Morning Herald*. Sydney.

Baker, K. 2001a. 'The first slum in America'. *The New York Times*. New York.

Baker, P. 2001b. 'Vodka's place in the russian soul: New museum to examine libation's role in the country's "National Tradition"'. *The Washington Post*. Washington D. C.

Barnes, M. 2009. 'Come on, feel the noise: Going up to 11 has long been a badge of honour in rock music. But there's a price to pay for those decibels'. *The Guardian*. London.

Barnes, S. 2005. 'Just like Morecambe and Wise, so sport and alcohol were meant to be together'. *The Times*. London.

Barquin, J; Luna, J; Hernandez, A. 2008. 'A controlled study of the time-course of breath alcohol concentration after moderate ingestion of ethanol following a social drinking session'. *Forensic Science International* 177: 140–145.

Barron, J. 2008. 'Medical examiner rules Ledger's death accidental'. *The New York Times*. New York.

Barton, L. 2007. 'Pressed to impress: Once it was a drink loved only by down-and-outs and teenagers wanting to get drunk as quickly as possible. But now cider is undergoing an amazing sales revival. It's even become sophisticated'. *The Guardian*. London.

Beccaria, F; Sande, A. 2003. 'Drinking games and rite of life projects'. *Young: Nordic Journal of Youth Research* 11: 99–119.

Beck, U. 1992. *Risk Society*. London: Sage Publications.

Beck, U. 1994. 'The reinvention of politics: Towards a theory of reflexive modernization'. In *Reflexive Modernization: Politics, Tradition and Aesthetics in the Modern Social Order*, Beck, U; Giddens, A; Lash, S., eds. Cambridge: Polity Press: 1–55.

Beckingham, D. 2008. 'Geographies of drink culture in Liverpool: Lessons from the drink capital of nineteenth-century England'. *Drugs: Education, Prevention and Policy* 15: 305–313.

Bee, P. 2008. 'How safe is your blast of caffeine?'. *The Times*. London.

Bell, D. 2008. 'Destination drinking: Toward a research agenda on alcotourism'. *Drugs: Education, Prevention & Policy* 15: 291–304.

Ben-Noun, L. 2002. 'Drinking wine to inebriation in biblical times'. *Israel Journal of Psychiatry and Related Sciences* 39: 61–64.

Benedictus, L. 2004. 'End of the affair: One pill now costs about the same as a pint of beer and is almost as easy to get hold of. But the youth of Britain is starting to turn its back on ecstasy. Leo Benedictus on how the drug of the 90s fell from favour'. *The Guardian*. London.

Benedictus, L. 2007. 'Way out west: This week a report revealed that unprecedented numbers of city folk are moving to south-west England. But life there isn't all clotted cream, surfing and sunshine'. *The Guardian*. London.

Bennett, D. 2005. 'Dr. Ecstasy'. *The New York Times*. New York.

Bennett, N. 2008. 'OLE!' *The Australian*.

Berlins, M. 2007. 'Hockney says the iPod has turned young people off art. So why are our galleries packed with children?'. *The Guardian*. London.

Bernstein, R. 2001. 'Stabbing the heart and soul with the savagery of truth'. *The New York Times*. New York.

Best, D; Manning, V; Gossop, M; Samantha, G; Strang, J. 2006. 'Excessive drinking and other problem behaviours among 14–16 year old schoolchildren'. *Addictive Behaviors* 31: 1424.

Bilger, B. 2001. 'For the love of potatoes'. *The New York Times*. New York.

Binyon, M. 2002. 'Putin promises to put Russia's house in order'. *The Times*. London.

Blakemore, C; Iversen, L. 2001. 'Cannabis – why it is safe'. *The Times*. London.

Blumenthal, R. 2006. 'Army moves to curb abuses in program for injured recruits. *The New York Times*. New York.

Blundell, G. 2005. 'Soap flakes'. *The Australian*.

Bogren, A. 2006. 'The competent drinker, the authentic person and the strong person: Lines of reasoning in Swedish young people's discussions about alcohol'. *Journal of Youth Studies* 9: 515–538.

Bogren, A. 2008. 'Women's intoxication as "dual licentiousness": An exploration of gendered images of drinking and intoxication in Sweden'. *Addiction Research & Theory* 16: 95–106.

Boodman, S G. 2008. 'Five Doctors, stumped; explanation for woman's fast-growing tremor turns out to be elementary'. *The Washington Post*. Washington.

Bostridge, I. 2006. 'The god of small things: Combining the eroticism of Wagner and genius of Schumann, Hugo Wolf's lieder are mini-masterpieces'. *The Guardian*. London.

Bowditch, G. 2006. 'The Enforcers'. *The Sunday Times*. London.

Boyce, F C. 2004. 'The patron saints of cinema – the London film festival starts today with tales of drunkenness, sex and violence – and that's just the saints. *The Guardian*. London.

Boyes, R. 2004. 'Nanny state fails to wean Swedes from the bottle'. *The Times*. London.

Bradfield, R. 2006. 'Intoxication and criminal responsibility'. *Law Reform Institute*. Hobart, Tasmania.

Brady, M; Nicholls, R; Henderson, G; Byrne, J. 2006. 'The role of a rural sobering-up centre in managing alcohol-related harm to Aboriginal people in South Australia'. *Drug and Alcohol Review* 25: 201–206.

Brantley, B. 2001. 'Leenane III, bones flying'. *The New York Times*. New York.

Brennan, P. 2002. '"Ulysses S. Grant": Rising to extraordinary challenges'. *The Washington Post*. Washington D. C.

Brewer, T. 2002. 'We the people, We the warriors'. *The Washington Post*. Washington.

Brick, J. 2006. 'Standardization of alcohol calculations in research'. *Alcoholism-Clinical and Experimental Research* 30: 1276–1287.

Briscoe, S; Donnelly, N. 2002. 'Young adults' experience of responsible service practice in NSW'. *Alcohol Studies Bulletin*: 1–16.

Britten, F. 2007. 'The hedonist's guide'. *The Sunday Times*. London.

Brody, J E. 2002. 'Hidden plague of alcohol abuse by the elderly'. *The New York Times*. New York.

Brody, J E. 2008. 'Curbing binge drinking takes group effort. *The New York Times*. New York.

Brooks, D. 2002. 'Why the U. S. will always be rich'. *The New York Times*. New York.

Brown, D L. 2000. 'High on gas and low on hope; in Canada's northeast, Innu children take up deadly addiction. *The Washington Post*. Washington.

Brown, D L. 2003. 'Left for dead in a Saskatchewan winter; a survivor's story exposes police abuse of indigenous Canadians'. *The Washington Post*. Washington.

Brown, M. 2007. 'Life and death on the island of despair'. *The Sydney Morning Herald*. Sydney.

Bruce, D. 2003. 'The wide main street of Oamaru with its central trees is one of the town's most attractive features, but it also becomes unattractive after a night on the town by some young people'. *Otago Daily Times*. Dunedin.

Burchill, J. 2001. 'The pleasure principle'. *The Guardian*. London.

Burns, J. 2001. 'The tiger loses its tolerance'. *The Sunday Times*. London.

Burstin, F. 2003. 'Message in a bottle'. *Herald Sun*. Melbourne.

Button, J. 2005. 'There goes the hood'. *The Sydney Morning Herald*. Sydney.

Calhoun, V; Carvahlo, K; Astur, R; Pearlson, G. 2005. 'Using virtual reality to study alcohol intoxication effects on the neural correlates of simulated driving'. *Applied Psychophysiology and Biofeedback* 30: 285.

Cameron, D. 2007. 'Moderation generation'. *The Sydney Morning Herald*. Sydney.

Cameron, D; Thomas M; Madden, S; Thornton, C; Bergmark, A; Garretson, H; Terzidou, M. 2000. 'Intoxicated across Europe: In search of meaning'. *Addiction Research* 8: 233.

Carr, C. 2000. 'Nor Any Drop to Drink'. *The New York Times*. New York.

Chaudhuri, A. 2003. 'Falling down'. *The Sunday Times*. London.

Chazan, G; Whalen, J; Higgins, A. 2002. 'Putin's plans to repair russia are damaged by hostage crisis'. *The Wall Street Journal*. New York.

Chrisafis, A. 2004. 'Ireland tries to end its love affair with drink: Rise in prosperity blamed for increase in alcohol-related accidents and deaths'. *The Guardian*. London.

Clemens, S; Matthews, S; Young, A; Powers, J. 2007. 'Alcohol consumption of Australian women: Results from the Australian longitudinal study on women's health'. *Drug and Alcohol Review* 26: 525–35.

Coleman, L M; Cater, S. 2004. 'Fourteen to 17-year-olds' experience of "risky" drinking – a cross-sectional survey undertaken in south-east England'. *Drug and Alcohol Review* 23: 351–353.

Cornwell, J. 2006. 'A head for trouble'. *The Sunday Times*. London.

Cotter, H. 2000. 'An iconoclast to whom the personal is always political. *The New York Times*. New York.

Crace, J. 2008. 'The reluctant guru: The historian turned his back on academia because he couldn't bear attracting clones'. *The Guardian*. London.

Critchley, C. 2008. 'Think before you drink'. *Herald Sun*. Melbourne.

Daley, S. 2001. 'Europe making Sweden ease alcohol rules. *The New York Times*. New York.

Dao, J; Barringer, F. 2006. 'Miners went by book, but time and air ran out'. *The New York Times*. New York.

De Visser, R O; Smith, J A. 2007. 'Young men's ambivalence toward alcohol'. *Social Science & Medicine* 64: 350–362.

Dean, A. 2002. 'History, culture, and substance use in a rural Scottish community'. *Substance Use & Misuse* 37: 749–765.

Delaney, S. 2007. 'Brand designs: From Duff Beer to Red Apple Cigarettes, fictional products are all over our screens. But can they survive in the cut and thrust world of business reality?'. *The Guardian*. London.

Demant, J. 2009. 'When alcohol acts: An actor-network approach to teenagers, alcohol and parties'. *Body Society* 15: 25–46.

Demant, J; Järvinen, M. 2006. 'Constructing maturity through alcohol experience – focus group interviews with teenagers. *Addiction Research & Theory* 14: 589–602.

Demant, J; Ostergaard, J. 2007. 'Partying as everyday life: Investigations of teenagers' leisure life'. *Journal of Youth Studies* 10: 517–537.

Depalma, A. 2007. 'Medical examiner, differing on ground zero case, stands his ground'. *The New York Times*. New York.

Devine, M. 2008. 'Alcohol law's unseemly costs'. *The Sydney Morning Herald*. Sydney.

Dingwall, G. 2007. 'Intoxicated mistakes about the need for self-defense (United Kingdom)'. *Modern Law Review* 70: 127–138.

Dingwall, G; Koffman, L. 2008. 'Determining the impact of intoxication in a desert-based sentencing framework'. *Journal of Criminology and Criminal Justice* 8: 335–348.

Dixit, J. 2005. 'Joey Gay's excellent adventure'. *The New York Times*. New York.

Dixon, R; Spinak, J. 2004. 'Common law liability of clubs for injury to intoxicated patrons: Cole v South Tweed Heads Rugby League Football Club Ltd'. *University of New South Wales Law Journal* 27: 816–825.

Dodd, C. 2005. 'Kids are mad for it'. *The Times*. London.

Doesburg, A. 2004. 'Alcohol's cultural hangover; few people would deny there is a binge-drinking problem in New Zealand, but there is disagreement about how to solve it'. *New Zealand Herald*. Auckland.

DSM-IV-TR 2000. '303.00 Alcohol Intoxication'. In *Diagnostic and Statistical Manual - Text Revision DSM-IV-TR™ 2000*. First, M B., editor. Washington, D. C., American Psychiatric Association.

Dudman, G. 2005. 'Media: "All the newspapers carried the same story": Other papers published slurs about Hillsborough, so why, asks Graham Dudman, will Merseyside not forgive the Sun'. *The Guardian*. London.

Edemariam, A. 2004. 'Profile: The new Monroe doctrine: Joyce Carol Oates: The first member of her family to finish school, she won a scholarship to university and went on to become a remarkably prolific writer – she has two novels out this year. She has been described as America's "true proletarian novelist" but she has also faced vituperative criticism. Interview by Aida Edemariam'. *The Guardian*. London.

Edmundson, M. 2006. 'Freud and the fundamentalist urge'. *The New York Times*. New York.

Eldridge, A; Roberts, M. 2008. 'A comfortable night out? Alcohol, drunkenness and inclusive town centres'. *Area* 40: 365–374.

Elgar, F; Roberts, C; Parry-Langdon, N; Boyce, W. 2005. 'Income inequality and alcohol use: A multilevel analysis of drinking and drunkenness in adolescents in 34 countries'. *European Journal of Public Health* 15: 245.

Elliott, J. 2000a. 'Panel reviews laws rejected by the courts'. *The Wall Street Journal*. New York.

Elliott, J. 2000b. 'Sober truth: Law fails to curb drunken driving'. *The Wall Street Journal*. New York.

Elvin, J. 2008. 'Intoxication, capacity to consent, and the Sexual Offences Act 2003 (United Kingdom)'. *King's Law Journal* 19: 151-157.

Fahrenthold, D A. 2006. In 'A beer in the belly can get youths arrested; possession is redefined to cover alcohol already consumed. H, N., author. *The Washington Post*. Washington.

Farke, W; Anderson, P. 2007. 'Editorial: Binge drinking in Europe'. *Adicciones* 19: 333–340.

Farouque, F. 2007. 'Gotta drink, it's part of growing up'. *The Age*. Melbourne.

Farrant, D; Ambrose, T. 2000. 'The color of justice'. *The Age*. Melbourne.

Farrelly, E. 2007. 'New ways to whet the appetite'. *The Sydney Morning Herald*. Sydney.

Feix, J; Wolber, G. 2007. 'Intoxication and settled insanity: A finding of not guilty by reason of insanity'. *Journal of the American Academy of Psychiatry and the Law* 35: 172–182.

Felten, E. 2006. 'How's Your Drink? What Teddy Sipped'. *The Wall Street Journal*. New York.

Felten, E. 2008. 'How's Your Drink? Do They Taste of Trumpets?'. *The Wall Street Journal*. New York.

Ferentzy, P. 2001. 'From sin to disease: Differences and similarities between past and current conceptions of chronic drunkenness'. *Contemporary Drug Problems* 28: 363–389.

Fields, G. 2007. 'Defense reservations: Native Americans on trial often go without counsel – quirk of Federal law leaves a justice gap in tribal court system. *The Wall Street Journal*. New York.

Figes, O. 2002. 'Who Lost the Soviet Union?'. *The New York Times*. New York.

Fillmore, M; Roach, E; Rice, J. 2002. 'Does caffeine counteract alcohol-induced impairment? The ironic effects of expectancy'. *Journal of Studies in Alcohol* 63: 745–754.

Finch, E; Munro, V. 2007. 'The demon drink and the demonized woman: Socio-sexual stereotypes and responsiblity attribution in rape trials involving intoxicants'. *Social & Legal Studies* 16: 591–614.

Finn, P. 2005. 'For Russians, police rampage fuels fear; one town draws attention to widespread torture and killings. *The Washington Post*. Washington D. C.

Fitzgerald, J. 2008. 'Culture of intoxication'. *The Age*. Melbourne.

Fitzgerald, R. 2007. 'Twelve steps forward'. *The Australian Literary Review*.

Ford, C. 2008. 'Parents: If this scares you, GET READY FOR THIS'. *Herald Sun*. Melbourne.

Frankel, G. 2005. 'Prince Harry's Nazi blunder burns old blighty'. *The Washington Post*. Washington.

Freeman, H. 2007. 'Road to redemption: Although described as "the purest living prose stylist", Edward St Aubyn was best known for his troubled past. A favourite for last year's Booker, he is now getting the recognition he deserves'. *The Guardian*. London.

Gaughwin, M. 2008. 'Addictions fought by facing demons'. *The Australian*.

Gerrard, N. 2004. 'Parents: Let them go!: On the eve of Glastonbury, Nicci Gerrard has some advice for anxious parents'. *The Guardian*. London.

Giddens, A. 1990. *The Consequences of Modernity*. Cambridge: Polity Press.

Giddens, A. 1994. 'Living in a post-traditional society'. In *Reflexive Modernization: Politics, Tradition and Aesthetics in the Modern Social Order*, Beck, U; Giddens, A; Lash, S., eds. Cambridge: Polity Press: 56–109.

Gill, J; Donaghy, M; Guise, J; Warner, P. 2007. 'Descriptors and accounts of alcohol consumption: Methodological issues piloted with female undergraduate drinkers in Scotland'. *Health Education Research* 22: 27–36.

Gold, R. 2002. 'Another round? Honing their craft, some police want to get you drunk – cops learn roadside tests for alcohol and drug use by studying live subjects – scouring a heavy-metal crowd'. *The Wall Street Journal*. New York.

Goldenberg, S. 2006. 'Battle lines: After two privileged white students were charged last month with raping a black stripper at a spring break party, it turned into a scandal that rocked America. Once again, the US finds itself divided on the basis of race, class and gender'. *The Guardian*. London.

Goodsite, B; Klear, L; Rosenberg, H. 2008. 'The impact of behavioral signs of intoxication on bartender service'. *Drugs-Education Prevention and Policy* 15: 545–551.

Goodwin, J. 2000. 'Go ye into all the World'. *The New York Times*. New York.

Gordon, M R. 2000. 'The Grunts of grozny'. *The New York Times*. New York.

Graham, K. 2005. 'Public drinking then and now'. *Contemporary Drug Problems* 32: 45.

Graham, M; Ward, B; Munro, G; Snow, P; Elliss, J. 2006. 'Rural parents, teenagers and alcohol: What are parents thinking?'. *Rural and Remote Health* 6.

Grattan, M. 2003a. 'Life of the party in the balance'. *The Age*. Melbourne.

Grattan, M. 2003b. 'What shall we do with a drunken Democrats leader?'. *The Age*. Melbourne.

Gray, C. 2001. 'A tale of two designations: Landmarked and not'. *The New York Times*. New York.

Graycar, A. 2001. 'Crime in twentieth century Australia'. *Year Book Australia*. Australian Bureau of Statistics.

Green, C; Polen, M; Janoff, S; Castleton, D; Perrin, N. 2007. '"Not getting tanked": Definitions of moderate drinking and their health implications'. *Drug and Alcohol Dependence* 86: 265–273.

Griffith, G. 2008. 'Intoxication and the criminal law'. In *New South Wales*, S. P L R., editor. Sydney: NSW Parliamentary Library.

Grose, J. 2007. 'Before Lindsay or Paris, there was Mrs. L—fle'. *The New York Times*. New York.

Gruley, B. 2003. 'Watered down: How one university stumbled in its attack on alcohol abuse – as industry resisted change, Florida State's President focused on campus image – "Beer Pong" and Phony IDs'. *The Wall Street Journal*. New York.

Guise, J; Gill, J. 2007. '"Binge drinking? It's good, it's harmless fun": A discourse analysis of accounts of female undergraduate drinking in Scotland'. *Health Education Research* 22: 895.

Guivarra, F E. 2008. 'The survival of public drunkenness laws in Victoria'. *Indigenous Law Bulletin* 7: 19–22.

Gustin, J; Simons, J. 2008. 'Perceptions of level of intoxication and risk related to drinking and driving'. *Addictive Behaviors* 33 (4): 605-615.

Halliday, C. 2007. 'School's out… forever'. *The Age*. Melbourne.

Hamad, A. 2005. 'The intoxicated pedestrian: tortious reflections'. *Tort Law Review*, 13: 14–39.

Hamilton, A. 2003. 'Irish are ordered to crack down on the craic'. *The Times*. London.

Hamilton, W L. 2001. 'Sex, drugs and seed catalogs'. *The New York Times*. New York.

Hammersley, R; Ditton, J. 2005. 'Binge or bout? Quantity and rate of drinking by young people in the evening in licensed premises'. *Drugs: Education, Prevention & Policy* 12: 493–500.

Hardy, R. 2008. 'Quiet please: Noise pollution causes sleep disturbance, raises blood pressure and can lead to heart disease. Rebecca Hardy on how to survive in an increasingly noisy Britain'. *The Guardian*. London.

Harnett, R; Thom, B; Herring, R; Kelly, M. 2000. 'Alcohol in transition: Towards a model of young men's drinking styles'. *Journal of Youth Studies* 3: 61–77.

Harrison, E; Fillmore, M. 2005. 'Social drinkers underestimate the additive impairing effects of alcohol and visual degradation on behavioral functioning'. *Psychopharmacology* 177: 459.

Hastings, M. 2008. 'If we endorse yob behaviour in role models, we'll become a yob nation: Every time TV chef Gordon Ramsay screams obscenities on screen, he kicks civilised values between the legs'. *The Guardian*. London.

Hayward, K; Hobbs, D. 2007. 'Beyond the binge in "booze Britain": Market-led liminalization and the spectacle of binge drinking'. *British Journal of Sociology* 58: 437–456.

Haywood, B. 2005. 'School's out forever'. *The Age*. Melbourne.

Healy, M. 2002. '"Just drive", said the road, and the car responded'. *The New York Times.* New York.

Heaney, M. 2003. 'Through a glass darkly: Interview with Shane MacGowan'. *The Sunday Times.* London.

Helliker, K. 2006. 'A test for alcohol – and its flaws – a new screen detects Sunday's gin in Monday's urine but it may be ensnaring some innocent people too – beer or hand sanitizer?'. *The Wall Street Journal.* New York.

Henley, J. 2008. 'Bonjour binge drinking: The French are famous for their sophisticated cafe culture and sensible approach to drinking. So why have their teenagers suddenly developed a taste for British-style boozing?' *The Guardian.* London.

Herring, R; Berridge, V; Thom, B. 2008a. 'Binge drinking today: Learning lessons from the past'. *Drugs-Education Prevention and Policy* 15: 475–486.

Herring, R; Berridge, V; Thom, B. 2008b. 'Binge drinking: An exploration of a confused concept'. *Journal of Epidemiology and Community Health* 62: 476–479.

Higgins, A. 2000. 'Russian empires: Putin's push for order pits local "Oligarchs" against political bosses – In Kirov, Governor does battle with a TV tycoon; both claim to be Kremlin allies – Pictures with the President. *The Wall Street Journal.* New York.

Higson, R. 2008. 'A look back at our ale and hearty past'. *The Australian.*

Hjul, J. 2006. 'Half measures will fuel alcohol abuse'. *The Sunday Times.* London.

Hodge, A. 2003. 'Town full of tension'. *The Australian.*

Hoel, S; Eriksen, B M; Breidablik, H J; Meland, E. 2004. 'Adolescent alcohol use, psychological health, and social integration'. *Scandinavian Journal of Public Health* 32: 361–367.

Honeysett, S. 2008. 'Final drinks for league's longest pub crawl?' *Weekend Australian.*

Hoolihan, R. 2003. 'Public drunkenness in Townsville: The way forward'. *Indigenous Law Bulletin* 5: 9–10.

Horowitz, A. 2005. 'Hoodies and baddies'. *The Times.* London.

Horwitz, T. 2000. 'In Sydney, the games are hot; oh, there's also those Olympics – Australian host city revels in vice; themed brothels and no agony over ecstasy'. *The Wall Street Journal.* New York.

Howie, R. 2004. 'Relevance of voluntary intoxication to criminal liability'. *Judicial Officers Bulletin* 16: 57–59.

Hsu, S S. 2002. 'Funds drying up in the war on wall art; understaffed crews work to fight surge of drawing'. *The Washington Post.* Washington D. C.

Hufford, M R. 2001. 'Alcohol and suicidal behavior'. *Clinical Psychology Review* 21: 797–811.

Hunt, T. 2004. 'After 13 centuries of binge-drinking we've found a new excuse'. *The Sunday Times.* London.

Hutchinson, S. 2003. 'Under-age, overproof'. *The Australian.*

ICAP 2002. 'Blood Alcohol Concentration Limits Worldwide'. *ICA Reports 11.* Washington D. C., International Centre for Alcohol Policies.

Jack, I. 2005. 'For whom the closing-time bell tolls: Will changing pub hours civilise our drinking habits'. *The Guardian.* London.

Jackman, T. 2000. 'Bitterness nearly rivals grief; fears that justice won't prevail in hit-and-run case fuel father's effort'. *The Washington Post.* Washington.

Jackman, T. 2002. 'Family Sues Over Man's Death in Police Hood'. *The Washington Post.* Washington.

Jackman, T; Montgomery, L; Reeves, T A; Mosk, M. 2000. 'Metro in brief'. *The Washington Post.* Washington.

Jacobsen, G. 2003. 'Last orders, please'. *The Sydney Morning Herald*. Sydney.

Jacques, M. 2006. 'Imperial overreach is accelerating the global decline of America: The disastrous foreign policies of the US have left it more isolated than ever, and China is standing by to take over'. *The Guardian*. London.

Järvinen, M; Gundelach, P. 2007. 'Teenage drinking, symbolic capital and distinction'. *Journal of Youth Studies* 10: 55–71.

Jayne, M; Holloway, S L; Valentine, G. 2006. 'Drunk and disorderly: Alcohol, urban life and public space'. *Progress in Human Geography* 30: 451.

Jayne, M; Valentine, G; Holloway, S L. 2008. 'Geographies of alcohol, drinking and drunkenness: A review of progress'. *Progress in Human Geography* 32: 247–263.

Jenkins, S. 2000. 'A cocktail of double standards, Mr Straw'. *The Times*. London.

Jenkins, S. 2001. 'Twin-track approach to the new prohibition'. *The Times*. London.

Jenkins, S. 2002. 'Why drugs policy is a mind-bending substance'. *The Times*. London.

Jenkins, S. 2006. 'Another victory for Britain's insufferable paternalists: The vote to ban smoking in public places reflects the government's preference for central control over local option'. *The Guardian*. London.

Jenkins, S. 2007. 'The state has only aided our seasonal spates of thuggery: The August news vacuum amplifies violent Britain. But politicians can't shirk the blame: They have torn apart local leadership'. *The Guardian*. London.

Jesella, K. 2008. 'Detox for the camera. Doctor's order!'. *The New York Times*. New York.

Johnson, P B; Richter, L; Kleber, H D; McLennan, A T; Carise, D. 2005. 'Telescoping of drinking-related behaviors: Gender, racial/ethnic, and age comparisons'. *Substance Use & Misuse* 40: 1139–1151.

Jones, J. 2004. 'Disposable cameras: We can't trust photographs. In fact, we never could. In an exclusive interview, David Hockney tells Jonathan Jones why painting creates a more reliable record of the truth'. *The Guardian*. London.

Kane, P. 2001. 'When the music stops'. *The Sunday Times*. London.

Kang, M. 2006. 'Under-age cocktail'. *The Sydney Morning Herald*. Sydney.

Kearney, S. 2007a. 'Rough road ahead'. *The Australian*.

Kearney, S. 2007b. 'Territory for hope'. *The Australian*.

Kenneally, C. 2002. 'The peace that passeth'. *The New York Times*. New York.

Kerr, W; Greenfield, T; Midanik, L. 2006. 'How many drinks does it take you to feel drunk? Trends and predictors for subjective drunkenness'. *Addiction* 101: 1428–1437.

Kiley, K. 2001. 'State considers limits on teenage drivers'. *The New York Times*. New York.

Kilgannon, C. 2002. 'Drinking young'. *The New York Times*. New York.

Killingsworth, B. 2006. '"Drinking stories" from a playgroup: Alcohol in the lives of middle-class mothers in Australia'. *Ethnography* 7: 357–384.

Kingsnorth, P. 2005. 'The great British pub is both cultural icon and community bolthole. But as closures and style bar makeovers loom, how long is it safe'. *The Guardian*. London.

Kloep, M; Hendry, L B; Ingebrigtsen, J E; Glendinning, A; Espnes, G A. 2001. 'Young people in "drinking" societies? Norwegian, Scottish and Swedish adolescents' perceptions of alcohol use'. *Health Education Research* 16: 279–291.

Knight, I. 2008. 'Put shame back into boozing'. *The Sunday Times*. London.

Knightley, P. 2001. 'Users and abusers'. *The Sunday Times*. London.

Koch, T. 2004. 'Bitter paradise'. *The Australian*.

Kovaleski, S F; Chan, S. 2001. 'D. C. Agencies For Homeless Miss 3 Deaths'. *The Washington Post*. Washington.

Kurtz, H. 2006. 'After Bode Miller's downhill turn, two weeks on the lift. *The Washington Post*. Washington D. C.

Kypri, K; Langley, J; Stephenson, S. 2005. 'Episode-centred analysis of drinking to intoxication in university students'. *Alcohol and Alcoholism: International Journal of the Medical Council on Alcoholism* 40: 447.

Kypri, K; Paschell, M; Maclennan, B; Langley, J. 2007. 'Intoxication by drinking location: A web-based diary study in a New Zealand university community*'. *Addictive Behaviors* 32: 2586.

Lane, S D; Cherek, D R; Pietras, C J; Tcheremissine, O V. 2004. 'Alcohol effects on human risk taking'. *Psychopharmacology* 172: 68–77.

Lange, D P. 2000. 'A morning-after pill for hangovers?'. *The New York Times*. New York.

Lange, J; Voas, R. 2001. 'Defining binge drinking quantities through resulting blood alcohol concentrations'. *Psychology of Addictive Behaviors* 15: 310–316.

Langton, M. 2008. 'Optional intervention gives choice to people'. *The Australian*.

Laville, S. 2004. 'Tension and fear in town hit by violence: Algarve as 33 fans are deported, traders and holidaymakers count the cost'. *The Guardian*. London.

Lee, J; McDonald, D. 2003. 'Rape – is the drink talking?'. *The Sunday Times*. London.

Legge, K. 2008. 'Clubland'. *The Australian Magazine*.

Leifman, H. 2002a. 'A comparitive analysis of drinking patterns in six EU countries in the year 2000'. *Contemporary Drug Problems* 29: 501.

Leifman, H. 2002b. 'The six-country survey of the European comparative alcohol study: Comparing patterns and assessing validity'. *Contemporary Drug Problems* 29: 477–502.

Leland, J. 2001. 'Psychodelia's middle-aged head trip'. *The New York Times*. New York.

Levi, R; Valverde, M. 2001. 'Knowledge on tap: Police science and common knowledge in the legal regulation of drunkenness'. *Law & Social Inquiry* 26: 819–846.

Levitt, A; Sher, K J; Bartholow, B D. 2009. 'The language of intoxication: Preliminary investigations'. *Alcoholism–Clinical and Experimental Research* 33: 448–454.

Lewin, T. 2005. 'Clean living on campus'. *The New York Times*. New York.

Lindsay, J. 2006. 'A big night out in Melbourne: Drinking as an enactment of class and gender'. *Contemporary Drug Problems* 33: 29–61

Lindsay, J. 2009. 'Young Australians and the staging of intoxication and self-control'. *Journal of Youth Studies* 12: 371–384.

Link, T. 2008. 'Youthful intoxication: A cross-cultural study of drinking among German and American adolescents'. *Journal of Studies on Alcohol and Drugs* 69: 362–370.

Lintonen, T; Konu, A. 2004. 'The misperceived social norm of drunkenness among early adolescents in Finland'. *Health Education Research* 19: 64–70.

Lintonen, T; Rimpelä, M. 2001. 'The validity of the concept of "self-perceived drunkenness" in adolescent health surveys'. *Journal of Substance Use* 6: 145–150.

Lintonen, T; Rimpelä, M; Vikat, A; Rimpelä, A. 2000. 'The effect of societal changes on drunkenness trends in early adolescence'. *Health Education Research* 15: 261–269.

Liptak, A. 2002. 'Judge's drug use at issue in 2 death sentences'. *The New York Times*. New York.

Lisante, J E. 2001. 'When the kid's in cuffs, what's a parent to do?; what might seem like the end of your world may really be the start of his shaping up'. *The Washington Post*. Washington.

Lourie, R. 2002. 'Liquid grapes'. *The New York Times*. New York.

Lueck, T J; O'Donnell, M. 2004. 'L. I. driver, 82, was drunk, the police say'. *The New York Times*. New York.

Lyall, S. 2004. 'British worry that drinking has gotten out of hand'. *The New York Times*. New York.

Lyall, S. 2006. 'Ever since Falstaff, getting sloshed is cricket'. *The New York Times*. New York.

Lyall, S. 2007. 'How the young poor measure poverty in Britain: Drink, drugs and their time in jail'. *The New York Times*. New York.

Lyall, S. 2008. 'Some Britons too unruly for resorts in Europe'. *The New York Times*. New York.

Lyons, A C; Willott, S A. 2008. 'Alcohol consumption, gender identities and women's changing social positions'. *Sex Roles* 59: 694–712.

Macaskill, M. 2008. 'Generation sex'. *The Sunday Times*. London.

Macaskill, M; Gordon, T. 2007. 'Drink problem'. *The Sunday Times*. London.

Macaskill, M; McKendry, M. 2007. 'Crime: Clean up or a cop-out'. *The Sunday Times*. London.

Macaulay, S. 2000. 'Dried out but not so dusty'. *The Times*. London.

Macintyre, B. 2005. 'Macho drink culture keeps Britain apart from Europe'. *The Times*. London.

Macleod, A. 2005. 'Hard facts on number of Scots drinking themselves to death'. *The Times*. London.

Mahoney, E. 2001. 'Have you got the bottle to quit?'. *The Sunday Times*. London.

Mäkelä, P; Fonager, K; Hibell, B; Nordlund, S; Sabroe, S; Simpure, J. 2001. 'Episodic heavy drinking in four Nordic countries: A comparative survey'. *Addiction* 96, 1575–1588.

Mangan, J. 2004. 'That old chip'. *The Age*. Melbourne.

Mann, S. 2008. 'Inquest puts spotlight on police duty of care'. *The Age*. Melbourne.

Margolis, S A; Ypinazar, V A; Muller, R. 2008. 'The impact of supply reduction through alcohol management plans on serious injury in remote Indigenous communities in remote Australia: A ten-year analysis using data from the royal flying doctor service'. *Alcohol and Alcoholism* 43, 104–110.

Markon, J. 2007. 'Driver in fatal beltway crash had .14 alcohol level'. *The Washington Post*. Washington D. C.

Marrin, M. 2002. 'Today's football roar can be tomorrow's Nazi rant'. *The Sunday Times*. London.

Marrin, M. 2003. 'Oh joy, now everyone can be a holiday hooligan'. *The Sunday Times*. London.

Marrin, M. 2007. 'To understand Britishness, watch rugby'. *The Sunday Times*. London.

Martin, A. 2004. 'Grain of truth: A global guide to beer has Andrew Martin licking his lips: The complete guide to world beer: What's brewing from Abbaye des Rocs to Zatec by Roger Protz, 240pp, Carlton, £19.99'. *The Guardian*. London.

Maslin, J. 2002. 'The poor little rich art collector'. *The New York Times*. New York.

Mason, N. 2001. '"The sovereign people are in a beastly state": The Beer Act of 1830 and Victorian discourse on working-class drunkenness'. *Victorian Literature and Culture* 29: 109–127.

Mayer, A. 2001. 'On sober reflection...'. *The Guardian*. London.

Mayes, I. 2004. 'Open door: A poet, the press and a lottery grant: The readers' editor on... attempts to catch and correct a runaway story'. *The Guardian*. London.

McAlpine, J. 2008. 'We need drinking lessons from America, not France'. *The Sunday Times*. London.

McCloskey, M S; Berman, M E. 2003. 'Alcohol intoxication and self-aggressive behavior'. *Journal of Abnormal Psychology* 112: 306–311.

McCreanor, T; Barnes, H M; Kaiwai, H; Borell, S; Gregory, A. 2008. 'Creating intoxigenic environments: Marketing alcohol to young people in Aotearoa New Zealand'. *Social Science & Medicine* 67: 938–946.

McFadden, R D. 2006. 'Off-Duty officer is shot by police during fight in bronx'. *The New York Times*. New York.

McKinley Jr, J C. 2001. 'Agreement on a tougher drunken-driving standard'. *The New York Times*. New York.

McMahon J; McAlaney, J; Eedgar, F. 2007. 'Binge drinking behaviour, attitudes and beliefs in a UK community sample: An analysis by gender, age and deprivation'. *Drugs: Education, Prevention & Policy* 14: 289–303.

McMillan, J. 2008. 'Australian Federal Police: Use of powers under the Intoxicated People Act'. Canberra: Commonwealth of Australia.

Measham, F. 2006. 'The new policy mix: Alcohol, harm minimisation, and determined drunkenness in contemporary society'. *International Journal of Drug Policy* 17: 258–268.

Measham, F. 2008. 'The turning tides of intoxication: young people's drinking in Britain in the 2000s'. *Health Education Research* 108: 207–222.

Measham, F; Brain, K. 2005. '"Binge" drinking, British alcohol policy and the new culture of intoxication'. *Crime, Media, Culture* 1: 262–83.

Midanik, L. 2003. 'Definitions of drunkenness'. *Substance Use & Misuse* 38: 1285.

Middendorp, C. 2004. 'We're here because there's beer'. *The Age*. Melbourne.

Midgley, C. 2001a. 'I have to get off my face'. *The Times*. London.

Midgley, C. 2001b. 'Why drink? Because we enjoy it'. *The Times*. London.

Milburn, C. 2002. 'Trying to curb the teen binge rampage'. *The Age*. Melbourne.

Miles, A. 2002a. 'A criminal waste of time – inside the police'. *The Times*. London.

Miles, A. 2002b. 'Is this how to beat crime – inside the police'. *The Times*. London.

Miles, H; Winstock, A; Strang, J. 2001. 'Identifying young people who drink too much: The clinical utility of the five item Alcohol Use Disorders Identification Test (AUDIT)'. *Drug and Alcohol Review* 20: 9–18.

Miller, J W; Naimi, T S; Brewer, R D; Jones, S E. 2007. 'Binge drinking and associated health risk behaviors among high school students'. *Pediatrics* 119: 76–85.

Minogue, K. 2001. 'Cosmopolitan women'. *Herald Sun*. Melbourne.

Mitchell, G. 2008. 'Police war on gangs'. *Herald Sun*. Melbourne.

Moerk, C. 2006. 'Ciao, Edie: Warhol girl gets 15 more minutes'. *The New York Times*. New York.

Mol, A; Law, J. 2002. 'Complexities: An introduction'. In *Complexities: Social Studies of Knowledge Practices*, Law, J; Mol, A., eds. Durham: Duke University Press: 1–22.

Monshouwer, K; Smit, F; De Zwart, W M; Spruit, I; Van Ameijden, E J C. 2003. 'Progress from a first drink to first intoxication: Age of onset, time-windows and risk factors in a Dutch national sample of secondary school students'. *Journal of Substance Use* 8: 155–163.

Montemurro, B; McClure, B. 2005. 'Changing gender norms for alcohol consumption: Social drinking and lowered inhibitions at bachelorette parties'. *Sex Roles: A Journal of Research* 52: 279–288.

Montgomery, L; Leduc, D. 2001. 'Crime, punishment – shaped by one man; loopholes undo mandatory sentences'. *The Washington Post*. Washington D. C.

Moore, S; Shepherd, J; Perham, N. Cusens, B. 2007. 'The prevalence of alcohol intoxication in the night-time economy'. *Alcohol and Alcoholism: International Journal of the Medical Council on Alcoholism* 42: 629–634.

Morris, S. 2001. 'Cocktail of problems as drinks firms zero in on youngsters'. *The Guardian*. London.

Morzorati, S L; Ramchandani, V A; Flury, L; Li, T –K; O'Connor, S. 2002. 'Self-reported subjective perception of intoxication reflects family history of alcoholism when breath alcohol levels are constant'. *Alcoholism: Clinical and Experimental Research* 26: 1299–1306.

Mosher, J F; Toomey, T L; Good, C; Harwood, E; Wagenaar, A C. 2002. 'State laws mandating or promoting training programs for alcohol servers and establishment managers: An assessment of statutory and administrative procedures'. *Journal of Public Health Policy* 23: 90.

Mullen, K; Watson, J; Swift, J; Black, D. 2007. 'Young men, masculinity and alcohol'. *Drugs: Education, Prevention & Policy* 14: 151–165.

Munro, I. 2001. 'Reluctant role models living on the edge'. *The Age.* Melbourne.

Mydans, S. 2003. 'African students' harsh lesson: Racism is astir in Russia'. *The New York Times.* New York.

Nader, C. 2008. 'Grieving over its lost youth, a Victorian town turns to action'. *The Age.* Melbourne.

National Health and Medical Research Council (NHMRC). 2009. Australian Guidelines to Reduce Health Risks from Drinking Alcohol. Canberra.

National Institute on Alcohold Abuse and Alcoholism (NIAAA). 2004. *NIAAA Newsletter.*

Neilan, T. 2000. 'World briefing'. *The New York Times.* New York.

Neumann, T; Spies, C. 2003. 'Use of biomarkers for alcohol use disorders in clinical practice'. *Addiction* 98: 81–91.

New Zealand Herald. 2003a. 'Louts, taggers and beggars will be losers'. *New Zealand Herald.* Auckland.

New Zealand Herald. 2003b. 'Message in a bottle: Alcohol in New Zealand'. *New Zealand Herald.* Auckland.

New Zealand Herald. 2004. 'Taxpayers still struggle'. *New Zealand Herald.* Auckland.

New Zealand Herald. 2006a. 'Addicts saved by ambush'. *New Zealand Herald.* Auckland.

New Zealand Herald. 2006b. 'Back in the chain gang'. *New Zealand Herald.* Auckland.

New Zealand Herald. 2007a. 'Cracking down on problem kids'. *New Zealand Herald.* Auckland.

New Zealand Herald. 2007b. 'Mission to rescue the children'. *New Zealand Herald.* Auckland.

New Zealand Herald. 2007c. 'Women hit the drink'. *New Zealand Herald.* Auckland.

New Zealand Herald. 2008a. 'America's secret sickness exposed'. *New Zealand Herald.* Auckland.

New Zealand Herald. 2008b. 'Open and informed debate the first step'. *New Zealand Herald.* Auckland.

New Zealand Herald. 2008c. 'Territorial armies'. *New Zealand Herald.* Auckland.

Newburn, T; Shiner, M. 2001. *Teenage kicks? Young People and Alcohol: A Review of the 'Literature'.* York: Joseph Rowntree Foundation.

Newman, A. 2002. 'Ex-officer guilty of manslaughter in crash following drinking bout'. *The New York Times.* New York.

Nicholls, J. 2006. 'Liberties and licences: alcohol in liberal thought'. *International Journal of Cultural Studies* 9: 131–151.

No Author. 2009. 'Alcohol is too cheap, says Victorian Premier John Brumby'. *The Australian*, 27 August 2009. Accessed 25 April 2010. Available at: http://www.theaustralian.news.com.au/story/0,25197,25988996-5006785,00.html.

Nogrady, B. 2008. 'Alcohol abuse eclipsing heroin'. *The Australian.*

Nordlund, S. 2008. 'What is alcohol abuse? Changes in Norwegians' perceptions of drinking practices since the 1960s'. *Addiction Research & Theory* 16: 85–94.

Nowra, L. 2007. 'Culture of denial'. *The Australian.*

Nusbaumer, M R; Reiling, D M. 2002. 'Environmental influences on alcohol consumption practices of alcoholic beverage servers'. *American Journal of Drug and Alcohol Abuse* 28: 733–742.

Nussbaum, D. 2001. 'It's a fast, cheap high with a big price tag'. *The New York Times*. New York.

O'Hara, M. 2004. 'Mary O'Hara reports on how the case of a woman with a serious drink problem is raising questions about the government's key weapon in the war against antisocial behaviour'. *The Guardian*. London.

O'Reilly, E. 2003. 'Alcohol culture will be undoing of us all'. *The Sunday Times*. London.

Ogle, R L; Miller, W R. 2004. 'The effects of alcohol intoxication and gender on the social information processing of hostile provocations involving male and female provocateurs'. *Journal of Studies on Alcohol* 65: 54–62.

Okie, S. 2002. 'Drinking lessons; as alcohol problems grow, colleges seek new remedies'. *The Washington Post*. Washington.

Otago Daily Times. 2003. 'Persecution will not save lives'. *Otago Daily Times*. Dunedin.

Otago Daily Times. 2004a. 'A high-speed chase which began on State Highway 1 about 1.30pm on July 25 brought a man before the Dunedin District Court yesterday on two driving charges'. *Otago Daily Times*. Dunedin.

Otago Daily Times. 2004b. 'Quark'. *Otago Daily Times*. Dunedin.

Otago Daily Times. 2005a. 'A Brighton man was so drunk when he crashed his car into a tree'. *Otago Daily Times*. Dunedin.

Otago Daily Times. 2005b. '"This was a determined spree of offending during which you had little regard for the effects on anyone else. It was selfish and self-centred," Judge Emma Smith said sentencing John Lewis Rogal 41, unemployed, to 21 months jail and denying him leave to apply for home detention'. *Otago Daily Times*. Dunedin.

Otago Daily Times. 2006a. 'Discussion about student behaviour in Dunedin's north end'. *Otago Daily Times*. Dunedin.

Otago Daily Times. 2006b. 'A man who drove with an excess breath-alcohol level on January 22, and again five days later, was remanded on bail for sentence next month when he appeared in the Dunedin District Court yesterday'. *Otago Daily Times*. Dunedin.

Otago Daily Times. 2006c. 'Nightlife in Dunedin… "emotional moderation is not the ready hallmark of the tired, of adolescence or young adulthood, or of the intoxicated"'. *Otago Daily Times*. Dunedin.

Ozick, C. 2006. 'A youthful intoxication'. *The New York Times*. New York.

Partanen, J. 2006. 'Spectacles of sociability and drunkenness: On alcohol and drinking in Japan'. *Contemporary Drug Problems* 33: 177– 204.

Patterson, J. 2005. 'Make mine a double bill: From the snobby tipplers of Sideways to the kamikaze boozing of Barfly, Hollywood likes its drunks guilty and troubled. John Patterson offers a toast'. *The Guardian*. London.

Perham, N; Moore, S; Shepherd, J; Cusens, B. 2007. 'Identifying drunkenness in the night-time economy'. *Addiction* 102: 377–380.

Perkins, H W; Dejong, W; Linkenbach, J. 2001. 'Estimated blood alcohol levels reached by "binge" and "nonbinge" drinkers: A survey of young adults in Montana'. *Psychology of Addictive Behaviors* 15: 317–320.

Phillips, M. 2000. 'Why should gays have the right to public sex?'. *The Sunday Times*. London.

Philp, C. 2008. 'Young men in Zanu shirts roam the streets, eyes wild with intoxication'. *The Times*. London.

Phipps, C. 2004. 'Why pick on us?': Claire Phipps, we don't start fights. But like some leering bloke in a pub, the government won't leave women drinkers alone'. *The Guardian*. London.

Plant, M L. 2008. 'The role of alcohol in women's lives: A review of issues and responses'. *Journal of Substance Use* 13: 155–191.

Polizzotto, M; Saw, M; Tjhung, I; Chua, E; Stockwell, T. 2007. 'Fluid skills: Drinking games and alcohol consumption among Australian university students'. *Drug and Alcohol Review* 26: 469–475.

Pollan, M. 2003. 'The (Agri)Cultural Contradictions Of Obesity'. *The New York Times*.

Poulsen, M B; Jakobsen, J; Aagaard, N K; Andersen, H. 2007. 'Motor performance during and following acute alcohol intoxication in healthy non-alcoholic subjects'. *European Journal of Applied Physiology* 101: 513–523.

Power, B. 2007a. 'Drink no reason to get away with murder'. *The Sunday Times*. London.

Power, B. 2007b. 'Give alcoholics support, not excuses'. *The Sunday Times*. London.

Pradarelli, M. 2000. 'Driving simulator: Chills and spills, all in the name of safety'. *The New York Times*. New York.

Price, M. 2006. 'All is not lost for remote communities'. *The Australian*.

Pryor, C. 2001. 'Safety is a night locked up'. *The Australian*.

Pryor, C. 2008. 'Alcohol and us: A drink to your health? Maybe not: For some, the recommended 14 to 21 units a week may seem unrealistic. So how are the limits set? And what happens if you exceed them?' *The Guardian*. London.

Putt, J; Payne, J; Milner, L. 2005. 'Indigenous male offending and substance abuse'. *Trends and issues in crime and criminal justice* 293. Australian Institute of Criminology. Canberra

Quinn, D. 2001. 'Irish artists have so much to talk about, so little to say'. *The Sunday Times*. London.

Rabin, D. 2005. 'Drunkenness and responsibility for crime in the eighteenth century'. *Journal of British Studies* 44: 457–477.

Raitasalo, K; Knibbe, R; Kraus, L. 2005. 'Retrieval strategies and cultural differences in answering survey questions on drinking: A cross-national comparison'. *Addiction Research and Theory* 13: 359–372.

Ramos, D. 2000. 'American hero'. *The New York Times*.

Reid, S; Ukoumunne, O; Coffey, C; Teesson, M; Carlin, J; Patton, G. 2007. 'Problem alcohol use in young Australian adults'. *Australian & New Zealand Journal of Psychiatry* 41: 436–441.

Reiling, D M; Nusbaumer, M R. 2006. 'When problem servers pour in problematic places: Alcoholic beverage servers' willingness to serve patrons beyond intoxication'. *Substance Use & Misuse* 41: 653–668.

Remini, R V. 2000. 'Union man'. *The New York Times*.

Reynaud, M; Schwan, R; Loiseaux-Meunier, M –N; Albuisson, E; Deteix, P. 2001. 'Patients admitted to emergency services for drunkenness: Moderate alcohol users or harmful drinkers?'. *The American Journal of Psychiatry* 158: 96.

Rhodes, D. 2004. 'Unhappy hour: Patrick Hamilton's novel The Midnight Bell contains a comic self portrait of a man hopelessly addicted to whisky and a girl'. *The Guardian*. London.

Richter, M; Leppin, A; Gabhainn, S. 2006. 'The relationship between parental socio-economic status and episodes of drunkenness among adolescents: Findings from a cross-national survey'. *BMC Public Health* 6: 9.

Riddell, M. 2003. 'Who let the yobs out?'. *The Guardian*. London.

Riding, A. 2004. 'Globe-trotting Englishwomen who helped map the world'. *The New York Times*. New York.

Roche, A; Watt, K. 1999. 'Drinking and university students: From celebration to inebriation'. *Drug and Alcohol Review* 18: 389–99.

Roginski, A. 2006. 'Dipso facto'. *The Age*. Melbourne.

Room, R. 2001. 'Intoxication and bad behaviour: understanding cultural differences in the link'. *Social Science & Medicine* 53: 189–198.

Room, R; Bullock, S. 2002. 'Can alcohol expectancies and attributions explain Western Europe's north–south gradient in alcohol's role in violence?'. *Contemporary Drug Problems* 29: 619.

Room, R; Makela, K. 2000. 'Typologies of the cultural position of drinking'. *Journal of Studies on Alcohol* 61: 475.

Rosen, J. 2000. 'Zero tolerance: When good policing goes bad'. *The Washington Post*. Washington D. C.

Rosenburg, H; Nevis, S A. 2000. 'Assessing and training recognition of intoxication by university students'. *Psychology of Addictive Behaviors* 1: 29–35.

Ruane, M E; Duggan, P. 2006. 'Promise thrown away; two decades after cocaine killed U-Md. basketball star Len Bias, a candlelight vigil spotlights the toll of drug abuse'. *The Washington Post*. Washington.

Rumney, P; Fenton, A. 2008. 'Intoxicated consent in rape: Bree and juror decision-making'. *The Modern Law Review* 71: 271–302.

Safire, W. 2002. 'Going to pot'. *The New York Times*. New York.

Salusinszky, I. 2004. 'Shooting star'. *The Australian*.

Sande, A. 2002. 'Intoxication and rite of passage to adulthood in Norway'. *Contemporary Drug Problems* 29: 277.

Saner, E. 2006. 'Drunk young things: Teenage drinkers don't just risk making fools of themselves. Doctors now say that binge-drinking in your youth can cause long-term health damage'. *The Guardian*. London.

Saner, E. 2008. '"The women? They're far worse in fights": The number of women being arrested for late-night drunken behaviour, particularly in the West Midlands, is soaring. But are they really becoming more violent – or are the police just treating them more harshly?'. *The Guardian*. London.

Santana, A. 2001. 'Officer who killed colleague faces uneasy return to work; White D. C. policeman's black peers voice distress'. *The Washington Post*. Washington.

Santora, M. 2002. 'A drink, and maybe trouble, around every new york corner'. *The New York Times*. New York.

Satel, S. 2001. 'Drugs: A decision, not a disease'. *The Wall Street Journal*. New York.

Scarscelli, D. 2007. 'Consumption patterns of alcoholic beverages in two cohorts of Italian men'. *Contemporary Drug Problems* 34: 313.

Schmid, H; Bogt, T; Godeau, E; Hublet, A; Dias, S; Fotiou, A. 2003. 'Drunkenness among young people: A cross-national comparison'. *Journal of Studies on Alcohol* 64: 650–661.

Schuckit, M A; Smith, T L; Kalmijn, J. 2004. 'Findings across subgroups regarding the level of response to alcohol as a risk factor for alcohol use disorders: A college population of women and Latinos'. *Alcoholism–Clinical and Experimental Research* 28: 1499–1508.

Schulte, B. 2005. 'Critics say district's DUI policy goes too far; jailing drivers for 1 drink called wasting resources'. *The Washington Post*. Washington.

Sciolino, E. 2003. 'Iran veers between admiration and resentment of American power'. *The New York Times*. New York.

Scott, A O. 2003. 'Cannes, where palms are made of gold'. *The New York Times*. New York.

Scott, L; Donnelly, N; Poynton, S; Weatherburn, D. 2007. 'Young adults' experience of responsible service practice in NSW: An update'. *Alcohol Studies Bulletin*: 1–8.

Searle, A. 2007. 'The fun of filth: Hogarth may not have been a great painter, but who cares? The world he gave us is rich, rude, teeming with life – and wonderfully familiar'. *The Guardian*. London.

Sengupta, S. 2007. 'India's Whiskey-Drinking Elite Make Room for Wine'. *The New York Times*. New York.

Service, R. 2000. 'The many faces of Boris'. *The Sunday Times*. London.

Sexton, R L. 2001. 'Ritualized inebriation, violence, and social control in Cajun Mardi Gras'. *Anthropological Quarterly* 74: 28–38.

Shanahan, D. 2007. 'A cultural sea change in Indigenous thinking'. *The Australian*.

Shaver, K. 2007. 'Vintage bureaucracy; Montgomery doesn't make it easy to buy fine wine, restaurateurs say'. *The Washington Post*. Washington D. C.

Shepherd, J. 2008. 'The party's over: Students tend to be portrayed in the media as hard-drinking hedonists. But that's simply no longer the case. Jessica Shepherd finds out why sober is becoming cool'. *The Guardian*. London.

Shin, J M; Sachs, G; Kraut, J A. 2008. 'Simple diagnostic tests to detect toxic alcohol intoxications'. *Translational Research* 152: 194–201.

Shore, J H; Spicer, P. 2004. 'A model for alcohol-mediated violence in an Australian Aboriginal community'. *Social Science & Medicine* 58: 2509–2521.

Sieghart, M A. 2001. 'It's time to take the crime out of drugs'. *The Times*. London.

Simester, A P. 2009. 'Intoxication is never a defence'. *Criminal Law Review*: 3–14.

Simic, M; Tasic, M. 2007. 'The relationship between alcohol elimination rate and increasing blood alcohol concentration – calculated from two consecutive blood specimens'. *Forensic Science International* 172: 28–32.

Simic, M; Tasic, M; Stojiljkovic, g; Budakov, B; Vukovic, R. 2004. '"Cognac Alibi" as a drunk-driving defense and medico-legal challenge'. *Medicine and Law* 23: 367–78.

Simper, E. 2007. 'If the booze disappears, other ills will follow'. *The Australian*.

Sirmans, F. 2001. 'The no-tech way toward art-making'. *The New York Times*. New York.

Skehan, C. 2003. 'Now for an inquiry into Solomon's strife'. *The Sunday Age*. Melbourne.

Skelton, R. 2006. 'This is the grave of teenager Jenissa Ryan, great grand-daughter of painter Albert Namatjira. We can't show her face, but we can tell her shocking story'. *The Sunday Age*. Melbourne.

Skelton, R. 2007. 'Rescue realities'. *The Age*. Melbourne.

Smith, P. 2001. 'And now, a word from our sponsors…'. *The Australian*.

Smith, R. 2002. 'How Masks Can Amplify as Well as Conceal'. *The New York Times*. New York.

Smith, R. 2005. 'Into the drink – an unabashed proponent of alcohol may pour it on a little freely at times, but he has some incisive things to say about the American way of booze'. *The Wall Street Journal*. New York.

Sontag, D. 2002. 'When politics is personal'. *The New York Times*. New York.

Sontag, D; Alvarez, L. 2008. 'Combat trauma takes the witness stand'. *The New York Times*. New York.

Squires, S. 2000. 'The dope on drugs; how the most popular substances affect your brain, body and behavior'. *The Washington Post*. Washington D. C.

Stapleton, J. 2004. 'Hope the true victim on Redfern's streets'. *The Australian*.

Stark, J. 2007. 'Heading for a hangover'. *The Age*. Melbourne.

Steinberg, P. 2002. 'Target the bingers, not campus drinkers'. *The Washington Post*. Washington.

Steinhausen, H; Eschmann, S; Heimgartner, A; Metzke, C. 2008. 'Frequency, course and correlates of alcohol use from adolescence to young adulthood in a Swiss community survey'. *BMC Psychiatry* 8: 12.

Stewart, C. 2006. 'The party's over'. *The Australian.*

Stewart, C; Power, T G. 2003. 'Ethnic, social class, and gender differences in adolescent drinking: Examining multiple aspects of consumption. *Journal of Adolescent Research* 18: 575–598.

Stolberg, V. 2006. 'A review of perspectives on alcohol and alcoholism in the history of American health and medicine (Author abstract)'. *Journal of Ethnicity in Substance Abuse* 5: 39 (68).

Stone, R. 2008. 'Day tripper'. *The New York Times.* New York.

Stowe, S. 2005. 'Students accept drinking rules, but the alumni strike back'. *The New York Times.* New York.

Strauss, N. 2001. 'The loose ends of last year'. *The New York Times.* New York.

Strickland, K. 2003. 'Getting into the party spirits'. *The Australian.*

Stuttaford, D T. 2001. 'Cannabis? It's a real killer'. *The Times.* London.

Stuttaford, D T. 2005. 'Warnings go up in smoke'. *The Times.* London.

Sulkunen, P. 2002. 'Between culture and nature: Intoxication in cultural studies of alcohol and drug use'. *Contemporary Drug Problems* 29: 253–277.

Summers, A. 2008. 'Binge drinking something to wine about'. *The Sydney Morning Herald.* Sydney.

Sutherland, J. 2007. 'Message in a bottle: Was John Cassavetes a genius in spite of his alcoholism, or because of it? John Sutherland on a director who made art out of addiction'. *The Guardian.* London.

Sweeney, C. 2008. 'A carnival day that descended into night of drunken mayhem'. *The Times.* London.

Syed, M. 2008. 'Playing away: What goes on tour stays on tour'. *The Times.* London.

Taylor, N; Bareja, M. 2005. '2002 National Police Custody survey: Overview'. Canberra, Australian Institute of Criminology.

The Guardian. 2004a. 'Become a good driver – admit you're bad – new spouse price panic'. *The Guardian.* London.

The Guardian. 2004b. 'Will bladdered Britain ever sober up?'. *The Guardian.* London.

The Guardian. 2006. 'There are many kinds of expert on alcohol abuse'. *The Guardian.* London.

The New York Times. 2001. 'Metro briefing'. *The New York Times.* New York.

The Sunday Age. 2001. 'Smoking and the demon drink'. *The Sunday Age.* Melbourne.

The Sunday Times. 2004. 'There's one road they'll never keep him off'. *The Sunday Times.* London.

The Times. 2003a. 'Culpability depends on defendant's perception of risk'. *The Times.* London.

The Times. 2003b. 'Many agree that the Greeks are right to crack down on British revellers, but what is to blame for such behaviour?'. *The Times.* London.

The Times. 2005. 'Call for review of law on all aspects of murder'. *The Times.* London.

The Washington Post. 2002. 'Fairfax crime watch'. *The Washington Post.* Washington D. C.

Thombs, D; Olds, S; Snyder, B. 2003. 'Field assessment of BAC data to study late-night college drinking'. *Journal of Studies on Alcohol* 64: 322.

Thompson, C W; Ly, P. 2000. 'Shootings by D. C. Police decline 66 percent in 1999; Chief credits new lethal-force policy, expanded training'. *The Washington Post.* Washington.

Thomson, H. 2007. 'Festive spirits: Every year, 30,000 pilgrims converge on a remote Peruvian glacier for one of the strangest – and coldest – festivals on earth. Hugh Thomson joins the celebrations: It was like a rock festival without the bands, with enough food stalls to feed an army'. *The Guardian*. London.

Thorpe N. 2004. 'Please don't force me to drink'. *The Sunday Times*. London.

Tindall, B. 2008. 'Just one more to calm the nerves…: Classical musicians are not paragons of virtue – but are recent tales of drink and drug abuse in the pit realistic, asks oboeist Blair Tindall'. *The Guardian*. London.

Tippet, G. 2000. 'Too much playing the man'. *The Age*. Melbourne.

Tippet, G. 2008. 'One victim, blood all over, and 200 spectators'. *The Sunday Age*. Melbourne.

Tolmie, J. 2001. 'Alcoholism and criminal liability (United Kingdom)'. *Modern Law Review* 64: 688–709.

Tomsen, S. 2005. '"Boozers and bouncers": Masculine conflict, disengagement and the contemporary governance of drinking-related violence and disorder'. *Australian and New Zealand Journal of Criminology* 38: 283–297.

Toohey, P. 2008a. 'Life and death of a crisis'. *The Australian*.

Toohey, P. 2008b. 'The war against grog'. *The Australian*.

Törrönen, J. 2003. 'The Finnish press's political position on alcohol between 1993 and 2000'. *Addiction* 98: 281.

Totaro, P; Coultan, M. 2004. 'Make mine a double standard'. *The Sydney Morning Herald*. Sydney.

Toynbee, P. 2005. 'Only raising prices will end our love affair with booze: Arguing over opening hours won't remove the fetishism from drink'. *The Guardian*. London.

Travis, A. 2007. 'Alcohol: Party's over? Curbs planned on cheap drink to beat binge culture: Ministers ready to outlaw cut-price promotions to make young sober up'. *The Guardian*. London.

Tryggvesson, K. 2004. 'The ambiguous excuse: Attributing violence to intoxication – young Swedes about the excuse value of alcohol'. *Contemporary Drug Problems* 31: 231–261.

Tryggvesson, K; Bullock, S L. 2006. 'Is it a fight or are they just drunk? Attributions about drunken behaviour in a hypothetical male-to-male aggression scenario'. *Journal of Scandinavian Studies in Criminology and Crime Prevention* 7: 61–77.

Tuller, D. 2004. 'Britain poised to approve medicine derived from marijuana [Corrected]'. *The New York Times*. New York.

Turner, V. 1969. *The Ritual Process: Structure and Anti-structure*. Ithaca: Cornell University Press.

Van Wersch, A; Walker, W. 2009. 'Binge-drinking in Britain as a social and cultural phenomenon: The development of a grounded theoretical model'. *Journal of Health Psycholology* 14: 124–134.

Vedantam, S. 2005. 'Inhalant abuse on the rise among children'. *The Washington Post*. Washington.

Vitello, P. 2006. 'Alcohol, a car and a fatality. Is it murder?'. *The New York Times*. New York.

Voas, R; Romano, E; Peck, R. 2006. 'Validity of the passive alcohol sensor for estimating BACs in DWI-enforcement operations (driving while intoxicated)'. *Journal of Studies on Alcohol* 67: 714–721.

Vonghia, L; Leggio, L; Ferrulli, A; Bertini, M; Gasbarrini, G; Addolorato, G. 2008. 'Acute alcohol intoxication'. *European Journal of Internal Medicine* 19: 561–567.

Vulliamy, E. 2002. 'Liberated US girls hit the bottle'. *The Guardian*. London.

Waldie, D J. 2001. 'California's golden dream goes dark'. *The New York Times*. New York.

Waldman, A. 2002. 'Sweet but deadly addiction is seizing the young in India'. *The New York Times*. New York.

Wang, G –J; Volkow, N D; Fowler, J S; Franceschi, D; Wong, C T; Pappas, N R; Netusil, N; Zhu, W; Felder, C; Ma, Y. 2003. 'Alcohol intoxication induces greater reductions in brain metabolism in male than in female subjects'. *Alcoholism: Clinical and Experimental Research* 27: 909–917.

Warner, M. 2004. 'In a savage landscape'. *The Times*. London.

Warren, S. 2007. 'Spring break is a legal specialty for Ben Bollinger – Florida lawyer enjoys a spike in his business; defendants in flip-flops'. *The Wall Street Journal*. New York.

Waters, J. 2004. 'What's the crack?: An economist report states that Ireland is the best country in the world to live in. But what with the nation's gangsters, high suicide rates and debts, Irish Times columnist John Waters is sceptical'. *The Guardian*. London.

Watson, P. 2004. '"You're not drunk if you can lie on the floor without holding on": Alcohol server liability, duty, responsibility and the law of torts'. *James Cook University Law Review*: 108–131.

Weatherburn, D J. 2008. 'The role of drug and alcohol policy in reducing Indigenous over-representation in prison'. *Drug and Alcohol Review* 27: 91–94.

Wechsler, H. 2000. 'Binge drinking: should we attack the name or the problem?'. *The Chronicle of Higher Education* 47 B12 (1).

Wechsler, H; Kuo, M. 2000. 'College students define binge drinking and estimate its prevalence: Results of a national survey'. *Journal of American College Health* 49: 57.

Weinberg, L; Wyatt, J P. 2006. 'Children presenting to hospital with acute alcohol intoxication'. *Emergency Medicine Journal* 23: 774–776.

Weisgall, D. 2002. 'A hard man who saw art as power and vice versa'. *The New York Times*. New York.

Wells, S; Graham, K; Purcell, J. 2009. 'Policy implications of the widespread practice of "pre-drinking" or "pre-gaming" before going to public drinking establishments – are current prevention strategies backfiring?'. *Addiction* 104: 4–9.

Welsh, I. 2002. 'Feeding off the naked lunch'. *The Times*. London.

Wertheimer, A. 2001. 'Intoxicated consent to sexual relations'. *Law and Philosophy: An International Journal for Jurisprudence and Legal Philosophy* 20: 373–401.

Westmass, J; Moeller, S; Woicik, P. 2007. 'Validation of a measure of college students' intoxicated behaviors: Associations with alcohol outcome expectancies, drinking motives, and personality'. *Journal of American College Health* 55: 227.

White, E. 2002. 'After they were stars'. *The New York Times*. New York.

Whitlock, C. 2000. 'Police rule was ignored before death; Pr. George's manual says to get suspect on drugs help'. *The Washington Post*. Washington.

Whitlock, C; Fallis, D S. 2001. 'Official secrecy shrouds fatal arrests; Prince George's police hamper prosecutors'. *The Washington Post*. Washington.

Whittell, G. 2004. 'Bladdered on Broad Street'. *The Times*. London.

Whyte, J. 2006. 'This is New Zealand's dark secret'. *The Times*. London.

Wild, T C. 2002. 'Personal drinking and sociocultural drinking norms: A representative population study'. *Journal of Studies on Alcohol* 63: 469–475.

Williams, D. 2000. '"A matter of survival"; Russian women fill void left by alcoholic men'. *The Washington Post*. Washington D. C.

Wilson, A. 2002. 'Mild on the streets'. *The Australian*.

Wilson, A. 2006. 'Inquest told how system failed to protect baby'. *The Australian*.

Wilson, D; Glater, J D. 2006a. 'Files from Duke rape case give details but no answers'. *The New York Times*. New York.

Wilson, D; Glater, J D. 2006b. 'Prosecutor's silence on Duke rape case leaves public with plenty of questions'. *The New York Times*. New York.

Wines, M. 2003. 'Reports of rape and torture inside Zimbabwean militia'. *The New York Times*. New York.

Wolf, N. 2007. 'The image of helplessness'. *The Washington Post*. Washington D. C.

Wolksa, B; Saggers, S; Hunt, L. 2004. '"Now we can drink, too": Changing drinking practices among Polish–Australian women'. *Health Sociology Review* 13: 65–73.

Wood, J. 2006. 'A fresh view: When his work was first exhibited, Cezanne was shunned by the art world and it took writers – including Virginia Woolf, Zola and Rilke – to recognise his genius'. *The Guardian*. London.

Workman, T A. 2001. 'Finding the meanings of college drinking: An analysis of fraternity drinking stories'. *Health Communication* 13: 427–447.

Wright, N. 2006. 'A day at the cricket: The breath alcohol consequences of a type of very English binge drinking'. *Addiction Research & Theory* 14: 133–137.

Writer, L. 2005. 'One day at a time'. *The Australian Magazine*.

Yang, S; Lynch, J; Raghunathan, T; Kauhanen, J; Salonen, J; Kaplan, G. 2007. 'Socioeconomic and psychosocial exposures across the life course and binge drinking in adulthood: Population-based study'. *American Journal of Epidemiology* 165: 184–193.

Yardley, J. 2008. 'The story of booze, hooch, brew and the veritas in vino'. *The Washington Post*. Washington D. C.

Zaborskis, A; Sumskas, L; Maser, M; Pudule, I. 2006. 'Trends in drinking habits among adolescents in the Baltic countries over the period of transition: HBSC survey results, 1993–2002'. *BMC Public Health* 6: 67.

Zhao, Y. 2003. 'With death penalty sought, trial unfolds'. *The New York Times*. New York.

Index of names

Index of subjects